DON'T LET ME DOWN

A Memoir

ERIN HOSIER

ATRIA PAPERBACK

New York   London   Toronto   Sydney   New Delhi

ATRIA
PAPERBACK

An Imprint of Simon & Schuster, Inc.
1230 Avenue of the Americas
New York, NY 10020

Copyright © 2019 by Erin Hosier

Most names and certain identifying details have been changed.
Photographs are from the author's personal collection.

All rights reserved, including the right to reproduce this book or portions thereof
in any form whatsoever. For information, address Atria Books Subsidiary Rights
Department, 1230 Avenue of the Americas, New York, NY 10020.

First Atria Paperback edition February 2020

ATRIA PAPERBACK and colophon are trademarks of Simon & Schuster, Inc.

For information about special discounts for bulk purchases, please contact Simon
& Schuster Special Sales at 1-866-506-1949 or business@simonandschuster.com.

The Simon & Schuster Speakers Bureau can bring authors to your live event. For
more information or to book an event, contact the Simon & Schuster Speakers
Bureau at 1-866-248-3049 or visit our website at www.simonspeakers.com.

Interior design by Amy Trombat

Manufactured in the United States of America

1   3   5   7   9   10   8   6   4   2

The Library of Congress has cataloged the hardcover edition as follows:

Names: Hosier, Erin, author.
Title: Don't let me down : a memoir / Erin Hosier.
Description: First hardcover edition. | New York : Atria Books, [2019]
Identifiers: LCCN 2018016389 (print) | LCCN 2018016918 (ebook) | ISBN
9781451644975 (ebook) | ISBN 9781451644951 (hardcover : alk. paper) |
ISBN 9781451644968 (pbk. : alk. paper)
Subjects: LCSH: Hosier, Erin. | Fathers and daughters—Ohio—Geauga
County—Biography. | Rock music—Ohio—Cleveland Region—Influence. |
Beatles—Influence. | Coming of age. | Young women—United States—
Biography. | Literary agents—New York (State)—New York—Biography. | Baby
boom generation—Ohio—Geauga County—Biography. | Fundamentalists—
Ohio—Geauga County—Biography. | Geauga County (Ohio)—Social life and
customs—20th century.
Classification: LCC F497.G2 (ebook) | LCC F497.G2 H67 2019 (print) | DDC
977.1/336043—dc23
LC record available at https://lccn.loc.gov/2018016389

ISBN 978-1-4516-4495-1
ISBN 978-1-4516-4496-8 (pbk)
ISBN 978-1-4516-4497-5 (ebook)

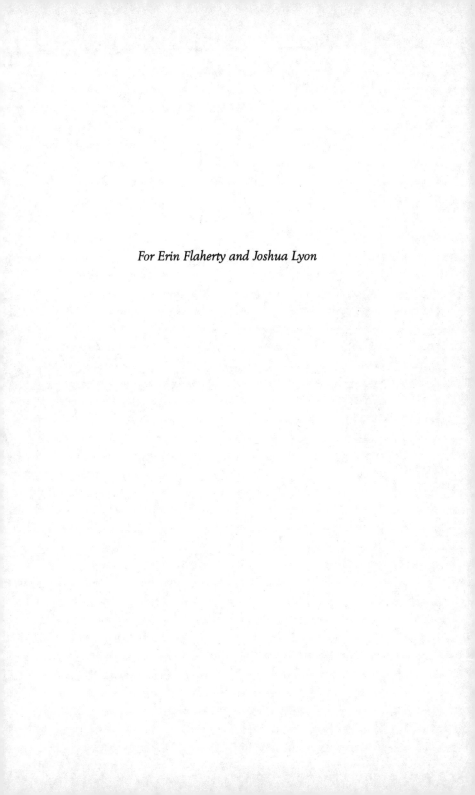

For Erin Flaherty and Joshua Lyon

Chris Farley to Paul McCartney: Remember when you were in the Beatles and you did that album *Abbey Road* and at the very end of the song it goes, "And in the end, the love you take is equal to the love you make"? You remember that?

Paul McCartney: Yes, Chris.

Chris Farley: Is that true?

—*Saturday Night Live*

CONTENTS

PRELUDE: YESTERDAY

THREE DEJECTED-LOOKING BOXES WERE STACKED on a modest utility trailer in my parents' old garage. I contemplated them with dread. Mom was moving, cleaning out the house; she said I needed to find room for anything I wanted to keep. The trunk of my borrowed '91 Corolla was already brimming with stuff I was taking back to Brooklyn. The small back seat was already filled with boxes, two fur coats, and some battered artwork, along with laundry, loose paper, and books I was planning to donate.

I had to make room for these last three boxes. Inside were years and years' worth of photographs I'd never been able to part with—and every letter anyone had ever written me, at least through 2001.

That was the year my dad died. Now here I was, in Ohio, eleven years later, on a break from the city after another failed love affair, dusting off the cobwebs from a lifetime of memories before my mom sold our childhood home. At my father's memorial service, we had sainted him, praised his boundless generosity, his heroism, his heart. When the minister reminded us that Jack hadn't been a perfect person—no one could be—we all laughed knowingly, on cue, secure in the knowledge that he'd certainly come close. All these things were true, but hidden beneath idyllic childhood remembrances was something much more complicated, a darker, truer truth . . . If daddies defined love for their daughters, and all you needed was love, why was I still alone?

Dad was a mass of contradictions: a pacifist and a tyrant, an optimist with demons, a hippie and a conservative, a proud father and a jerk, a boy and a man. A businessman with a closet full of elegant suits, he preferred the ease and comfort of khaki golf shorts paired with white socks that hit just above the ankle: Don Draper meets Clark Griswold. He exposed me to the great art and music the world had to offer and had an extensive knowledge of history, geography, and culture (he always won at *Trivial Pursuit*). But he was a world explorer with no passport, and his international travel was limited to Canada and the Caribbean. For all his communication savvy, for all the sparkling copy he wrote, all the client meetings he aced, all the accounts he won, he was a spectacular failure when it came to consistency of message with his family, with me. He was both hero and villain; he was both sides of a record.

The term "daddy issues" often refers to the baggage of a woman who dates significantly older men, men who can take care of her. But I went for the boy-man every time. I was chasing my own childhood dream of love. My dad had done the same thing. Jack Hosier never grew up, and before I could, he died. And that's where I got stuck.

When I think about my father now, I hear only the music that was my legacy: rock 'n' roll. I remember the times he pushed me to fight back, to question authority, to tell him he was full of shit and I wasn't gonna take it anymore. He was the Man I grrrl-ed against. Back then, he was cool. But as I got older and lived the kind of life I thought might make him proud, I realized that I wasn't done with him.

I looked through the boxes. Why had I hung on to this stuff? Assorted Valentines from third-grade classmates (Snoopy, DC Comics, Care Bears). Random elementary school report cards. A dingy woven friendship bracelet from no one I remembered having as a friend. My senior term paper, meant to be a kind of memoir at forty pages—I'd gotten a B– for saying it in thirty. "Well-written, but incomplete." (Apt.) A too-small T-shirt from Record Revolution circa 1992 emblazoned with two pharaoh heads and the words DON'T TOUCH MY TUTS. A stack of fanzines from the early nineties—*Franklin Zine, Rollerderby, ANSWER Me!, Asshole Weekly, The Severed Cow, The Debaser, The Bob Ross Counterculture,* and *Forced Exposure.* A diary of high school acid trips, some poems torn from loose-leaf notebooks, amethyst crystals and fortunes culled from the centers of cookies: *You are free to invent your life.*

A thousand ticket stubs from shows, many of which I attended with Dad. Neil Young and Sonic Youth at Blossom Music Center. Also the venue for a Bob Dylan appearance that was both brief and awful. Our first big show together: Paul McCartney at the Cleveland Stadium. Our last show together: Fleetwood Mac at the Gund Arena. Lollapalooza 1992 featuring the Jesus and Mary Chain and Ice Cube. The Violent Femmes headlining End Fest (miraculously appearing at Burton's own Geauga County Fairgrounds). Nirvana at University of Akron, Fugazi at Kent State, Hole in Columbus, My Bloody Valentine in Akron. Suckdog at Euclid Tavern. The Grifters at the Grog Shop.

Three boxes filled with irony. You could smell the flannel. The only thing missing was a DVD of *Reality Bites.*

I imagined that these boxes would stay in the car until I invested in another eighteen-gallon Rubbermaid tub to keep in my landlady's garage. I popped the trunk to confirm what I already knew: there was no more space for the last big box, the heaviest one, the one with Dad's records. I bent at the knees and heaved, then carefully set it back down.

The box was folded closed, not taped, at the top. Opening it, I was hit with the familiar scent of mildew, cedar chips, and vinyl. If the scent were a Demeter perfume it would be called Record Store. When I inhaled I got a blast of dust. I scanned the collection of records within, then leaned down and breathed them in again. The Who's *Tommy.* The Beach Boys' *Pet Sounds.* Joni Mitchell's *Clouds.* (Every

Joni Mitchell record, actually.) Seemingly everything Neil Young recorded before 1980, George Harrison's *Concert for Bangladesh*, the Lennon stuff, Wings. Faces, the Band. *The Very Best of the Byrds*. Something called Poco. This would be kind of a cool collection for someone to discover. I could leave them on a curb where some kid might find them, or drop them off at the vintage shop on the way out of town.

There was the Rolling Stones' *Sticky Fingers*, absent its infamous Andy Warhol–designed cover, no doubt a victim of a church-endorsed weeding-out for the protection of impressionable minors. Some kids had *Pat the Bunny*, but I preferred the denim-clad crotch of Mick Jagger (or his proxy) with a real metal zipper that revealed his underwear beneath. The record itself was pretty great, too, probably my favorite Stones album, still.

The Beatles records were still all together. They had provided the soundtrack to our lives and seen us through every great joy and tragedy. Dad and I used those songs to both connect with and escape from each other, to both understand and rebel against each other. The parallel messages of coming together and pushing apart were always there—throughout my parents' courtship, at their wedding, *yeah, yeah, yeah*–ing along to my conception. A dozen rotated records accompanied every picnic and party with friends, and provided a distraction from the daily drudgery of lawn mower maintenance, the ironing of oxford shirts, and homework. The music seeped into the walls of the house, made us dance, encouraged us to love and dream and grieve. Ultimately the lessons and diversions provided by just ten years of compositions by Lennon and McCartney (and Harrison and Starr) proved more powerful than the ones provided by my parents' church. Rock 'n' roll transcended religious faith. I'm willing to bet that when Dad saw the light, the face of God was Lennon's.

This band of British cartoon characters called the Fab Four sang songs for kids when I was a kid. Beatles songs had hand claps, made-up words not even grown-ups could spell, harmonies, sighing, riddles, rhymes, and lullabies. They had repetition: Who doesn't like to sing "Na na na, na na na na" from "Hey Jude" at the top of their lungs? And they had opposition: Who doesn't delight in the contradiction of *You say goodbye, and I say hello?* The songs told stories and had characters with chewy names like Eleanor Rigby, Mean Mr. Mustard, and Bungalow Bill. Technicolor imagery (Tangerine dreams! Marmalade skies!), a talking walrus. "Octopus's Garden," Ringo's version of "Yellow Submarine," a sweet, simple song about the virtues of living under the sea that epitomized childhood.

But as I grew up, so did my taste in Beatles songs and my understanding of their meaning in my life. The walrus, I knew, was Dad, but that was still a song that made no sense.

I had clearly tried to organize this box of records a few times before, as its contents were in alphabetical order. Here was Dad's copy of *Yesterday and Today*—a later pressing than the infamous "butcher" cover, which featured the band members draped in plastic baby doll parts and raw steak; this cover showed them posing with luggage. And there was the White Album, still intact but missing all its neat interior artwork, which I'd posted on my teenage bedroom walls. None of Dad's records ever could have been collectible. He had a terrible habit of signing his name—JACK—in red Sharpie on the upper right-hand corner of the cover (like a mother writing a kid's initials in his underwear—but worse, in my opinion).

Mixed in with the vinyl were some curious artifacts: a random how-to booklet on playing Frisbee and one of his old résumés. Sandwiched between Van Morrison's *Saint Dominic's Preview* and Jimi Hendrix's *Electric Ladyland* was an unframed sign on parchment paper. Written in calligraphy on the trumpet blast of an angel, above a hand-painted image of a house surrounded by flowers and birds, it read:

Bless This House
The Hosiers
1975

No one had seen fit to do anything with it, but here it was in near-perfect condition, though yellowed by age just like the record sleeves. I liked the sentiment of it. This had been a housewarming gift when my parents bought the place—the year after I was born. In 1975, it was just me and them.

I carefully put the papers back in the box, then folded the flaps over each other. There was no way I could part with all of it. What had I been thinking? (And by the way, where was my record player?) It wasn't just that these albums were my birthright. They were also a permanent record, proof of my primary education in music. They were full of the smells and sounds of my childhood, the images that first made me appreciate visual beauty, the men who first made me love men. I went back to the car and rearranged the stuff in the trunk to make room. Even if I never listened to another album in analog form, I'd always love the memory of the sound of the needle on the record, its whirring like breathing.

If this is the last of my father's baggage that I'll need to carry, I thought, *I might just be okay.*

But it was just the beginning.

SIDE ONE

JACK

1

A DAY IN THE LIFE

IF YOU GO BY THE NOW-CLASSIC FORMULA of adding your first pet's name to the name of the street you grew up on, my porn star name would be Dusty Rider. Dusty was a shaggy terrier mix who barked incessantly and chased cars, and Rider Road was a dead end. That dog had the dubious distinction of being run over four times—twice on Rider, and twice on nearby Route 87—sometimes by my own parents. Yet it was natural causes that eventually took him when I was fourteen.

Northeast Ohio had four seasons: Tornado, Oppressive, Blizzard, and Bitter. The weather famously tried your morale, especially in a town such as Burton that was downwind from Lake Erie and smack-dab in the middle of the snowbelt. Residents lived under constant threat of snow and ice that plagued the area. Between Blizzard and Bitter, our unpaved wraparound driveway required cars to either have four-wheel drive or gather enough momentum coming around the corner to make it up the snowy hill to the house. You could always tell who was coming over by how well they knew the quirks of the driveway. Unsuspecting Jehovah's Witnesses had been known to get stuck.

There were three acres of yard, with neighbors to the front and left side of us. The opposite side of Rider Road had no houses at all, just woods and wetlands and a branch of the Cuyahoga River. Hundreds of acres were designated a privately owned hunting preserve. Shotgun blasts were constant during deer season (also during bird season, and during shotgun season). If a little kid were to wander off, there was potential danger everywhere. You didn't need to walk very far.

My parents met when my father had just graduated from Ohio State. His college roommate happened to have grown up with my mother in suburban Cleveland, and fixed them up. My father's declared major had been child psychology. Years later, his textbooks were still on our bookshelf upstairs next to his hardcover Stephen King novels and Mom's dog-eared Christian motivationals. I distinctly remember noticing *The Developing Child* and other psych books when we were at odds with each other and thinking, *Who the hell do these belong to?*

My mother was intrigued and a little concerned by the fact that this guy had starved himself down to a frighteningly skeletal 115 pounds in order to avoid the draft. A picture of them on their first date was typical of dozens of later portraits: A man who would one day be responsible for the upbringing and downfall of a modest family of five looked stoked sitting in the back seat of a Volkswagen Beetle next to the hottest chick he'd theretofore been lucky enough to date. He appeared to look directly into the camera, proudly wrapping his arm around his future wife, who sullenly squinted into the distance like a vampire unused to the light, her long brown hair falling loosely down her arms. She stared off; he connected.

Those were the days when you married the first boyfriend who asked. My mother wasn't bowled over with options for how to begin her life. It was the year 1970, and her going to college or planning for a career wasn't the default priority for her parents. A daughter could make the transition from childhood bedroom to marital bedroom even quicker than a son could earn a bachelor's degree. Why fight the inevitability of a husband and children?

There had been two teenage boyfriends; one was a milquetoast American prom date, and the other was a high school dropout with a motorcycle. Having grown up in a relatively sheltered environment with two brothers, where her own father repeated the mantra "Never trust men; they are rotten to the core," she lacked the confidence and worldliness to know how to maneuver through the sex, drugs, and rock 'n' roll of the sixties. She was more comfortable jumping horses over four-foot fences than flirting with boys.

I suspect that my mother was drawn to my father because he was the perfect mix of reliable and reckless. He'd seen the Beatles live in '66, the Doors in '67, and Jimi Hendrix in '68 when he opened with a cover of "Sgt. Pepper's Lonely Hearts Club Band"—all while he was still in high school. He'd been a drummer. He always had a lot of expertise to impart, the kind of person who made you feel smarter by association. He'd managed to find a job right out of college, and had a positive energy that impressed my mother's parents. They didn't know he'd actually been kicked out of school for a semester for flagrantly displaying large marijuana plants on his fraternity's float in the annual Ohio State homecoming parade. Meanwhile, he introduced their daughter to the drug culture and took her to the kind of concerts where junkies overdosed in the crowd. But Mom liked the music and she liked that Dad did enough talking for both of them. They dated for a year before he told her that his search was over and he wanted to get married.

Neither of my parents considered themselves religious then, but my mother's family occasionally attended a local Episcopalian church. It was there, before their wedding, that they engaged in a kind of premarital counseling session. When the minister asked them pointedly what had brought them together, and why they believed the marriage would last, they were unprepared to answer. They looked at each other as if considering this question for the first time, then giggled and simultaneously announced that they both loved the Beatles. The minister, appalled, rephrased the question. "It's because you love *each other*, right?"

Indeed, the wedding almost didn't happen. They had a fight just a couple of days before the big day. Mom had cold feet, a sinking feeling that she would regret not going to college. Maybe she'd loved the one with the motorcycle, maybe she'd never been in love; maybe she wasn't in love now. She told him how she felt, and the man who would become a father lost his temper and bared his teeth in her face, pointing his finger aggressively between her eyes. She was afraid to be alone with him. The next day she told her parents what had happened, that she wanted to call off the wedding, or at least postpone it. Their response was that relatives would be traveling long distances, the reception hall was already paid for, and it was time to grow up; all couples are tested in times of stress, but things would settle after the big day.

They walked down the aisle to "Here Comes the Sun."

———————

Two years before they had me, my parents rented a cottage on the river. When it rained and the river was up, they'd float right out of their garage on yellow rubber rafts and spend lazy days smoking and drinking with friends. As soon as Mom got pregnant, it was time to grow up, and they moved to a red farmhouse built in 1870 with a lot of "potential." They planned to fix it up and sell it in five years. (Neither of those things would happen.)

In the early days of their marriage, Dad sold audio equipment to stoners on Coventry Road, the Haight-Ashbury of Cleveland Heights, the perfect job for someone so crazy about music. But by the time I was a year old, Dad had gotten serious and started an ad agency in Cleveland with another stereo salesman. Because they were hippies, they called themselves Azure Blue (the color of a cloudless sky), and they set up offices above a jazz bar. Their first account was a head shop that manufactured its own paraphernalia. The ads ran in the back pages of *High Times*: "Hi/Lo Rolling Papers: Get High on Low Prices." Eventually the agency grew to a team of twenty. They never won a Clio Award, but they were living the dream. The company would last a few years, but eventually shuttered to make way for my dad to take an executive position at a big corporate agency. More visibility with less risk.

Mom was particularly earthy then, and Dad kind of tried it on for a while. He still wore bell-bottoms, but at heart he was too much of a capitalist to ever maintain the appearance of the counterculture. Mom, meanwhile, made my baby food from scratch with ingredients grown in our yard. She kneaded bread dough and baked carob cookies, filling the kitchen with the scent of wheat and honey. Dad chopped firewood, and together they tended a garden in the yard, or swatted at bats that made their home in our chimney. The thwapping of tennis rackets—used exclusively for this purpose—could often be heard from my room upstairs after dark.

Decidedly thin by any standard, Dad was nevertheless a giant to me at five foot seven. He had thick, sandy hair that swooped like a Ken doll's, his teeth pearly and straight; his smile was as winning as a talk show host's, and often followed by a vigorous handshake. Mom was classically pretty—apple-cheeked with symmetrical features and hair that did what she wanted it to—but to me he was the glamorous one. In the seventies he had a Tom Selleck mustache; in the eighties he wore a tie *and* a vest to the office; on the weekends it was the same blue-and-yellow-striped rugby shirt and the worn-in and faded size 28 jeans I'd co-opt thirteen years later, forever preferring to steal his clothes over my mother's.

————————

Like many little girls, I liked to watch Dad shave in the mornings: the curious white foam from the striped red-and-blue can, how he held his breath as he leaned into the mirror over the sink. Sometimes if he made a mistake and nicked his skin with the razor, he'd suck in his breath and pucker his cheek. *It's okay, I'm okay.* It was a tiny thing, nothing to worry about, easily remedied by a minuscule piece of toilet paper applied right to the spot, a speck of blood holding the tissue that would remain affixed throughout breakfast like paper stuck to a cherry popsicle.

He worked long days, leaving at the crack of dawn and not coming home until eight o'clock at night. Every morning I would hear the clock radio go off around six thirty, always tuned to the notorious Cleveland rock station, "*WMMS: Home of the Buzzard.*" But Dad didn't tend to get up right away, so by the time he reached consciousness he was usually running late. I'd hear his feet hit the hardwood floor of my parents' bedroom, followed by the screech of hangers sliding across the metal rod of the closet as he selected the suit he would wear that day. He'd then thump down the uncarpeted stairs, sometimes at a jog, to our only bathroom, located off the kitchen, and turn on the shower, the pipes echoing their strange House of Usher whine. Mom often didn't bother to get up to make him breakfast, since he never had time to eat anyway and preferred to grab an Egg McMuffin and coffee for the hour-long commute.

Some mornings, the ritual was diverted at the closet.

"Paige, where is my blue shirt?"

"I'm sorry," Mom would try, "I washed it for you but I haven't had a chance to get the ironing done."

"Aw, *nuts*, Paige! I work constantly to provide for this family." He'd lambast her, saying she had only one job around here—to keep the house, take care of the family, cook, and do the laundry! (Technically that was four jobs.) "I can't believe you can't at least make sure I have clean clothes to wear to the office."

Mom would dutifully slump toward the kitchen, set up the ironing board, and press the shirt. I'd sit in the corner, twisting a lock of hair in my ear or sucking my thumb, a coping mechanism I'd use until I was eight years old.

Whenever Mom got in trouble, I felt guilty. I knew I could have helped her more by putting my toys away as soon as I'd finished playing with them, but it would be at least a decade before I'd find joy in organization. And Mom seldom talked back to her husband. She was curiously silent through every rebuke, though once I did catch her middle finger "talking" to my father's back.

————————

Ohio bred a certain kind of redneck. Living in Yankee territory, they longed to hang a Confederate flag in the backs of their pickup trucks. This wasn't everybody, but they were easy to spot. The mullet peeking out under a sweat-stained baseball cap, the deep-fried cuisine, the NRA bumper stickers, the ubiquitous sight of homemade spittoons in the form of Dixie cups that littered the runways of the county fairgrounds. There was a general defensiveness among folks about the merits of country versus city living. ("City slickers think their shit don't stink" was the observation that set me on a quest to one day become a city slicker myself.)

Even if you didn't count the rednecks, the whole town of Burton was living in the past. In the center of the one square mile that constituted the village (population 1,400) sat a log cabin replica of Abraham Lincoln's birthplace. It was an active maple sugar house, where maple sap, the local cash crop, had been boiled into syrup since 1931. Our town's motto, "Where History Lives," referred to the eighteenth century. Across the square, you could take a walking tour of Century Village Museum, a living replica of a town settled in 1798 that didn't change much in the following hundred years. Highlights included the actual home of the town's first settlers, a one-room schoolhouse, and a general store where you could buy penny candy while watching a re-enactment of the Civil War on a thoughtfully arranged battlefield. At the twentieth-century grocery store, our hatchback shared a parking lot with horses and buggies belonging to the Amish.

As soon as I could run, I followed close behind my dad during summer evening jogs around our property. There are pictures of me trailing adorably at his heels like a puppy, and then pictures of me far behind but still chasing. Indeed, I loved being an only child. When I was four and my parents delivered the news that there would be a new member of the family in the form of a baby brother, my heart sank. I knew that this would change things; my parents and I were a package deal. I was the only one who could understand them, and I didn't want to share them with a gurgling, glistening new person.

Dad tried to make me feel special, often taking the opportunity to remind me that I would always be their first, the one who had made them so happy that they'd wanted to have another. I would love being a big sister, everyone promised. But their assurances couldn't seem to quell my anxiety. Since I'd begun attending preschool I'd made a habit of spontaneously hyperventilating until I passed out right where I was standing. The first time it happened I was walking on the sidewalk with my mother to the car. She was going to drop me off somewhere I didn't want to go. I only remember the instant before waking up on a patch of grass. *You're going to fall*, I thought, and then I went down. I opened my eyes moments later to the sun and my mother's panicked face hovering above, trying to eclipse it.

It happened many times after that, but I never again felt the spell coming on. I didn't even have to be breathing heavily; the stress of having to remember to breathe proved to be too much and I'd turn blue and lose consciousness. A doctor couldn't pinpoint the cause. Sometimes kids just cried until they couldn't cry anymore, he said, or held their breath without meaning to. It was thought to be a reaction to stress or big life changes. It was the first time I sensed that my parents believed I was prone to overreacting, that I created these states by sheer force of will in order to get my way. It was true that I craved the special attention that followed grand gestures. If I stumbled it was still their job to pick me up.

One weekend morning before the baby was born, I was in the car with Dad and we were out running errands. Sitting in the back seat, I could see his face in the rearview mirror, his thumbs tapping along on the steering wheel to the song on the radio. He absentmindedly hummed in his inimitable way—through his teeth, as if mimicking the sound of a jazz cymbal—*tsss, tsss-tsss, tsss*. While waiting in line in the drive-through of the Huntington Bank, I was overcome by a need to break up his reverie and speak my mind.

"Daddy, I love you *so much more* than I love Mom." There was a pause, and then I saw him grin in the mirror, which filled me with pride.

"That makes my day, E, but we probably shouldn't tell your mom. It might hurt her feelings," he said, still smiling.

He needn't have worried, as I was already plotting a similar line favoring her.

2

BLACKBIRD

MOM WAS LONELY AND ESTRANGED, inexperienced and scared. Most days her husband was a world away in the city, we were isolated in the farmhouse, and there was only so much bread a person could bake for three and a half people. How to fill a day: "You Are My Sunshine" took up only about four minutes, even when she added two extra ad-libbed verses and repeated the chorus five times. "Itsy Bitsy Spider"? Tedious, but good for a couple minutes more. There were always chores like vacuuming the inherited Oriental rugs, chipping away at old wax on the linoleum kitchen floor with a butter knife, and dusting her grandmother-in-law's Victrola from 1922. There were casseroles to bake and tomato sauce to can for the winter. She took me to ballet class once a week, and maybe attended the odd Tupperware party. *General Hospital* killed an hour each day at three o'clock. I always looked forward to hearing the swirl of the ambulance siren that served as its theme song; it meant I could watch beautiful nurses with faces as sad as my mother's (just wearing more lip gloss).

But sometimes Mom spent too much of the day in bed. Sometimes she cried by herself in the kitchen, her head on top of folded arms on the dinner table, hair falling limp around her shoulders, great heaving sobs racking her throat. I'd climb up on the chair next to her and stroke her hair as she wept. This only made her cry harder.

She needed an outlet—friends, and human contact with a person whose diaper didn't constantly need changing. My brother Simon had been born when I was four, and he was still in diapers. It was 1979, and the diapers were *cloth*, which was a commitment to say the least: She had to remove the saggy, fetid, soiled cotton square, the contents of which were deposited into a nearby toilet, the diaper itself into a separate pail to be dealt with later. Disposable wipes weren't on the market yet, so to de-shitify the baby, she used a wet washcloth, which, like the diaper, would need to be washed the same day. Into the pail it went. Time to fetch a freshly laundered but gray cotton square, employ the kite fold, or the trifold, whatever fold did the job, then pin the sides to fasten, and apply rubber pants to prevent any leaks. Launder. Repeat (ten times a day). She was twenty-six years old, and our father never once offered to help.

Dad wasn't the guy who knew how to fix stuff. Besides the handling of the firewood that would sustain us through winter, the one household chore that he regularly completed was mowing the grass in the summer. He spent hours every weekend tinkering with his Sears lawn tractor, filling it with gas, topping off the oil, then driving back and forth, back and forth across two fields of crabgrass. I could gauge instantly whether or not it would be a good day depending on the tractor's initial sound effects. If Dad climbed into the seat and turned the key only to be met with a rhythmic whine instead of the thunderclap of successful ignition, it was game over. He'd open the hood, jiggle some wires, try again, procure a wrench, loosen some things and tighten some things, all the while becoming more and more exasperated. If Mom dared poke her head out the door to the garage and ask if she could help—"Maybe it's a spark plug"—he didn't take it well. I often saw him clench a wrench in his fist like a murder weapon.

Though he was often smiling in public, Dad was just as quick to cloud up and rain all over you if he was in a bad mood. His tone of voice could go from casual to a punch in the face in the time it took for him to misplace his keys. A private rage seemed to fester just below the surface, and it didn't take long for him to access it.

One of my parents' early arguments became part of family lore. It was summer, and we kids were in the yard. Dad had been pruning bushes with hand clippers. Simon was tooling around on his Big Wheel. Mom had just set the picnic table for lunch and had fired up the charcoal grill for burgers. When smoke from the grill began pumping toward the house, she attempted to close the rickety old wooden garage door, which often came off track. There were a lot of things in the house that Dad told us to never, ever touch, and the garage door was number one.

Suddenly there was a screech of rusty metal and a bang from a large spring slamming into wood.

In that moment the whole world seemed to stand still. The clippers stopped clipping, the Big Wheels stopped turning. Before I saw Dad's face, I saw Mom's. Her eyes were wide with surprise as she tried to find whatever had come unhinged from the door. I heard the clippers hit the dirt and the awful pause before Dad's fury. He could never scream without spitting, and he waved his arms like he was trying to get the attention of an airplane in the sky. "What did you *do*? What did you DO! I told you never to touch the garage door!" he roared. "You are so stupid!"

Mom usually cowered when confronted, but this time she wasn't going to take it. "This is *not* my fault. I was trying to help!" she screamed. "Stop yelling at me!" The anguished look on her face gave way to one of determination. They circled each other, Dad's anger mounting, Mom not backing down. I stood in front of Simon, ready for anything. Then, with astonishing agility, Mom swiped a full bottle of ketchup from the picnic table, gripped its base, and swung it like a Louisville Slugger, the red sauce splattering all over the front of Dad's white cotton T-shirt. For a moment we all stared, stunned, then Mom grabbed our hands and we scrambled into the house.

From the kitchen window we watched as Dad picked up his chainsaw, yanked the pull cord, and cut down an apple tree in the yard, looking as if he were covered in blood. Later, this memory would remind me of the scene in *Mommie Dearest* where Faye Dunaway screams, "Tina, bring me the axe!" This would be a tale we'd tell at family dinners for decades to come—the time Mom fought back with condiments. There were a lot of domestic battles we'd laugh about once some time had passed. And there were some things I'd never find funny again.

———————

Mom was creative and needed an outlet. She knew how to knit and sew pretty well and thought she could expand her repertoire by taking a class. Before Simon was born she'd responded to a classified ad in the county newspaper *Good News* inviting interested ladies to a stitchery workshop in the home of a local artist named Jane. Mom noted that all of Jane's work depicted stories and verses from the Bible. In fact she was *in love with Jesus*, Jane said, and she couldn't help wanting to share what she knew with the world.

Jane had a daughter my age and understood the loneliness that could befall a housewife. Her husband, Lou, was not a churchgoer, but a beefy guy who rode a Harley and drank beer in the garage while listening to the Allman Brothers. The church frowned on marriages to nonbelievers, but it was Jane's mission to help bring the father of her children to Jesus.

Becoming born again appealed to my mother. It meant a clean slate for the soul and hope for a fresh start. The saved aren't your average believers; they're evangelical. It's not enough to believe in God, go to church on Sunday, and be a good person. You have to accept that God, a benevolent father, loves you unconditionally, in spite of your inherent flaws. In order to enjoy eternal life after death, you must enjoy a personal relationship with the Lord Jesus Christ, himself the

Son of God and heaven's property manager. Once you've accepted that Jesus is The Way, it really doesn't matter what awful things you've done or imagined doing; as long as you truly believe and actively help indoctrinate new members into the flock, you'll never be lonely again. Soon Jane was the shepherd, and Mom was her lamb, eating from her hand all the riches of the gospel. Eventually this art class would evolve into its own mini revival.

Jane adorned herself in bright colors and extra shoulder pads. She had a bold and sassy short haircut that drew attention to the enormous clip-on earrings she had to remove in order to answer the telephone. Her daughter, Sarah, was more of a tomboy, but Jane always made me feel lucky to have been born a girl. She had a trunk full of dress-up clothes: silk scarves, embroidered shawls with fringe, satin and tulle ballerina dresses from the fifties, a midnight-blue kimono printed with flaming orange koi, a red petticoat fit for square dancing, a white feather boa, a crystal tiara, velvet opera gloves. There was a proper dressing table in her bedroom, on top of which sat a GE Lighted Makeup Mirror (with four light settings for day, office, home, and evening). A silver tray held a selection of glass bottles—perfumes and creams and nail polishes galore. Stray sequins and tiny iridescent beads were forever being coughed up by their family cat. The occasional speck of glitter danced in the sunshine that streamed through the windows of her bedroom.

While our mothers stitched away, Sarah and I would build forts out of cardboard boxes in the basement, or Jane would set us up in her art studio at a big table spread with long sheets of butcher paper, individual bottles of Elmer's glue, and jars and jars of shiny things. Jane made organic Play-Doh out of flour, water, and salt for us to create sculptures, which she baked in the oven like cookies. She taught us how to tie-dye our T-shirts and puff-paint our Keds, and she didn't even freak out when we used the same techniques to decorate every pair of white underwear we could find in the basement dryer.

One New Year's Eve in the early days of Mom's joining Jane's church, Dad invited all his fun-loving agency friends to a party at our house. I could tell by the way she seemed angry with the dishes that she was not in the mood to play hostess. I'd been dispatched to my parents' bedroom upstairs, my arm still throbbing from the bruise of a booster shot obtained earlier that day. Not at all sleepy and in quite a lot of discomfort, I laid my ear to the vent on the floor and listened to my parents' familiar arguing. Mom was especially irritated this evening— she did not want drunk people crashing overnight, did not want dope in the house anymore. Did he really want to make her feel uncomfortable in her own home, especially with a feverish child upstairs? She had already begun planting the rumor to some mutual acquaintances that the party had been called off. Dad, not to be outdone, immediately got on the phone to cancel Mom's cancellations. Consequently, she was overruled, and no one got much sleep that night.

The ever-present cigarette in Dad's hand was another cause of their arguing. Dad liked to spend his weekends watching Browns games or golf tournaments, which enabled him to chain-smoke and drink the adult beverage of his choice. Even alone he would shout at our small TV screen if things weren't going his way. I had a fierce desire to understand what he found so interesting, this game that agitated him as much as my mother did.

One Sunday I made a place for myself on the couch next to him and pretended to understand what was happening on television. I followed his lead and reacted passionately to a player's fumble, and shouted along to his cheers as someone scored a field goal. Something happened on the screen and Dad leaned forward so quickly that he inadvertently singed the palm of my hand with his cigarette. The feeling was so surprising, sharp like the sting of a wasp, that I sucked in my breath and held it all the way to the kitchen, my only instinct to get to my mother.

Mom was washing dishes when I approached the sink, my hand

outstretched, the blister already forming underneath the circle of ash. She quickly replaced her hand with mine under the cold tap water and threw ice in a sandwich baggie. Sitting me down at the table with instructions to hold the makeshift ice pack tightly, she stormed off to the living room. Everything had happened so suddenly that I didn't know whose fault it was.

Mom returned with Dad's soft pack of Winstons and quietly emptied the box on the table in front of me. She held up a cigarette and broke it in half, encouraging me to do the same, and continued to methodically destroy each one. I refused and waited for the thunder of his footsteps down the hall, but instead he appeared sheepishly in the doorway, averting his eyes when he saw my hand.

"Apologize to your daughter," Mom commanded, angrier than I'd ever seen her. "You burned her hand!"

I was afraid to look in his direction and stared straight down at the table instead. I was angry at my mother for breaking the rules and the cigarettes. How many times had I heard him desperately cry out to anyone within earshot about the fate of his cigarettes? If he had to go without, if he'd unknowingly smoked the last of the second pack he kept in the glove compartment of the car, or if, God forbid, he'd misplaced the pack he'd just had—*No, it was right here a second ago, goddammit, did you not just see the last one in my hand?*—or failed to remember the cigarette behind his own ear, he very quickly melted down. His smoking disgusted my mother and she openly complained about it. But I'd never seen her actually make good on a promise to break a cigarette in half before, or flagrantly destroy the lot of them, not to mention interrupt a man watching a football game.

But instead of screaming like I was expecting, Dad sat down next to me at the table, looking more wounded than I felt.

"I'm sorry, E. I didn't do it on purpose." It was the first time he'd ever apologized to me, and I didn't know what to do with it. Did dads apologize?

Mom interjected, addressing him more than me. "Your father is going to quit smoking so this will never happen again," she said, eyeing him as he contemplated the pile of broken cigarettes—all cotton, paper, and dust. It might as well have been a shredded pile of money.

Mom went to the garbage bin under the sink and wordlessly swept the butts into the bag. We watched as she walked over to the can of Genesee Cream Ale that sat on a TV tray on the counter, meant to accompany the roast beef sandwich she'd just made him, and dumped its foamy contents into the bin overtop. As if in slow motion she crumpled the can with her hand and tossed it in with the rest, pausing to make eye contact with Dad before taking the whole mess outside.

I was so embarrassed. I thought that I'd just created all that waste. The waste and the defeated look on his face. Somehow the fact that he wasn't fighting back made me feel worse. Couldn't she have just fixed me without him knowing? I didn't run to tell him every time she was crying.

Dad asked if he could see my hand. I released my grip on the dripping plastic bag and we surveyed the damage together.

"It doesn't even hurt," I said, turning the ice over to him. I didn't need it anymore.

"You didn't do anything wrong, kiddo. I wasn't paying attention and I should have been. Your mother is right about the smoking. It's a bad habit." He leaned down and kissed the top of my head. "Do you want to punch me as hard as you can?"

It was something he did sometimes when I was hurt through no fault of my own (or his). He would squat down at my level, brandish his biceps, and invite me to hit him there, so that way we'd be equal. I started to make a fist but thought better of it when I felt the friction from the burn. I didn't want to hit him anyway. Experience told me that it actually hurt the hitter to hit someone as hard as you could, something that also occurred to me whenever one of my parents said, *This will hurt me as much as it hurts you* before a formal spanking.

I shook my head no. I didn't want to punch my father.

After a while we went for ice cream, the three of us and my baby brother, up the road a mile or so to our usual place, the frozen custard stand known as Dairy King. We ate our cones and watched the sun set over the road. Mom was quiet when Dad announced that we would all go to church together from now on, starting next Sunday. And that's just what we did. He would give her church, and she would concede to him his smoking, as long as he did it outside.

It would be a couple of years before Dad would develop a spiritual identity of his own, and even then it was hard to know what was really in his heart. But in the early days of Mom's conversion, she built a community through Jane's church and had other women to talk to about her discontent at home. Ironically, her newfound allegiance to this church meant that Dad—as head of the household—would only benefit from her subservience. Husbands—even the nonbelievers—were to be nurtured by their wives, who showed their devotion by quiet example.

Even before our dad came around, when Mom took up with what would become Fellowship Bible Church, she managed to convert her parents and her brothers. There had been the perfunctory Episcopalian church attendance back when she was a girl, but it wasn't until Mom started talking to them about the real spiritual change she was experiencing that they began seriously reading the Bible. Both my uncles were looking for a change in their lives. My grandmother traded smoking Larks during bridge night for helping to organize church potlucks. My grandfather wanted to leave painful memories of the Korean War behind him and get in touch with the concept of an afterlife. By the time I was learning to read, both my grandparents had been recently baptized.

At age five, I thought that Jesus had always been among us, and most of the people around me talked to and about Him all the time. I was young enough to still be pure in the eyes of God, already washed in the blood of the Lamb, so filled with the hyperbole of the Holy Spirit that it bubbled up and overflowed. You couldn't hide my "light under a bushel," *I was gonna let it shine.* The thing about Jesus was that you never saw Him, but He was always listening. And all pronouns attributed to Him were to be capitalized.

When I was six, it became important to me to get saved. I wanted to do it myself, to have my own conversation with the Father, ask if He could take away my sin so I could be born again. I memorized my little prayer and took it to the bathroom for a private chat—just us guys. *Dear Heavenly Father, I'm sorry I'm bad. I want to invite You into my heart so that I can be a beacon. In Your name, amen.* After I asked Jesus to come into my heart, I tried to imagine Him watching me, proud the way grown-ups were proud whenever I did something right. I tried hard to feel the love. After a time I got the urge for some feedback and went to tell my mom and grandmother about what I had just accomplished. "I just got born again!" I said.

My grandmother clapped her hands up under her chin with delight, letting loose her patented "Oh, Erin!" She and my mother had been deep in conversation but both seemed pleasantly surprised by my revelation. I liked their response so much that I announced I was going to go and do it all over again, just to make sure He'd heard. All that talk of saving, needing a savior—I pictured Jesus as a handsome superhero, Superman in a crown of thorns. No wonder we were always in trouble. It was kind of fun to imagine being rescued.

Following Jane's example, Mom began to attend special luncheons, prayer groups, and conferences to learn how to better glorify God in her home, and sometimes she brought me along. The largest such gathering was called Women Anew. The guest speakers were jaunty ladies who traveled cross-country from church to church wearing silk neckties and opaque taupe panty hose with sensible pumps. They'd come to share personal stories of feminine transformation and how you, too, could learn the careful art of submission. Long experienced in the evangelistic ministries, the speakers always began with a deceptively contemporary, Erma Bombeckian bon mot meant to bond the group—something like "All of us have moments in our lives that test our courage. Taking children into a house with a white carpet is one of them." The speakers were greeted with good-natured laughter and audible *Amens*.

Most of the women focused on the importance of being married, as man and wife were the foundation of any family. Divorce was a huge bummer for Jesus—you were allowed to leave your marriage only if your spouse was a nonbeliever who was abusing you into a spiritually bankrupt lifestyle. But frankly, if the abuse was in keeping with scripture, and it was being dispensed by a godly man, then there might be a problem with your definition of obedience, and you should do all you could to follow through with God's plan for you.

A woman was meant to be a helpmate to her husband, his biggest fan, a "creative counterpart." *Creative Counterpart* was also the title of one of my mother's handbooks on maintaining a Christian marriage, of which there were several. These were owners' manuals for homemakers that promoted the idea that husbands were created in God's image, and God was meant to be followed, served, and obeyed.

Creative Counterpart, *Fascinating Womanhood*, and *Disciplines of the Beautiful Woman* were some of the most dog-eared of Mom's collection. (It's worth noting that all three of these books are still in print, each with updated editions.) Their marginalia revealed an earnest young woman's quest to be a better wife and mother, a more pliant supplicant. A common theme among these books was a focus on the importance of organization as a key virtue. "If you forget to do something your husband asks you to do and he becomes angry, accept it as God teaching you that you should write things down so you won't forget them," advised the authors of another guide to happiness called *The Fulfilled Woman*. It was essential to keep a daily planner in which to record your to-do lists, topics for prayer, appointments, and snippets of scripture to be analyzed; a good Christian woman's notebook was invariably awash in the ink of a thoughtful highlighter.

Mom listed in the margins several Bible verses that referred to dutiful humility—citations from Romans, Isaiah, and Proverbs. Even before one's earthly husband, God was woman's "Heavenly Bridegroom."

In *The Fulfilled Woman*, she drew a circle around a paragraph declaring that a man's actions are almost always the result of a woman's attitude toward him.

I was beginning to see the light.

From *Creative Counterpart*, here's a list of (paraphrased) lessons one could take away from Mom's course of study on human husbands:

1. Men need quiet.
2. Men need not be nagged for failing to put discarded clothes in the hamper or for any other reason related to their right to comfort.
3. Men need sex on demand.
4. Men need you to look and smell your best. Think of yourself as God's secretary.
5. Men need you to be super organized so they don't have to be.
6. Men need you to look the other way and keep your opinions to yourself.
7. Men need you to create an atmosphere befitting the king of the world.
8. Men need you to take care of the kids.
9. Men need you to build them up and make them feel like they can win a beauty contest.
10. Men are always right, even when they're clearly insufferably deluded.

And here's the (official) list of a wife's "priorities" in order of importance, to be pasted prominently in your notebook, according to author Linda Dillow.

1. God
2. Husband

3. Children
4. Home
5. Yourself
6. Community

In order for this to work there had to be an underlying assumption among women that men could be manipulated into competence (thus women were really the ones in control). Smart women knew that men needed to believe that they were the main event, that all the good ideas were theirs to begin with. Men worked too hard not to be the shining star in the relationship. If you really deserved it after a long day of raising children and keeping house, your husband might throw you a bone once in a while in the form of a handful of long stems, or, if he was feeling particularly grateful, a trip to Epcot. (Wherever you were lucky enough to go on vacation, insist your husband choose the destination.)

Dad was glad to see that his wife was finding herself through all this transformation, but not as enthusiastic about affiliating himself with any church. He considered himself to be a progressive thinker; he knew that everybody needed something to believe in. Once Mom's pleading for him to participate became more insistent, he seemed to get that it was important to their relationship; it was important for their children to know that they were of one mind.

My father really got into enthusiastic church attendance when Mom and Jane started a singing ensemble. The fledgling church did not have a choir, so the two of them decided that, rather than complain about it, they'd start their own. After Jane's invitation during announcements one Sunday for any women interested in accompanying her in "making a joyful noise unto the Lord," four more women joined the efforts. That's how His Harmony, a contemporary praise sextet, was born.

Mom had grown up in a musical family, and spent her high school years singing in Glee Club. That she was a born performer came as somewhat of a shock to me—Dad seemed more likely to be the one onstage—but soon she was taking voice lessons and, inspired by her favorite Beatles ballads, was moved to develop her considerable skills as a songwriter. She eventually wrote more than fifty songs. Before long, the group would take their show on the road to perform at other churches, nursing homes, and weddings. They would ultimately keep it going for six years, and in all that time Mom missed only one practice—the night she gave birth to my little brother Greg in 1980.

The group was a perfect addition to Fellowship Bible Church, which would become known for employing the arts in order to be distinctive and attract the next generation of Christian soldiers. The congregation was growing and with it the idea that more people could be spiritually moved through a theatrical sketch or an interpretive modern dance performance than could be by the same old solemn hymns. Like the Supremes before them, the ladies of His Harmony wore coordinating outfits, each donning a different take on the same colorful theme. (Darlene wore cap sleeves, Jane three-quarter length, Mom long sleeves with a puffy shoulder.) My favorite of His Harmony's oeuvre was an early Christian rap duet meant to speak to the youth. The chorus:

It's hot, It's hot
In the fire of Hell it's hot
Well, I don't wanna go there, how 'bout you?

Before long, Dad became the group's George Martin—he would contribute by offering his production skills as their soundman, and even booked space at a recording studio in Cleveland for them to cut a demo. He beamed from the back of the church as he fussed with the mixing board and bragged about his beautiful wife and her many talents. He bought her first guitar, and gazed at her like she had a halo when she played. It didn't matter that it wasn't rock 'n' roll; the fact that they were songs about love was enough. I'd never seen him happier.

3

CRY BABY CRY

ONE DAY, MOM'S CHURCH FRIEND CINDY came over with a gift for the house. We all gathered around and watched as Mom gingerly unwrapped the surprise. Inside the paper was a two-foot-long wooden paddle, lovingly hand-hewn in oak by Cindy's husband. It featured six round holes drilled into its lower half, known to reduce wind resistance for a faster swing and memorable impact. Inscribed in black Sharpie, one side read *Dare to Discipline*; the other, *Spare the Rod, Spoil the Child*. From that point forward this weapon would hang in plain sight on the kitchen wall next to the mustard-yellow rotary phone, replacing the belt or wooden spoon as the preferred method of punishment in the house. But mostly it just sat there as a threat.

As a child, I wasn't really "bad," but I didn't exactly do everything I was told to do, and Mom spent a lot of time trying to reason or negotiate with me to no effect. A typical exchange when I was a kid:

"Erin, put away your toys."

(No response.)

"Erin, if you put away your toys, I'll make your favorite cookies."
(Not worth it.)

"Erin, I know you can hear me!"

If she grabbed my arm and gave me a swat on the butt, I'd sit on the floor and scream as loud as I could, huge tears gushing, and then sequester myself for a nap. Either way, my mother picked up my toys in the end.

———————

One Sunday after service, when we were waiting for Dad to pull the car around, a woman named Helen approached Mom and me, her eyebrows furrowed, ferret-like, over two black beads of eyes. Helen personified the color beige and had the posture of a dictator, aided by her unfeminine brown flats. She was dour—certainly nothing like Jane—and didn't wear any makeup, which increased my distrust.

Years later I'd imagine Helen as Margaret White, the batshit crazy maternal force in Stephen King's *Carrie*, coincidentally published the year I was born. Her devotion to penance, to constantly reminding children that a voice was something to be shushed, that there was no such thing as an intelligent question, that your body was the vessel against which pain and suffering must be wrought—these were the tropes of Helen's faith. I found her boring. What kind of grown woman, having finally achieved full agency and the ability to acquire cosmetics whenever she wanted, would choose to go out in public without lip color?

"Paige, some of the other moms and I have noticed that you seem to be having a little trouble with Erin," she said to my mother. "She's awfully willful." Helen turned her gaze to me. Mom was adjusting the straps on my brother's car seat; I had been pulling on her skirt.

"Well, she's six," Mom said, sifting through her purse for a little box of raisins for me, a promised reward for sitting quietly through service.

"Yes, and it's not too early to introduce corporal punishment. I have found it's a very effective deterrent to defiant behavior. Children can be very manipulative, especially daughters, but who's in control here? If you spoil her she'll never learn her place," Helen lectured.

Mom was already insecure about her parenting skills—in those days, there was no way to know if you were doing it right. I didn't exactly snap to attention when she told me to do something, and I didn't always come when I was called. I was living in a dream world. I had a tendency to isolate and challenge my mother when I didn't want to do something (and also to sleepwalk and pee in bedroom wastebaskets, to confess to one of my more anomalous behaviors). In contrast, Helen's two boys were perfectly behaved. They were quiet and polite, and there was never a wrinkle in their clothes.

"Naturally you've got your hands full with the baby. Let me take Erin for the weekend for a little Bible boot camp. I'm not apt to be as charmed by her as you are."

———————————

The following weekend Mom dropped me at Helen's, where I would stay while her husband was away on a business trip and her own children were at their grandma's. Mom and Dad would have a long weekend alone to nurture their marriage. Right off the bat I felt like I was in trouble. Being banished to a tower whose custodian was a miserable grump was not my idea of a good time. I couldn't imagine why I had to go by myself and why I was permitted to bring only one toy from home. Would Helen have colored pencils, paper for drawing, books to read?

Helen's house was full of uncomfortable furniture that left the backs of my legs imprinted with crosshatching after even a short sit. After prayer in the morning, followed by an hour of Bible class, Helen had me organize her kids' Lego stash. Then it was time for carrot sticks and milk. The peanut butter and jelly sandwich Mom had packed from home had disappeared completely. "In our house, you'll eat what I eat," Helen had said after I'd asked for pancakes that morning. "Too much sugar is part of what's wrong with you," she'd added ominously. Was there no way to please her? After lunch, I was sent to take a nap, something Mom didn't ever force on me. If I was sleepy, I would sleep; otherwise I was permitted to play quietly in my room. But here, rules were rules.

The first night I was there, *The Wizard of Oz* was on television, and I rejoiced and clapped my hands at the sight of ruby slippers. Helen frowned and asked, "What do you know about it?"

"My mom lets me watch it. It's a kid's movie!" I said. Mom and I had watched it together when it aired annually on network television. We sang along to the songs the Munchkins sang and I hid my eyes when the Wicked Witch of the West made her appearance.

"It most certainly is not for children," Helen spat, looking past me toward the television. "And I don't think you should watch any more television tonight. It rots your brain."

Helen seemed hell-bent on making me feel bad about being alive, about deigning to exist. I was sent to bed early, where I could hear her watching the adventures of Dorothy from the bedroom down the hall.

The next morning after breakfast Helen told me a Bible story in the kitchen. Abraham had so much faith in God that he waited one hundred years to be given a son, Isaac. As a test of Abraham's faith, God told him to take Isaac to a mountain and kill him as proof of his devotion. Even though it made him sad, Abraham did as he was told and set about sharpening his knife. Just as he was about to kill Isaac, an angel appeared to call it off—Abraham had passed the test of faith, so Isaac's life would be spared and both of them rewarded with riches. Helen asked me if I understood how difficult it must be for a father to have to hurt the child he loved. I nodded. "But when God tells us to do something," she said, "we shouldn't question it, but trust that He knows what is best."

The confusing thing about Helen was that she didn't appear to have mood swings like Dad. When I did something wrong, her tone of voice remained neutral; she was utterly unsurprised. She calmly told me to play with the Legos, then left the room. She returned a few minutes later to tell me to stop playing with the Legos and put them in the basket. The first time she asked me to stop I was so absorbed in the task at hand—putting the finishing touches on my stairway to heaven sculpture—that I don't think I heard her. Then she came over to where I was playing and quietly took the Legos out of my hand and said firmly, "In order for us to do what we're told we must be able to receive what God is telling us He wants. You must learn to listen." She took my hand and led me to the kitchen.

"Does your mommy have a wooden spoon?" Helen asked as she procured one from a drawer. I nodded.

"Do you know why I'm going to have to use the wooden spoon on you today?" I did not, and shook my head no.

"Because you disobeyed me by not stopping what you were doing when I told you to stop. It makes God very sad when you don't do what a grown-up tells you to do." Helen went on to say that she'd warned me of these consequences just that morning after breakfast. Had I already forgotten Abraham?

Helen told me to pull down my pants and put my arms above my head. With one hand she squeezed my hands together at the wrists and told me to count down from ten. Between each swat of the spoon I'd howl as Helen came down ever harder on the backs of my legs until I couldn't feel anything but the sting of sin and regret. Afterward, we prayed for forgiveness and Helen told me she felt really close to me. We had gone through something special together, something she knew I would never forget.

Among the sins I committed that weekend: not finishing my broccoli, failing to rinse my dish before putting it in the dishwasher, taking too long to emerge from a nap, forgetting to recite a daily Bible lesson, telling Helen that she was mean and I wanted to go home. Each time I'd be sent to procure the wooden spoon. Now I had to deliver the weapon of my own punishment. Each time I'd count down from ten. Each time she'd hold me afterward and tell me she forgave me, that God forgave us both.

When Helen returned me to my parents after three nights, I was badly bruised on my arms and legs and had fresh welts on my bottom. Mom was mortified by how much discipline I'd required, and felt like she had been punished, too—judged for being too lenient and not taking a firm enough hand with her children. But she was also disturbed by the way I had grown to interact with Helen. Upon returning, I was angelic in Helen's presence, not wanting to be separated from her, calling my own mother *ma'am* like a stranger.

Helen must have liked the feeling it gave her to break my spirit, to beat the child out of me. Though it was at her hands that I received the most physical pain, it was my mother I held responsible and blamed for outsourcing it. I expected the physical punishment to come from a man, because discipline was naturally a father's domain. But here was another woman doing the Lord's work while Mom preferred the passive approach; she was terrible at follow-through. She once cried in my arms on the bathroom floor after failed attempts to spank me with a hairbrush. She may have been inconsistent with hitting, but when I was old enough to start rebelling with language—committing the mortal sin of taking the Lord's name in vain—she had an easier time pushing my head under the bathroom sink to shove a memorable bar of Dial soap in my mouth.

It's in scripture—Proverbs 23:14: *Thou shalt beat him with the rod, and shalt deliver his soul from hell.* A permissive, nonspanking parent was a parent who hated her own child, and was in fact guilty of abuse by neglect. What better way for a kid to learn that disobedient actions yield painful consequences than to have the people who love you most in the world do the punishing? It was how our parents were brought up, and their parents before them, except back then it was way worse, and look, they had turned out just fine.

According to the literature on the subject at our house, the church provided some guidelines. Spanking was necessary to correct bad behavior and instill humility in an overconfident child. It was always meant to be a last resort after fair verbal warnings went ignored. In order to prevent added shame and embarrassment, it should never be carried out in public. If you were angry while you hit a child, it was thought that she might receive the confusing message that love and violence go hand in hand, thereby making her less likely to leave an abusive relationship down the road.

The proper protocol was to remove the child from the group and take her to a private room, ask her to acknowledge what she had done that required you to administer a spanking, tell her you felt betrayed by her disobedience but were glad to hear her admit responsibility. Tell her to lean over the bed, or your lap if she was too small, give her three hard swats with a board, communicate grief—cry if you feel like it, tell her it was for her own good, then hold her on your lap as she cries. She'd get the right message, which was that people who hit her did it *because* they loved her. (Which, in the end, it seemed to me, ultimately led to the same outcome: she would be less likely to leave an abusive relationship down the road.)

What always tripped Dad up was the one where you were never supposed to administer beatings while you were angry. His tendency was to accelerate from zero to out of control, spontaneously. Even his tone of voice changed at the moment of truth; you could hear the silent swearing behind every word of rebuke. The more I tried to squirm to prevent the impact of the belt and cover my ass, the angrier he got. "*I'm not going to tell you again. Move your hands . . . Move your hands. Move your hands!*"

I can remember only one formal spanking where he wasn't spitting with rage. I was much older when it happened, at puberty. The sin I'd committed was not cleaning the fish tank when I was told. When we discussed it beforehand I tried to bargain and come up with alternatives—perhaps we could skip it and not tell anyone we skipped it. But it was a foregone conclusion. I think it was awkward for both of us, the bending over the knee, the use of the hand; the embarrassment stung more than the hitting. I remember feeling that I had to win his love and respect all over again. When it was finished I thoroughly cleaned the fish tank and called him into my room to show him my work, looking for absolution, for him to forgive me.

After Helen, I began to distrust and avoid the adults responsible for my care. *Protect me*, I'd pray whenever I'd inevitably done or said another wrong thing. As I got older I would lie in the bathtub and try to clear my head by visualizing life after death and the infinity of space, the soul, the war between good and evil. Imagining burning in hell for all eternity made me feel both dizzy and defensive. Why would God have gone to the trouble of making me and giving me free will, if He knew all along that I'd just end up in hell?

I don't want to get involved was God's reply. *This is between you and your father.*

4

IF I FELL

IT WAS A BEAUTIFUL PURPLE SCHWINN with glittery silver handlebars and streamers falling from the handles. I was excited about all the
ways I could accessorize the thing before I even knew how to ride, still
believing that my first bike was going to be the best thing to ever happen to my seven-year-old social life. Though somehow I sensed that I
wouldn't have long to master this skill. Dad had little patience when
it came to slow learning.

A natural athlete, he loved to compete. He was captain of the
swim team in high school and as an adult skied cross-country and
downhill. In his midforties he would switch to snowboarding. Baseball, kite flying, Frisbee, cycling, throwing the football around the yard
with the guys from the office, even badminton—these were games he
played on the regular. I think Dad was disappointed that ballet turned
out to be the only physically strenuous activity I ever pursued in my
youth. He was looking for playmates, and he found them in Simon and
Greg, who would go on to enjoy many good times with him on skis

and on the golf course. Vail every winter, Pebble Beach every summer. Sports were the way they connected.

Maybe it was because I was the firstborn, but when it came to athletics, Dad held me to a higher standard than he did my brothers. With me, he was the throw-her-into-the-deep-end-of-the-pool type. *Swim!* With one exception: the time when I fell down my first bunny hill on skis. Then, he begged me not to move until he could make sure I wasn't hurt, got down on his knees, wiped the snow from my cheeks, and said, "You scared me."

Before I got my bike, I'd ridden a Big Wheel around the partially flat portion of the driveway, but never anything more sophisticated or upright. I was confident when operating a vehicle made of plastic and low to the ground, secure in knowing no one would ever be thrown from a Big Wheel. But the Schwinn was tall and made of metal; it had treaded tires and a kickstand.

"Where are the training wheels?" I asked Dad. My friend Katie's training wheels had stayed on for half a year while she was learning.

"Training wheels are for little kids," he said. "Completely unnecessary. It's so easy, and once you learn how to ride a bike you'll never forget it. It's a skill you'll have the rest of your life." Dad was using his rah-rah voice, the same one he used when he tried to get Dusty, our dog, to fetch.

He straddled the bike himself and demonstrated how to catch the ground with one foot and use it as a brake. He talked about balance, and showed me how to coast and ease to a stop by gently pushing backward on the pedals. We did lots of repetitive stops and starts—where I pushed off on the pedals but then dropped my foot flat on the ground—until I finally felt comfortable enough to proceed. I worried that I wouldn't be able to coordinate all my body parts in order to propel the bike while also steering, but Dad promised that he'd run alongside.

"Don't let go!" I yelped.

"Will you trust me?" he asked, holding the back of the bicycle seat.

"Don't let go—"

"You've got this. You're doing it," he said. I heard the big grin in his voice but didn't dare turn my head away from the front wheel of the bike. "That's good, that's good. Now turn just a little and lean into the turn."

I did what I was told but overshot when I realized his hand was no longer on the back of the seat. I quickly wiped out.

"What are you *doing*? . . . You had it!" His arms hung at his sides, palms out, his whole demeanor a question mark. "Pick up the bike and try again."

"You promised you wouldn't let go," I whined, but he wasn't listening.

"This time, I want you to go as far as you can without stopping, and when it's time to turn, I want you to turn, but not as sharply as before—just follow the curve of the driveway."

"But will you be there? Will you hold on like you promised?" I asked.

I wanted reassurance that I would not be expected to be perfect at this, that he wasn't going to let me fall.

"Goddammit, what is so hard about this? Just do it, Erin. Listen to what I'm saying to you, and do it." I could tell by the tone of his voice that I didn't have long to get it right before he'd lose his temper. "This time I want you to try it yourself, that way I can watch and see what you're doing wrong."

I got back on the bike, bit my lip, and pushed off, following along the curve of the driveway. But the act of looking up broke my concentration, and I lost control of the handlebars and steered off course.

"Straighten out," he called out, exasperated. "Do it again."

Again I got back up on the bike, and again I was too shy. Before long I slowed to a stop and lamely looked for guidance.

Dad was all out of patience. "I'm not going to tell you again. Either get up on that bike and ride it, or I'm going to take it away. Stop acting like you're going to cry or I'll give you something to cry about." I couldn't understand why I was so terrible at this bike-riding thing, but I was perfectly willing to set it aside for the day and try again another time, maybe with Mom.

"Pedal. Pedal. Pedal" was his refrain. "Pedal . . . Pedal, pedal, pedal.

Keep pedaling." The bike propelled forward for four easy turns of the wheel, but if I didn't stop or turn around I would have to go down the gravel-strewn hill of our driveway. Was this a trick?

"I can't do it," I said. "I'm stopping." No sooner had I popped off the back of the bike than Dad's hand came down on the back of my shorts, a spontaneous punishment I hadn't expected. I started to cry.

"You're acting like a baby," my father yelled, spittle flying, enraged. My incompetence disgusted him so much that he roughly grabbed the bike and headed back to the garage with it.

———————

By age nine, I'd finally mastered riding my little purple Schwinn, though the joys of cycling were still foreign to me. I rode my bike down our dead-end street when prompted, though that was spoiled, too, by the cruelty of nature, of rural living: Once I ran over a black snake that had stopped to sun itself on its way across our road. I wasn't able to avoid it at the time without crashing, so I picked up speed and screamed as loud as I could. I expected to feel the cruel *ba-bump* under my tires or perhaps swerve from the impact, but neither of those things happened. When I cycled back the snake was gone. How I longed for the absence of rolling hills, for the even smoothness of a parking lot. Pave "paradise," please: it would seem much safer.

Despite my basic competence, Dad insisted that better times awaited if I could just join him for epic rides on the back roads of Amish country, like Mom once did. That year, he'd started in on me about it after Christmas. It was time for me to get a *real* bike, he said. "It's so much better when you can switch gears. You'll really be able to go fast then."

I disliked being pressured to go fast, but to him going fast was the whole point: I'd see what I had been missing. As it happened, Dad had gotten Mom a companion Raleigh ten-speed racing bike with twenty-six-inch wheels, and she didn't seem to mind at all if I wanted to take her place on the road with him that spring.

I'd passed by the Raleigh a hundred times, and filed this bike under Things in the Garage That Don't Concern Me. Now that the silver monster stood before me, resting menacingly on its kickstand, I felt like I'd been handed a spaceship. It was a virtual replica of Dad's racing bike, slightly shorter. Still, the seat came up to my chest. The next thing that worried me was the presence of a "boy bar," the horizontal pipe that stood between your genitals and solid ground. I contemplated the curled handlebars as if they were ram's horns—ones that required you to maintain an unnatural forward bend if you were going to reach the brakes or gears. I'd never switched gears on a moving bicycle before; it seemed incredibly counterintuitive. Dad tried to explain the basics: The lever on the left side of the handlebars controlled the large derailleur (*de-what-eur?*); the lever on the right controlled the small one. Pushing a lever forward would make the bike more difficult to pedal; pushing it back would make it easier.

I searched Dad's face, looking for the punch line. "Why would I want to make it more difficult?" I asked.

"Because you just do sometimes, for fitness, or to pick up more speed, cover more distance. And you'll see—it gives you more control when you're going up and down hills." He was patting the bike seat like it was a saddle on the back of a horse, still another childhood obstacle I'd have to overcome in the name of fun.

"I really don't want to go faster," I said, pushing my arms deep in the pockets of my jeans and taking a few steps back. He couldn't possibly think I was going to be able to actually ride this thing. "Why can't I just ride my old bike?"

"Because you've outgrown your old bike, and I want us to be able to go on some real rides together. Come on, Erin, it's easy," Dad said. "This is the best part of growing up."

And so I climbed onto Mom's bike in our gravel driveway. The bike was so large he needed to hold it while I mounted, my feet barely reaching the pedals, with foot straps too loose to slide into. I held my breath and leaned forward, grasping the level top of the handlebars so tightly I could see the veins in my hands. We started on flat ground at the top of the hill and I cautiously pedaled forward, shakily rolling along the gravel, onto the grass, circling the very large apple tree and back onto the drive without falling, an amazing feat.

"That's great, I knew you could do it. I want you to do it again, except this time I want you to push the gear lever forward on your right side when I tell you to, and don't stop pedaling." Again I went around the apple tree, still feeling unsteady on the skinny tires, not meant for grass or crumbling terrain. I did manage to push the gear forward without falling, but the hollow space it left during the transition from one gear to the next made me feel like something had broken inside the bike, and I didn't like it. As I was moving around the loop, I moved my hands forward to slowly press on the brakes and was horrified to realize the left one was stuck. Before I could effectively figure it out I had moved past my father at the top of the driveway and soon found myself about to coast down the gravelly hill. Panicking, I started to scream.

"It's okay," Dad called after me. "You've got this, just gently press on the—"

"I can't stop! No brakes! No brakes!" I could feel the rush of speed picking up, I could hear him chasing behind.

"Squeeze the brakes!"

Finally I was able to push forward to brake, but by the time I got it I was already coasting down the hill of the driveway at full speed. As soon as the brakes took effect I flew right over the handlebars into the ditch just before the road, which was buffered by thickets of blackberry bushes. I ended up with a stinging thrash of gravel and scratches from prickers and thorns. Too shocked to feel any pain, I lay on my side in the ditch above the dusty road, pine, maple, and the craggy arms of the hickory tree rising to my left. I rolled onto my back and Dad's face flopped down from the sky, tree limbs shooting out from his head in all directions like lightning bolts. His face was still too dark to see from where I lay twisted in the brambles, but I could hear him as clear as the voice in my head.

He was laughing.

5

TWO OF US

WHEN GREG BEGAN TO FORM INTO AN ACTUAL PERSON, at age three or so, Simon and I bonded over our resentment of him. As far as babies went, Greg had been the delightful kind. He rarely cried and his joy could not be contained; every day was a good day to be alive for the bouncy swing. When Mom sang in church he would smile and kick his feet while Simon and I cringed with boredom. He constantly inspired praise from every adult lucky enough to encounter him.

When he began to talk, Greg said the darnedest things. When Mom laughed and called him "goofy" for sticking his finger in his belly button in order to connect with outer space, he paused before answering, "I'm not Goofy, I'm Mickey." He had a thing for hats. During one summer family vacation, we went to an amusement park on Lake Erie and stayed overnight in the resort hotel. All weekend Greg refused to take off the new sailor cap that Mom had picked up from the gift shop. He preferred to sleep in it, but when Mom finally convinced him the hat needed to rest, too, he slipped it under his pillow for safekeeping. Early the next morning, we were at the exit gate before Greg realized that his hat was no longer on his head. He wept hysterically until Dad ran back to the hotel to find it. *What a baby*, I thought to myself, about a baby.

It was hard not to be jealous of such an innocent human. I couldn't remember at what age little kids crossed over into being sinners. I'd started early, to be sure, but I sensed that Greg had what it took to maintain his perfect record with both our parents, as well as with the big guy in the sky.

Sometimes when I was supposed to be having quiet time with God, an imposter's voice would take over and tell me to do something that ended up displeasing Him. Like the time I hid in the coat closet in my fourth-grade classroom for the first half of the day just to see what would happen, to see if anyone would notice. I wanted to know what it was like to be God Himself, the quiet observer of all things. I stood behind the accordion doors, through math and reading and social studies. The coats hanging on hooks smelled like winter and delousing agents, with top notes of cat.

When recess finally convened, I simply met my classmates on the blacktop. My name had been on the attendance sheet; I had simply not been missed. And yet, after spying on my class all morning, I felt like a creep. I reasoned that at least I had heard the lessons, so it was almost as if I'd been there. Only God knew that I was a fraud.

According to my teacher that year, I was much too vain. She told my parents that I spent too much time in front of the mirror at home and not enough in front of my reading assignments. By the looks of it, I had a rich fantasy life, she said, but a poor grasp of what was really important. She accused me of cocking my head to the side in class to make my hair look longer after I'd gotten an unfortunate haircut. She failed to realize that the haircut was an homage to a Bonne Bell lip gloss ad I'd seen in *Seventeen* magazine—it was asymmetrical on purpose. Still, it felt like God—using Ms. Murphy as a conduit—wanted me to feel ashamed for wanting to be seen.

It was under the gaze of Dad's camera that I was most in his thrall.

Even when I was going through an awkward, uncute stage in my adolescence, I would will myself to be pretty. I would do my damnedest to project prettiness in spite of what I knew was at best totally average, gawky, and unspecial. I wanted the responsibility that beauty required, to be on at all times because one never knew who, or what, one might inspire. I wasn't content to just be—I wanted supplicants. I was the girl who would throw herself a grade-school graduation party in our backyard, invite the entire class, and perform a dance routine to Madonna's "Material Girl"—complete with lifts provided by two male classmates. That's the self-esteem boost I was given every time I saw myself through my father's eyes.

Dad liked to walk around on the weekends with his 35mm Pentax around his neck, wearing his old jeans faded to perfection and his Nikes (when he said this word, it rhymed with "bikes"). He took moody, cinematic pictures of my mother and me as if they might appear in a feature on our family for *Life* magazine. He always crouched down to my level, making himself kid-sized.

Me as a blue-eyed baby with a head of tousled brown hair, learning to prop myself up on my favorite blanket, a patchwork quilt hand made by my hippie godmother, Greta.

Me holding newborn bunnies in an ivy patch in the yard, my hands cupped to gently cradle the little bodies, fretting that I'd be responsible for their deaths. I'm wearing my OshKosh denim overalls, my bangs exactly the same as the ones I'll have more than thirty years later.

Me in plié in fifth position, my arms in second.

I learned to pose without posing, sometimes interacting, sometimes not. In pictures I am often contemplative, lost in thought or deep in concentration. Or I am looking into the camera, the thing that yields another way to be loved.

Meanwhile, Mom was so unguarded that you could see her plain unhappiness, and yet Dad made each photo of her look like a fashion still. Even when Mom looked bored or pissed off, she somehow became even more beautiful. If she happened to have been crying, all the better. Her vulnerability only added depth to the image, elevating it to art. She was nothing like Dad's secretary, who wore creamy silk blouses and a delicate ankle bracelet over her panty hose, which were a shade tanner than what I'd seen in church. She also wore perfume, something Mom abhorred; if she wanted to smell fresh she'd spritz herself with a tangerine peel. She didn't have to try.

Mom wearing a sheer gauze top, a scarf on her head, leaning in the doorway, eating yogurt out of a plastic cup, the sun streaming in through the screen door behind her, a halo of light around her pregnant stomach.

Mom, some months later, lying on the green velvet couch with our cat propped on her now enormous belly. The room glows red and yellow, Mom bathed in light from the lamp behind her, propped upright on the couch, her honey-brown hair tousled in her eyes, impossibly beautiful in her reverie.

One Friday night, when I was about seven, Dad came home from work and announced that he was taking me to the "playhouse" and that I'd better pick out my prettiest dress to wear. I wondered what kind of playtime ever asked you to dress as you would for church—wouldn't our clothes get dirty when we played? Most exciting of all was that there were only two tickets, and even though Mom had been standing right there, Dad had picked me. Even once I learned what really happened at a playhouse, even after many outings, I always felt very fancy and important—even famous—when I was accompanying him to the ballet, the symphony, or the theater.

The other thing that was just ours: On weekends I went with Dad to visit one of our neighbors, Mark, a musician in his twenties who had muscular dystrophy. I'd grown up knowing Mark. In the years before he relied on a wheelchair, he could still walk with help from his older brother, who would carry Mark's bass on his back and lift him up the stairway to our back door. He'd spend whole afternoons with Mom playing guitar. She had been taking lessons and obsessively practicing the chord progressions and picking rhythm of "Blackbird" in our living room. Her teacher suggested that she match the rhythm to the words "*grass-hop-per but-ter-fly, grass-hop-per but-ter-fly*," which she'd say aloud while playing.

Mark was one of us, an obsessive Beatles fan. During our visits, we would hang out in his bedroom and pore over his impressive collection of memorabilia. The walls were painted a dark color to better offset the professionally framed posters of John, Paul, George, and Ringo, as well as the various collectibles that were housed in a glass cabinet—original buttons, actual tickets to the two historic Cleveland concerts, trading cards, a yellow submarine keychain, Beatles dolls with synthetic hair that you could brush, and a Fab Four lunch box. He had every album in its first pressing, and a stack of image-heavy scrapbooks to look through.

I first started taking a particular interest in these visits around age ten. They made me feel older and more sophisticated, like I was going to an art museum. Even though I thought a lot of the stuff they would talk about was really boring and over my head, Dad was at once patient and enthusiastic about explaining the significance of each song, record, or piece of memorabilia. He didn't treat me like a kid or a little girl; he treated me like he treated any die-hard fan, like a friend. Even when I saw the first naked adults I had ever seen—the picture of John and Yoko holding hands on the cover of *Two Virgins*—the uncensored subject of rock 'n' roll was never off-limits. This was the place where I felt like I could hang with the guys.

These conversations changed the way I thought about music. Bands, to them, had stats like baseball teams, and these stats were something to be discussed at length. Dad and Mark solved the Beatles versus Stones conundrum (of course the Stones had that bluesy edge and, ultimately, longevity, but the Beatles revolutionized music in less than a decade), then they moved on to other debates: Which was the true final Beatles album, *Abbey Road* or *Let It Be*? (Consensus: *Abbey Road*.) What was the best album the band ever made? (Mark: *Revolver*; Dad: *The Beatles*, aka the White Album). Mono versus stereo? (Consensus: it depended on the album.) Who was the definitive

Beatle, the most important songwriter? (This argument was ongoing and circuitous, but I walked out of there leaning toward Lennon.) Best art direction on an album cover? (Me: *Sgt. Pepper*, hands down.) Mostly I just listened, but every time I expressed my opinion, I felt like I was finally fulfilling my father's expectations.

Before rhythm and blues, popular music was polite. The big-band stuff that old people danced to at weddings, or Frank Sinatra—that's what was topping the charts when my dad was a kid. As musicians, the Beatles took from Chuck Berry, Buddy Holly, Little Richard, and Fats Domino (and Jerry Lee Lewis and Elvis and the Shirelles) and created a sound that inspired pure emotional and physical mania the moment it graced its listener's ears. Then they grew and changed and reached their full potential in a decade's time, and we're all still listening.

My father taught me why "A Day in the Life" from *Sgt. Pepper* was the rare example of a perfect song, composed of two halves—one by Lennon, one by McCartney—that were totally different in sound, yet perfectly complementary. *And* the song featured an orchestra; the piano chord that closed it was more than a minute long. He'd remind me that John and Paul were still teenagers when they wrote "Please Please Me." I learned to identify a sitar because of "Norwegian Wood," and tape looping in "Tomorrow Never Knows." There were backward vocals in "Rain," the first time a band had used that recording technique in a pop song. My father could talk ad nauseam about the significance of the invention of artificial double tracking on the vocals on every song on *Revolver*. I preferred these "classes" to the ones I had to take about the Johns and Pauls of the Bible.

6

CARRY THAT WEIGHT

BY THE SUMMER OF 1984, our parents were finally a power couple in Christ. When Dad saw how much more smoothly the household was running once Mom had transformed herself into the kind of wife who prioritized her husband above herself, he came around to her way of looking at things. I think he had a genuine faith, and he was disciplined about church attendance and meaningfully involved with ministering the gospel, especially with the youth group. Even after His Harmony had disbanded, Dad stayed on as the sound engineer for Sunday services, sitting in the back of the chapel at a small mixing board, carefully adjusting the controls. We were a Christian family of five.

Now that I was almost eleven and Greg was entering elementary school, our parents began to spend more time away from home, working on music and attending more church functions. This was fine with my brothers and me. We had a good thing going with the other misfit kids of Rider Road, who tended to band together in order to have enough bodies to play a decent game of kickball or help each other search for crayfish in the creek.

The neighbor's house across the field, one house down, was a hotbed of adolescent activity. There lived Butch, fifteen, our de facto leader, and his fourteen-year-old stepbrother, Joel, who was usually there in the summer and sometimes on weekends. They both had actual muscles and shadows of scruff or dirt on their faces; they sweated like men. Down the road, a nine-year-old eccentric named Donnie lived with parents who often seemed too preoccupied to ask about his whereabouts. Donnie was a bit of a would-be juvenile delinquent, the kind of kid who killed frogs. The other girl child on Rider went by the name of Fat Nathalie—she was twelve. She had the most permissive parents, but she rarely left her house, though if you made the bike ride down, she would show you the R-rated video of Duran Duran's "Girls on Film."

I don't even remember a time when Butch wasn't like a big brother to us. He must have moved there four or five years before, when I was too young to know any different. His family had an edge ours didn't; I heard my parents refer to them as "secular," which I took to mean "lightly satanic." But they had an aboveground pool and an Atari console, and over the years our property lines just fell away. Sometimes when Mom was at Bible study and Dad was working late, Butch's older sister would babysit. Once she turned eighteen, she left home to join the army, and since none of us kids ever drowned in their pool or got into trouble, Mom eventually let us go next door whenever we wanted to. Maybe our Christianity would inspire Butch and his family to see the light.

That summer it seemed like Butch was always trying to get me alone. I'd vowed to stop going to the tree fort in the woods behind our houses by myself, even though I'd been granted special entry privileges. I didn't have to provide any passwords or secret knocks, and I had a key to the trunk that Butch kept locked in the corner. But since the school year had commenced some older friends of Butch's had been coming around. The usual collection of cassettes and paperbacks had been replaced with dog-eared porn magazines and crushed packs of Camels. The walls had been plastered with pictures of naked women with thickets of pubic hair and enormous nipples, their mouths open and pink and waiting for something.

The last time I'd gone to the fort I'd thought I was alone. It had been raining all week and it seemed an unlikely time for anyone to be there. After weather like that, the moldy plywood made for a soggy, mosquito-ridden shelter and the shag carpet remnants smelled of cat pee. The whole place felt grimy. But I liked to go up there after school sometimes to be by myself, listen to music, and generally plot my social ascension at Burton Elementary.

On heavy rotation in my Walkman that year were Michael Jackson and Prince. Butch had *Off the Wall* and *Purple Rain* on vinyl, which I'd listen to when visiting. Recently Dad had gotten me some kind of advance copy of *Thriller* on cassette, which immediately rendered him the coolest dad in the world. None of my friends' dads had any music connections.

The trapdoor in the floor was covered, the sign that no one was home. To enter, you had to climb the ladder and slide the makeshift handle to the side once you got to the top. Maneuvering the plywood by myself could be tricky, but I had lots of practice. I knew just where it would stick and when it would need an extra push to make space for my body to go through. Once halfway in, I used an inelegant hoist-and-flop maneuver with the floor as leverage to crawl up the rest of the way. All that mattered was that I could do it, but I was glad none of the guys was there to judge my technique.

I pulled myself up on my knees and slid my backpack off, squinting to adjust my eyes to the light.

"Hey, kid."

I turned my head to the corner of the room. Butch sat cross-legged on the floor under the lone window. The boom box was in his lap, but no music was playing. He wore the same T-shirt he always wore then—the cover image of the smoking baby from Van Halen's *1984*—the one we had taken turns shooting with Donnie's BB gun one day during a heat wave. As kids, our main mission in all activities was to destroy something. Guns, fire, water, explosives (however small), spray paint—we never lacked ways to leave a mark.

On top of the tackle box beside Butch was a lazy pyramid of empty beer cans. He didn't make a move to get up, and I couldn't tell if his eyes were open or closed.

"I'm sorry. I thought no one was up here." I started to move back down toward the light from which I'd just emerged, but Butch waved me over to him instead.

"Where you going? Come here."

I looked at his face and tried to read his mood. Why hadn't he opened the door for me? He must have heard me coming; it would have been impossible not to.

Even though he was only four years older than I was, Butch had always seemed like a man to me. He was taller than Dad and had the beginnings of a mustache. Butch knew how to build stuff and fix things and play sports with ease, and he always had a tan. I supposed that made him handsome. I sometimes tried to imagine what it might be like if, when I grew up, Butch wanted to be with me. I pictured us sitting in a hammock side by side, talking about our plans. He was a fireman, I was a nurse. A Dalmatian puppy sat between us.

Nathalie was always talking about the guys in Duran Duran being *gorgeous*, but maybe that was because they wore *women's makeup*. At the time, my dream man, if I had to think about future boyfriends, was Michael Jackson. Secretly a lot of my prayers lately had been MJ-centric. *Please, God, if he could just come to Cleveland, there might be a chance for us to meet.* Then I would remember that God could see me lustfully kissing my Michael poster before I went to bed every night, and I felt embarrassed and ashamed. But Butch wasn't like Duran Duran *or* Michael. He was a different kind of masculine.

There was a single mattress in the tree fort, a grimy pinstriped thing rescued from the curb, a rumpled and damp wool blanket its only cover. There was nowhere else to sit, but I looked around anyway.

Butch seemed really tired. I told him I didn't want to interrupt, that I'd just come here to read, and that I could easily return later.

"I'm glad you're here," he said. "That's why we built this place. You have just as much right to come here as I do."

I looked around at the porn and felt small. My body was still girlish and undeveloped and the women's bodies looked three-dimensional, almost inside out, from their places on the walls. I could not imagine what it might feel like to have breasts, to have hair under my arms or anywhere else. But the boys around me just kept developing, and sex was their main topic of conversation. Butch was watching and waiting for me to talk.

"Will you do something for me?" he asked, not looking me in the eye. "Will you trust me?"

"What do you mean?"

"Will you trust me if I want to do something?" he asked, then was already halfway on top of me, making himself heavy, spreading me out. And then his body eclipsed mine, and I held my breath and waited while nothing happened and nothing was said. He smelled like sour, dying things, and I didn't, in fact, trust what he was doing to me, so I held my breath some more. After a minute he adjusted his weight so that his arms were pinning my arms and I practiced thinking that this might be normal, and then I remembered that God was watching. He lay on top of me for so long that I worried he might fall asleep there, but after a while he sat up, and he let me sit up, and then he dusted himself off and said, "Thanks."

By the time school was out the following summer, our pack had reassembled in our adjoining yards, a typical day. I thought we were too old to be playing hide and seek, but there were younger kids around and Butch was trying to be inclusive. He grabbed me around the waist and threw me over his shoulders like a sack of potatoes in one dizzying motion.

"This one's on my team," Butch announced to the kids, and then he was running with me on his shoulders as if I were a flopping, oversize Raggedy Ann, then someone was counting in the distance, and someone else was telling us we'd better run. Nothing good ever came of hide and seek. Last time, Donnie's hiding place had intersected with a yellow jackets' nest and the wasps swarmed and stung him until he passed out.

I whooped and screamed and made my body as rigid as possible as I bounced along on Butch's shoulders. I both loved and hated the feeling of being picked up, hated the way it pulled and stretched at my muscles as I struggled to hold my stomach tight, and loved the abandon that came when I closed my eyes, exhilarated by the idea of falling. Or maybe I had just liked it as a baby, when I was truly small and it was Dad throwing me up in the air and catching me.

I pummeled Butch's shoulders with my fists until we were out of sight across the yard, and just as fluidly as he'd snatched me up, he let me down again, and then he was taking my hand and leading me toward the brush and the pines that surrounded the property and led to the woods beyond.

Something about this felt inevitable. Fated, I guess. I wasn't afraid, but I braced myself for anything as soon as he started whispering in my ear. *"Just keep really still."*

Stillness was something I'd been practicing since I was little. Sometimes I'd practice looking as close to dead as possible; did he know I could hold my breath till I passed out? Didn't he know that Jesus could hear through silence?

I was on my stomach and he was on my back. We'd crouched behind a wild briar patch that lined a part of my family's property, our house, only partially visible through a thatch of thorns and shrubs. I could feel the sap from the pine needles starting to stick to the cotton of my clothes. Butch had pushed me down gently, my body as low as it would go until I just turned my head to the side and rested my face on the bed of orange needles. It was futile to try to squirm away. He made himself heavier and nuzzled the back of my neck and made a shushing noise in my ear that signaled to me that I should just trust him and let whatever was going to happen happen. Afterward I would wonder why he hadn't just asked me for whatever it was he wanted to see, to know about, to take from me.

For some reason I thought of the opening theme from *The Muppet Show*, the last thing I was permitted to watch on television before bed. I still couldn't figure out how exactly the Muppets and the human guest stars coexisted. I thought it had something to do with a rehearsal process for actors and musicians; when John Denver wanted to get ready for a tour, he went on *The Muppet Show* to practice with puppets instead of real people.

It's time to play the music.

Butch licked my ear as he slid his hand down the inside of my jeans. I could smell the Skoal in his spit on my neck. I cursed my prepubescence. *He's going to want there to be hair down there and there is none*, I thought.

It's time to light the lights.

You think that if you know about a bad thing, you can somehow avoid it. If you prepare yourself with information about how difficult a situation might be, it can't happen to you, or at least if it does you'll know just what to do. There I was on the ground, cursing myself for not recognizing the signs, for not fighting harder to stop it.

I knew what was happening was called "being molested," and I was mortified that it was actually happening to me. I had won the shame lottery. I felt the scar of it burrowing through my skull and into my brain, recording it forever. What else is there to do when a man holds you down to satisfy his curiosity: whimper, say, *Hey, what . . .* , squirm politely, then lie perfectly still, counting. I stayed in my body and counted to somewhere in the three hundreds. By the time the *Muppet Show* theme song played once through, I knew that no matter how long I'd live, this would be a defining event in my story, the day I learned what women knew.

Immediately the following typography flashed like a billboard in my mind's eye: IT'S NOT YOUR FAULT. I was thinking of all the "very special episodes" or afterschool specials I'd seen on the subject, the embarrassed cops who came to our school annually to talk to us about the dangers of gangs and drugs and what to do if someone in your family was hurting you. It was the first moment in my life when I had the sense I was inhabiting a cliché, my own personal birth of irony.

After he had finished, the event was over almost as quickly as it began. Suddenly the tension in the air normalized. When his hands were out of my pants he dropped the faux tenderness routine and we were back to not being found during hide and seek. No one had even come looking.

"Come on, let's go find the others," Butch said, getting off me and sweeping leaves and burrs off us both.

"You cool?" he asked.

Was I cool?

"Yeah, sure," I said.

But I felt scalded on the places where his hands had been. I had a flash of panic that Mom would take one look at me and know. The thought of that was too much to bear. I pushed it out of my mind. Butch seemed to be acting already as if nothing out of the ordinary had happened. I would simply fall in line and do the same.

Afterward I sat on the edge of my bed in my room and thought hard. Okay, this thing had happened and it wasn't my fault. But. I had imagined what it might be like to kiss him before, hadn't I? Imagined our being together when I was older? Therefore I'd probably sent him a signal, an invitation. Hadn't I been experimenting with lip gloss and studying the "Guide to Flirting with Boys" in *Seventeen*?

But. What about all the secrecy around being alone, and the weird holding-me-down thing? Maybe what had happened was a test of some kind, the lead-up to a more adult relationship, an initiation into puberty.

I also worried I was being melodramatic. After all, it could have been worse. I could have been raped, but instead he'd been gentle. He'd said he would never hurt me, and except for the scalded memory, he'd kept his word. This seemed within the range of possibility of normal, even though I was young and weighed less than eighty pounds. Maybe my preternatural maturity and knowing sense of humor had belied my status as an elementary school student. Maybe he was confused by his feelings for me and felt terrible because he hadn't realized my true age (even though I'd known him since I was in the fifty-pound range), but now that he'd done it he'd know I was still a kid and leave me alone.

No matter what, it was an untellable tale. Not once was I tempted to tell my mother. She would die, I was sure of it. She'd blame herself and there would be so much talking and crying. And Dad—it was too much to imagine. What would he do? I thought of the space in my bedroom closet behind some family snowsuits and Stephen King paperbacks, on the high shelf. Sometimes Dad hid things from Mom there, usually just the Christmas presents, but then there were other things like the books and the Oreos and that gun. A shotgun wrapped in a towel above the clothes that hung in the closet. I'd never heard anyone mention it, didn't know how long it had been there, if it was loaded, what it was for, only that it was there. Just another reminder that adults lived by their own rules, and those rules were none of my business.

For once I kept my mouth shut.

———————

Soon after that, at twelve, I began to feel even weirder around boys. It seemed like there were more of them than there were of us girls, and neither group seemed to know its own strength. Fourth grade recess had turned sinister after Rusty Childs introduced the game known as Pussy Patrol to our schoolyard. Pussy Patrol was kind of like Smear the Queer. If you were a girl and "it," you had to run as fast as you could and slide into "safe" (usually a specific tree on the outskirts of the playground), but if you failed and the chaser caught you, he'd grab your crotch outside of your clothes as hard as he could and squeeze, all the while yelling "Puuuuussyyyyyyyy Patrrrrrroooooooool" at top volume. Afterward, the chaser would have license to report to friends on the outline and overall volume of what was between your legs. The existence of Pussy Patrol became a very good argument against wearing skirts.

Here was the thing about this game: it was exciting. Only certain girls seemed to get picked, and not the ones who couldn't handle it. Those girls were easily recognizable: the crybabies and the bed wetters and the ones with silk ribbons tying up pigtails, the ones who played in groups and pushed each other on swings, kicking their legs and squealing like baby pigs. The "it" girls, though, we were operating on a different level. We didn't scream or narc when a kid pulled his thing through his zipper and tried to scare us. We didn't say anything at all. When they stared at us, we stared back. We had skinned knees and scars under our chins and dirt under our fingernails. At sleepovers, we practiced frenching on each other, not just so we could be prepared for the "first kiss," but because we liked the way it felt. We knew our role was to run until we were caught.

I ran hard and almost always made the safety of the tree, but when Rusty, the avowed creator of the sport, took me down and grabbed me there, he barely grazed the area, only making it seem like he had grabbed me. He was careful with me, I believed, because he secretly respected me. He liked me and this was how he proved he could be trusted, just like he needed to pretend that he was hurting me to save face. The truth was I didn't mind being tackled by Rusty, not like I did with the other boys. He never screamed when he caught me, so I never screamed, in return. In that way, it was like we'd shared something. The other boys all treated that place between our legs like it was just another thing to bruise.

———

The summer before seventh grade, my best friend, Michelle, and I went to Geauga Lake, a just-okay amusement park not so far away from home. We liked to start with the ski lift ride that overlooked the grounds. That way we could scope out the lines for the Corkscrew and the Big Dipper, map out a plan for the afternoon. When we passed other riders as both sides of the conveyer merged, we scanned the chairlift for kids our age. One of the lifts held two bearded old men, doughy and smooshed together behind the safety bar. As they got closer, one stuck out his tongue and flicked it in and out of his mouth and the other openly stared and said to his friend, and to us, "Mmm, yum . . . young cunts."

We pretended not to hear them, just sipped our pops and waited, and when they had passed Michelle rolled her eyes and said, "Bikers are the worst." I didn't even know what a young cunt was, only that this was the way it was now. Something about a girl bothered some men, irritated them, caused them to stop and stare and comment on what they thought of the way we looked, or worse, the way they thought we should look.

"Smile!" the man at the mall told me when I noticed him staring at me as I waited for Mom outside Higbee's.

"Smile, it's not that bad," barked a guy in a hard hat at Michelle when she was walking home from school.

"You'd be so much prettier if you smiled, ladies," prompted the security guard as he held the door open for us at the bank.

When it came to social interactions with strangers on the street, neither of us could imagine a grown woman imploring us to smile. And what kind of person just went about her day grinning to herself like a lunatic? We got this request so frequently that when we were bored we would try to make up witty comebacks, the best of which was Michelle's:

"Why don't you give us a smile?"

"Because my mom is dead."

———————————

The summer before eighth grade, the only thing I was both young and old enough to do for money was babysit. Put me to work, I told our congregation. If I was qualified to be a big sister to two boys, I figured I could handle the responsibility. I'd augmented my résumé by receiving CPR training, but word of mouth wasn't leading to any gigs. It was still the eighties—the workforce was full of kids back then. I wanted a new peach-colored sweatshirt from Z. Cavaricci so I could go to the roller rink and learn how to be vulnerable in front of cute boys with long-distance phone numbers. My parents were not about to increase my lunch-money-size allowance, so I would need to get serious.

My father had a brilliant suggestion: put an ad announcing my skills in the local free newspaper that was always sitting in piles at the grocery store. So I wrote up a classified ad promoting myself as an experienced, responsible, literate teenager with first aid experience and a photographic memory for the poison control chart. Unfortunately, I was too young to drive and would need rides to and from clients' homes, but this seemed a reasonable exchange for three-dollars-an-hour child care. The ad went in the paper on a Wednesday, and within twenty-four hours I had a gig in a neighboring town with a four-year-old girl and her younger brother, still in diapers. Simon and Greg had once been two and four; how hard could it be to keep kids that age alive for a few hours?

"That sounds exciting!" my mother said after I hung up the phone in the kitchen. "What did she say?" The woman who'd called told me her name was Liz and that she'd be by to pick me up at three o'clock the next afternoon. Some adults were having a no-children-allowed party somewhere and I would have the kids all afternoon and until the middle of the night. They'd try to make it home as close to midnight as possible, and someone would drive me home after. But the children would go to sleep around eight and I'd have whatever videos I wanted from Video Time to keep me company. I'd already planned on renting *Beverly Hills Cop*, which I'd been forbidden to see till I turned seventeen.

When Liz came up our driveway, her Impala's exhaust was a sputtering black cloud of warning. There was practically a *dun dun dun dun* following her up the sidewalk and into our kitchen. Mom didn't seem fazed in the slightest by her appearance, which I immediately recognized as trashy. Liz's hair was thick and straight and oily, and hung down the middle of her back like a horse's tail. She wasn't wearing any makeup, and her teeth were snaggled and yellow. A red tank top stretched over her eight-months pregnant stomach, which unsettled me further, as if I'd also be responsible for the fetus. A fresh cigarette rested behind her ear. Chain-smoking while pregnant wasn't so uncommon in these parts, and maybe it was rude to judge any woman this far along in her pregnancy; she was doing God's work by even having it at all. We exchanged pleasantries.

"Have fun," Mom said as I was halfway out the door. "No R-rated movies, okay?"

The back seat of the Impala was littered with garbage and a too-long seat belt whose metal clasp shone in the sun. The stale and crusty remnants of McDonald's french fries and empty cigarette packs littered the floor. My thighs stuck to the vinyl. Another woman with blond hair was sitting in the front seat.

"Hey, girl, I'm Carla, Lizzy's sister-in-law," she announced, and turned to me in profile. I was relieved to see that she had a naturally pretty face and freckled cheeks. Beauty made everything a little lighter somehow. As we began the drive to the house, the women conversed about the upcoming party.

"There's a nigger's baby in my belly," Liz hollered back over the seat to me. "I guess you could say I got a weakness."

Carla snorted and whooped. "Damn right. You know what they say . . ."

"Once you go black, you *never* go back!" They shrieked in unison.

I didn't know what to say, so I stared out the window and braced myself.

As we drove, Liz and Carla talked to me about the children, whom Liz regarded as two snarling balls of *pick me up, more,* and *wah.* There were a few things I should know about the boy: Junior was enormous for his age, and seemingly possessed by a suicidal demon. When having a tantrum, he would sometimes knock his head into or against a wall. He had a knack for climbing out of his crib and up onto window ledges. Neither Liz nor Carla said the word "retarded," but at thirty-two months Junior had to wear a helmet pretty much every day, and sometimes to sleep. He had twice survived serious falls, once out of a moving car.

"Not this car. His daddy's van," Liz said casually. "If I were him I'da probably tried to jump out, too. Kid's got a psycho for a father." Carla shook her head in agreement, sighed, and turned up the radio.

The car sputtered and revved as Liz weaved it down a gravel drive lined with a few shacks and trailers, each on a small lot separated by chain-link fences, a makeshift trailer park. We pulled in to the largest house on the road, a charmless, ramshackle two-story structure held together with different-colored sections of aluminum siding. A leaf-strewn baby pool sat outside, a hose still snaked over to it, dripping at its edge.

Inside, Liz gave me a tour. The color scheme throughout was mostly brown and orange, a classic combination best described as "remnant," a theme in seventies furniture I think of as "GI tract." The rust-colored shag carpeting in the living room must have survived a few crime scenes, and it held an odor that reminded me of a camp-fire that had been snuffed out indoors. The kitchen was a nightmare. Despite a preponderance of natural wood in the house, wood-grained contact paper covered every surface but the floor—walls, cabinets, even the fridge was covered with that paper, which had a stucco of eggy crust. The surfaces were filthy and piled with dirty dishes and debris and crawling with bugs.

A lot of weird adults were milling around, too many to keep straight, but there were no children in sight. A blond woman with Far-rah Fawcett hair sat on her boyfriend's lap and was loudly regaling him with tales of her period. There was no door to the bathroom, though the woman using the toilet didn't seem to mind who saw her as she talked with a man who sat drinking a beer on the edge of the tub. A bald man wearing a black leather vest smoked a hand-rolled cigarette out a window and stared hard at the driveway. I wondered if I should be worried—or if I was worried enough, rather.

Liz told me the house rules, mainly that there were none except that her soon-to-be-ex-husband was Not Allowed Anywhere Near The Kids. If I saw him or his white carpet-cleaning van, I was to call the police first and ask questions later; the number was on the fridge. At first I thought this had to be some good-natured ribbing, a little hazing for the new babysitter, but no one laughed.

"I got an order of protection says I don't have to deal none with that son of a bitch," Liz announced, getting the attention of the smoking biker, who nodded his head solemnly and continued to fix his eyes on the yard.

"Or it's a restraining order . . . whatever . . . he ain't allowed in here." Liz pointed to a picture of him on the mantel next to an older son, who was now in prison. "Just so you know what to look out for." The man in the picture was thin and white and had a horseshoe mustache.

I finally laid eyes on the kids when Liz was showing me the bedrooms upstairs. The little girl appeared to spend her sleeping hours on a mustard-colored foldout couch not far across the room from the toddler's crib. (No sign of a helmet.) The kids were naked but for their diapers, their faces sticky with snot and Dr Pepper. The little boy was clearly doomed, but I was struck that there was nothing sweet about the little girl, either. These children were botched right out of the gate because this house was a petri dish for a serial killer. Everything was grimy, as if a family of gravediggers lived there and never once wiped up a mess or vacuumed a carpet. There appeared to be blood on the floor by the tub. Cheerios crunched underfoot; SpaghettiOs adhered themselves to the linoleum flooring in the kitchen. It was the filthiest house I'd ever seen, the filthiest family. Now I understood the meaning of the word "trash" as it applied to people.

After Liz and her friends left, I considered calling Mom and confessing that I was in over my head, but it was too late to turn back now. How would I even explain where I was, not knowing the roads? I couldn't even remember how long we'd driven to get there. Anyway, I was probably being a conceited brat, hoping for a posher setting. These kids didn't know any better than what they had, and I might as well just start cleaning up the worst of it and begin with the crusty

SpaghettiOs. I was putting on a happy face and searching for a bottle of Fantastik under the sink when I noticed a white van pulling too fast into the driveway.

I wasn't sure it was real until a man was already out of the truck and crashing up against the rickety screen door, thwarted by the mechanism that locked from the inside. In one clumsy motion he simply put his hand through the hole in the screen, reached down, and pushed the meager latch to the side.

I put the baby to my hip and grabbed the little girl's hand to usher them into the adjacent living room, cursing the fact that the only phone I knew about was back on the wall in the kitchen. By the time we moved through the room he was already inside.

For such a small guy, he had a big voice. "Who the hell are you?" he barked. The children seemed to know him, or at least nobody but me was flinching. The little girl dropped to her knees and started crawling on the floor.

"I'm the new babysitter; I'm just here to watch the kids tonight. Liz hired me. I'm sorry, but I don't think you should be here right now—she didn't mention expecting any visitors."

"Visitors? Girl, I ain't a visitor, that there's my baby son and I'm the only daddy that girl's ever known!" He started to address the kids, and I held on to the boy, who began to squirm wildly in my arms.

At the sight of me struggling, the man put both his hands to his head and grasped at his skull. "Listen, girlie. I need to have a talk with you in private. Put the boy down and let's you and me go upstairs for a minute." I wondered why he didn't seem to want to hold his son if he'd gone to the trouble of breaking the law to come over here.

"I'd feel more comfortable if we talked right here," I said, surprising myself at my directness.

"I don't give a shit where you feel comfortable, let's git up there, c'mon now . . ."

"Okay," I said, trying to appear normal. The baby was heavy and fussing. I set him down near his sister. "Will they be okay here by themselves?" I asked, wanting to do the right thing.

"Okay as they're ever gonna be," he said, and gestured for me to take the stairs before him. *He isn't much bigger than Dad*, I thought. I dutifully climbed the stairs to the second floor.

In the kids' room, he looked shaky, and I could see he was having a hard time focusing his eyes. That, or he didn't want to look me in mine. Our foreheads were both beaded with sweat. The air was stuffy and close, and the setting sun's light blazed through the bars on the windows into the room, dust dancing in its rays. I knew that most of what made dust was actually our dry skin shedding in the wind. Dead skin. Dandruff.

"Sit down," he instructed. There was nowhere to sit but on the bed. I sat on the edge of the pullout mattress, careful about my posture. A rubber sheet crinkled beneath me. If I pissed myself from fear, I wouldn't have been the only one that day.

The madman paced in front of me and ranted. He wanted me to know that his ex had taken unfair advantage, that he wasn't as bad as he'd been made out to be, and not half as bad as she was. All he wanted to do was see his kids, love his kids. He hadn't even known the baby she was carrying wasn't his till a few months ago. *That cheating whore caused the incident that led to the restraining order. She's the worst possible parent, a nigger lover to boot. And she should know that nobody can keep me out. A man can't be put out in his own pasture.*

I was sure he had brought me into that room to rape me, but as he ranted I noticed that he seemed very nervous, like this wasn't easy for him, like he wasn't sure what he'd meant to do, bringing me up here. Maybe I could connect with the father in him, like the way I wished Mom would try to defuse Dad when something stupid set him off. It seemed to me that if a woman could provoke a man's anger, she ought to be able to discourage it from escalating.

He stopped pacing and appeared to contemplate me for the first time. He cocked his head to the side and looked at me like he could tell what I was thinking.

"Is there something you want to tell me?" he said, his face an angry question mark. "Do you *know* something?"

"It's obvious that you really love your kids and kids need their dad," I heard myself say. "And nobody has to know you were ever here."

He turned away and stared at the bars on the windows.

"No one will be back for hours," I added, completely unaware of what I was giving him until the words had escaped my mouth.

"Why don't you have a visit with them now?" I continued. "I was just going to start cleaning up the kitchen." So normal. I tried to project that I wasn't the kind of babysitter who squealed, while also emanating a confidence that I was in it for the kids. For what seemed like minutes but was more like a long pause, he just stared into the middle distance in the direction of the window.

Finally he looked at me, his eyes twitchy silver pins. "You scared of me or something? Don't be. *You're* not worth the effort."

Just like that the trance was broken and he went back downstairs, picked up his kids one at a time and then put them down again. Then he called the place a dump and left, the van's tires spitting gravel at the baby pool as he peeled out of the drive.

I never mentioned it to Liz, never called my parents to ask for assistance or advice. I never told anyone but my best friend after the fact, believing I'd been spared any violence precisely because I'd known enough to bargain with a volatile man.

If someone would have asked me at the time if I'd ever been afraid of a boy or a man, or if I'd ever been victimized or traumatized by one, I would have said no. I would have denied it because first and foremost I didn't want it to be true. In one context, the threat that men posed to me seemed minor—I'd already proven to myself that I could take the pain of getting hit, so the mental stuff seemed all about endurance: don't dwell on the horror, and pat yourself on the back for being a good sport.

With Butch, I reasoned, it could have been so much worse. He could have hurt me, tried to make it scarier—but he obviously cared enough about me not to. I'd had it relatively easy, considering what happened to some girls.

Even much later, once I had more of an understanding of how

these experiences shaped the way I viewed my place in the world, I still shunned the idea that I was either a victim or a survivor. Who would want to be part of a club that conceded that initial defeat—that whoever he was, he got under my skin, even caused me a moment's trauma? Men were ticking time bombs—mentally, emotionally, and physically—so it was up to me to find a way to soften the blows, either by appearing perfect (and therefore worthy of respect and protection) or by hiding the truth of my own burgeoning power.

My father had taught me well.

7

RUN FOR YOUR LIFE

WITH PUBERTY CAME AN INCREASING AWARENESS of my rights as a person. Post-Butch, whom I'd been successfully evading for a couple of years, I was beginning to question my parents' judgment when it came to other people. I had a budding sense of feminism and felt I'd seen enough to know that my mother was a doormat. I had been watching *The Phil Donahue Show* after school, which I believed made me the most sophisticated member of the household. I'd learned from Phil Donahue that not all kids got smacked around at home, for one thing, and some so-called Christians behaved horribly all the time, such as to gay people with AIDS or to women who'd had an abortion. The news was littered with sex scandals involving prominent evangelicals, and no one at church could give me a straight answer about anything. *Christians make mistakes. As long as one truly repents, God will forgive.* It was too easy.

I had zero interest in becoming a member of the youth group. I knew it wasn't for me after I attended a session devoted to Jesus's thoughts on rock music, only to find that it was basically an ad for the Christian metal band Stryper—and that our "hip" spiritual adviser felt strongly that Bon Jovi's "Livin' on a Prayer" should have been retitled "Livin' on a Wish" because to use "prayer" in a nonspiritual context was blasphemous.

Once I entered puberty, my mother took me to more and more gatherings of Christian women designed to help me get in touch with my own personal "fascinating woman." Unfortunately, in the eighties, "fascinating" meant frosted lipstick and a permanent wave. Being a mascara-wearing Christian meant using Mary Kay cosmetics; with its signature powder-pink packaging, it was the godliest makeup on earth. The selling of Mary Kay was one of the few legitimate careers for women that felt sanctioned by the church. It was a way to make money while caring for children at home and socializing with friends. If you sold enough you could win a pale pink Cadillac for your family.

The Holy Spirit's beauty secrets appealed to me. It was important to know your "season," what colors flattered you most, the colors that He intended, whether you were an autumn, winter, spring, or summer. Did you look better in warm colors, such as cream and rust, or was stark white more reflecting of the glory of God? The draping of different-colored fabrics across my shoulder and against my skin revealed that I was a winter, but I had a tendency to dress in a spring palette. Royal violet was a winter's destiny, but I liked to wear powder blue.

I resisted modeling myself into Christ's girlfriend and embraced high fashion instead. Sneaking them between my textbooks at the local library, I inhaled *Vogue* and *Vanity Fair* and any other women's magazine I could find every month. The church ladies didn't have the option of cleavage, platinum hair, or a miniskirt. It seemed to me that there was no adventure in the natural look—in a funny way, there was no truth in it. The best part of being a girl was getting to choose to become the one to shun the neutrals in favor of reds.

As traditional as our church members could be about gender roles, at least my parents respected my right to express myself through the way I dressed; as I'd learned from Jane, style could be a virtue. But I sometimes found myself exposed to other, more hard-core denominations of the faith. I heard them referred to as "Old Testaments," the Baptist, Methodist, and Pentecostal churches, whose doctrines were more strident when it came to anything creative or fun, unless you considered speaking in tongues to be a viable pastime.

One day at some sort of interfaith picnic, my mother befriended a woman from a nearby Baptist church who had a kid my age. It seemed to please her that I was twelve, "such an important age," she assured me—not that I'd asked—and invited me to come to their family church's weekly youth group Bible class. One of the things I didn't know about the King James Baptists was that they were traditionally nitpicky about the way women and girls should look. The women in this church all had long hair that they'd officially stopped cutting for Christ, and wore a daily uniform of full skirts and long-sleeved blouses, the very picture of unadorned, vanilla modesty.

Maybe if I'd known this going in, I wouldn't have opted to wear my new favorite outfit: bubblegum-pink faux-leather pants by Gitano, paired with a white sleeveless shirt—to show off my perfectly tanned arms—and my mother's pink linen scarf, worn as a shawl, all topped off with several gold chains. The only difference between this look and one I'd wear to the roller rink was the pink feather roach clip I'd wisely deemed to be too much. I didn't know that some churches considered what I was wearing to be an act of cross-dressing, that I was implicitly advocating homosexuality or some other form of general deviance by being so conspicuous. I saw pink pleather and I thought "dressed up."

I must have looked to all in attendance like some kind of plant, put there to confuse the humble congregation of sheltered youth. There were only about a dozen of us in all, and the group leader decided to use my presence as a teachable moment, and commenced an impromptu sermon on what not to wear if you didn't want to look like a whore at church.

"Deuteronomy twenty-two, five, says, 'The woman shall not wear that which pertaineth unto a man, neither shall a man put on a woman's garment: for all that do so are abomination unto the Lord thy God.'"

Oh. *Pants.*

The pastor, who was wearing a brown polyester suit, went on to explain the roles of godly women in the family and in church. "It's not that you ladies are inferior to men in the eyes of God. It's that Eve was created after Adam for a reason—to show that her place is subordinate. Eve was created to support Adam by mothering his children and keeping him honest and spiritually inspired." He went on to tell us that the most important attribute of any woman was her virtue. After all, women hold all the influence. Because Eve first fell for Satan's forbidden fruit, then used her powers over Adam to convince him to join her in defying God's laws, the consequences were pain during childbirth for all of womankind, and eternal damnation for all mankind, unless we repented.

Vanity was a sin. Taking pride in one's looks or expressing oneself with ornamentation was immodest, and therefore a sin. Money should never be spent on worldly things such as showy jewelry or clothes. Short hair on a woman was disrespectful to God's vision of femininity; long hair on a man was disrespectful, too. I looked around at the other kids in the group. A striped polo shirt on a boy looked to be the most radical embellishment in the room. Nobody seemed fazed by the message, nor did anyone say anything to me about how I was dressed.

I tried to imagine back to the days of Jesus. Hadn't all the men back then worn what amounted to robes and gowns? They certainly hadn't worn *slacks* because those hadn't been invented yet. So I couldn't see why wearing pants, especially pink ones, could be seen as cross-dressing. And weren't the men of the period always depicted as either having long hair like Jesus or being bald like Yul Brynner in *The Ten Commandments*?

I spent the hour in silence, taking it all in, ready to burst out in protest. When I got home, I told my parents all about how I'd inspired the sermon. Both were amused and took the opportunity to praise our own church for its comparatively radical stance on such matters. As long as you loved Jesus, you could praise him in jeans and a T-shirt, or pink pants, they assured me.

I could not imagine a life without color, music, or fashion. What was the point? Dad agreed wholeheartedly. "Some people are just nuts," he said, by way of explanation. I appreciated that he'd taken my side, but this new church experience was definitely confusing. If all these Christians read the same Bible but interpreted the scripture so differently, what else were they wrong about?

———————

Sometimes "some people" were nuts, and sometimes just our dad was. Life at home was the very definition of cognitive dissonance. Dad's unpredictable moods kept us all on our toes. Sometimes he was the cool parent, the playful one. He had a prank he liked to pull with kids. "You want a Hertz donut?" he'd mumble while holding out an imaginary box of donuts. You'd either ask what he said or reach your hand toward the donuts, when suddenly he'd sucker punch you in the arm. "Hurts, don' it!" He'd cackle like a frat brother.

But a couple of times a week the conditions wouldn't be right, and he'd spring forward on his feet as if he were a boxer about to enter the ring, fists clenched at his sides, his face suddenly the kind of red it got after he had played eighteen holes on a clear day. Then he would spit-whisper the words *Whatdidyoujustsaytome?*—picking a fight— while cocking his head to the side like Robert De Niro in *Taxi Driver*, daring us to answer.

The first thing to change when he was angry was his posture. When Dad got mad he'd lunge and gnash his teeth, turn red and make fists, and usually retreat on cue once we cowered. The implicit threat was that we were going to get hit with the paddle that hung on the kitchen wall, which was prone to being knocked off its hook in his fury. Most times we got away, but sometimes we got hit as we fled, the worst damage accruing to our hands as we tried to fend off the board. My brothers were particularly adept at the art of the chase. Their skinny bodies could dodge and slither easily. Their high-pitched screams rang through the dining room as one or both of them ran to their room, where they'd hide out, lie low, and quietly construct a fort out of bunk bed sheets and afghans.

Life at home was a succession of family dinners that never gave Mom the feeling that we were a unit, that we actually loved each other. Her women's group stressed the importance of togetherness at the dining room table, but few things could be more tense than dinner at our house. Mom was a pretty good cook, but all our meals rotated around my father, who was a picky eater and liked routine. We typically had the same things on corresponding weeknights—Monday was fish sticks for us kids. Tuesday: roast chicken. Wednesday was tacos or pizza or a hasty trip to McDonald's, Thursday was all about casserole, Friday was pot luck (usually the leftovers of whatever we hadn't eaten on Wednesday), Saturday was spaghetti and meatballs (with absolutely no green peppers, per Dad's specification), and Sunday was pot roast with mashed potatoes and gravy.

In the spring of 1987, I had just taken an under-the-table job busing tables at a restaurant on Saturday mornings, and my weekdays already started early. Sunday was the only day all week I'd be able to sleep past six a.m. I decided to test the waters in my quest to take a day off at dinner that night. Addressing my mother, I casually mentioned I was thinking of skipping church in the morning. I hadn't been getting enough Z's lately, I said, in what I hoped was a very grown-up tone of voice. I tried to keep it cool, just stating a preference. Before Mom could respond, Dad sprang to attention.

"What are you talking about? You don't get to decide when you will and will not go to church, not while you live at this address. We go to church in this house as a family, and you're going tomorrow, end of discussion." He'd paused with his fork halfway between plate and mouth and the spaghetti unraveled pathetically.

I hated the way he used church to justify his bad mood, and how his personality seemed to shift with the changing tide. Where once had stood a long-haired dreamer now sat a culturally confused Republican. Recently Dad had taken to playing the "American Country Countdown" in the car on weekends, which confused me. Ronnie Milsap, Kenny Rogers, and the Judds did not fit my impression of my father's taste.

But there was a lot I didn't know about my dad. That past winter, Simon had asked me what "weed" Butch might have taken out of Dad's car. He'd overheard Butch whispering to Donnie that he'd swiped some from the glove compartment. I wondered why Butch (*and who else?*) had been rifling through our family car. If confronted, he probably would have tried to excuse himself by pointing out that the car was just parked there most nights, unlocked. I didn't want to believe the rumor about the pot was true, but what if it was?

"I think I'm old enough to decide whether or not I stay home from church," I said. "I'm old enough to decide for myself how and when to worship. Besides, if I pick up Sunday morning shifts I'll miss that service anyway."

Dad gripped his knife and fork in his hands and bared his teeth like a snarling dog. He relaxed his jaw, then repeated the scowl, looking feral in the eyes. It was like he was puffing himself up to go against a mountain lion. He was suddenly a big version of small. I stifled a laugh.

Bring it, I answered silently, making wolf eyes at my father. What could he do, hit me? He'd been hitting me as long as I could remember, and I'd finally reached the age where it could land both my parents in some kind of family court, I was sure of it. *Just push me one step further.* No sooner had I finished the thought than he lunged across the table and smacked me clean across the face. The fork in my hand ricocheted off the plate and onto the floor. I put my hands to my cheek, feeling the sting, and surveyed the table. Not one person met my eyes. Simon bit his bottom lip to keep from laughing. Greg sat frozen, suddenly alert. Mom buried her face in her hands and cried.

"WHY?" I screamed, and leaped from the table to run to the bathroom, slamming the door for emphasis. The bathroom was closer than my bedroom to the dinner table, and it was also my favorite room in the house. It was big enough for a sink, toilet, tub, and washer/dryer. Inside the cabinet above the washer/dryer were a bunch of poisons and items known to aid in family planning. We had cough medicines older than Simon and backups of all our personal-care products: chemical orange Jhirmack shampoo, the usual yellow bars of Dial soap, a single tube of Brylcreem. Cloth diapers—now rags used for cleaning, folded into squares; Kotex, Tampax Super Plus, and more bleach than was necessary. There was a large mirror over the sink in which I liked to watch myself cry.

The bathroom door also had a working lock, unlike my bedroom's, whose flimsy latches had been forced enough that the door barely closed all the way. Some of this damage was due to the drama I liked to invoke with a well-placed slam of the door, usually directed at my brothers or, increasingly, Mom. But Dad had come home from work one night and gotten wind that I had tried to shut out the world and kicked in my bedroom door's lock for good.

Next to the toilet I'd stashed a few lifesaving *Sassy* magazines under Dad's issues of *Arizona Highways* and *Golf* in a basket on the floor. If I'd have to stay here all night, I could. I put my hand to the hot sting of my cheek where Dad had smacked me. *Please, God, let it leave a mark.* He'd lost control in front of three witnesses, one of whom— our mother—was now openly weeping. Now I'd have license to be a bitch for a good twenty-four hours. And, I thought, there was no way they could force me to go to church now. Let's just see if they could get me out of the bathroom before I was ready.

I pressed my ear to the door. It was quiet.

It figures, I thought. Mom never stepped in between us. When psychosis came to visit Dad, she covered her eyes. Since I was too old now to be put over his knee, apparently I'd be taking it on the chin instead. Every time she cried in front of me I resented her a little more. Sulking wasn't the same as standing up to him.

When I got tired of reading back issues of magazines whose pages I'd already memorized, I skulked out of the bathroom and to my bedroom, which was across the darkened kitchen. Taped to my door was a note:

No more weekend work for you. You're going to camp in Texas, and you leave next week. No negotiations—it's this or you won't be cheerleading in the fall. See you for church in the morning. —Dad

8

DON'T LET ME DOWN

AND THAT'S HOW I FOUND MYSELF AT CAMP VICTORY, "a place to talk to Jesus," where I had to go to clean up my attitude and wipe that sarcastic smirk off my face. I liked being put on a plane by myself and loved being separated from my family, but Texas was hot and smelled like manure. I didn't feel prepared for weeks of social interaction with strangers, and I resented the opportunity to make new "prayer partners for life" with some random Christian knitter from another crappy little town.

I hated everything about Camp Victory except our counselor, Molly, America's sweetheart. It wasn't possible to merely pass over her with your eyes, you had to hold your gaze. She was nineteen and small like the rest of us, but for the womanly breasts hanging heavy in her bra. She looked like the models whose faces I'd memorized, all eyelashes, lip gloss, and a cascade of sweet-smelling chocolate waves. I couldn't wait to be her age, to live in a world where I would be the one to decide the best use of my summer vacation.

I sucked at camp. The arid heat and forced togetherness left me feeling claustrophobic. I hated the food, I hated the format. Two solid weeks of Bible study in the mornings, followed by various structured physical activities, then "Crafts for Christ" (which included a special course in the miracle of tie-dye), "Chill Time" at the pool before dinner, afterward a talent show or a theme party, followed every evening by focused reflection and prayer. The constant prying eyes, the degradation of the public shower, the flies, the horseshit. The pipe cleaner crafts (inevitably of Jesus on the cross, looking like an emaciated Gumby with an O-shaped mouth). The ball games: dodgeball, volleyball, softball, and soccer. The water sports: Marco Polo, water balloon relay, wet sponge Hot Potato, somehow intended to quench our spiritual thirst. Why were the followers of Jesus so concerned with competitive sports?

Everything was going according to plan until one Saturday afternoon, when I had only four days left at camp. Coming back to Destiny House from the canteen, my roommates and I discovered that our little cabin had been trashed. Someone had taken Del Monte Pudding Cups and smeared chocolate goo across the mirror that topped the large dresser we all shared. Our cotton panties and training bras littered the floor, as did a dog-eared Beverly Cleary paperback (*Ramona Quimby, Age 8*), a couple of inhalers, an army of plastic barrettes, a neon yellow scrunchie, and Nicole Vandimer's signature banana clip, my own contraband issue of *Seventeen*, and Mary Louise's secret stash of grape and strawberry Fruit Roll-Ups. Busted-up Hostess donuts left a powdery wake and generally just looked sad. The five of us stood dumbly surveying the damage and Nicole started to cry like a baby. "Who would *doooo this*?" she whined.

Molly, our glamorous counselor, asked if anyone had anything they wanted to tell her. We looked at each other with wide eyes and shook our heads no; we were stumped. Molly told us to sit tight and she would be back with help. We shouldn't touch anything until she returned with instructions.

When she left, one of the girls put an arm around Nicole to com-

fort her, and someone else made a move to pick up her hair accesso-
ries. One by one each girl quietly began collecting her possessions—it
seemed wrong to leave the underwear on the floor, in particular.
"Molly told us not to touch anything," I said. "Maybe we should wait?"
We awkwardly sat on our bunks and did so.

When Molly returned she was alone and stuck her head in the
door. "Erin, can I talk to you outside, please?" Every girl turned her
head and stared, first at me, then at each other, then down at the floor.
I could feel my cheeks burn in shame.

How could she suspect me?

"I know it was you who trashed the cabin, so please don't try to
blame it on the boys. I checked, and they've been in mandatory De-
votions at the chapel since Marksmanship after lunch. Only the girls
would have access to this side of the campus, and Mrs. Kunkle told me
that she excused you from Bible Boot Camp twenty minutes early so
you could go to the infirmary."

"I'm having my period," I blurted.

"Oh?" Molly said, waiting. I looked down at the ground. I hadn't
counted on being found out, on having to defend myself so soon. Was
I that transparent?

"If you don't admit what you did, I'll be forced to call your parents
and have you removed from camp," Molly said, her voice stern. "Please
just confess and we'll pray about it. I can help you."

I weighed my options. If I got kicked out of Bible camp for defac-
ing property, there was no telling what my punishment might be. I'd
definitely have to give up cheerleading in the fall. I could probably
say goodbye to any overnights with friends, and they might even look
into Camp V's live-in boarding school for further reform. I had to get
myself out of this.

I looked at Molly. "I hate this place. I hate being here. The other
girls think I'm a freak, and I don't relate to them. But if you tell my
parents, things will be bad for me. They sent me here because I stopped
wanting to go to church." Maybe if I leveled with her . . .

"When things get confusing with our parents, we need Jesus more than ever," Molly said. "He is the original Son of God. And you are a daughter of God. He wants you to think of Him as your Father. Your Heavenly Father."

All I knew about God was that I had enough to worry about with my earthly dad. Seriously, what was the point of talking to an entity you couldn't feel or see? I felt like everyone around me was suffering from some kind of psychosis (or maybe I was). But hey, if this father was forgiving, I was willing to try anything.

"The only time it's appropriate to express your anger by over-turning tables and destroying personal property is when someone is openly defying God, like when Jesus cleansed the temple when His house was desecrated by the mob in Jerusalem. Did the other girls do something that I don't know about?" Molly looked at me with gentle, searching eyes.

I looked down at my Converse. The black stripes were fading from the rubber near the soles.

"I don't feel right being here. The other girls all hate me," I blurted. I wasn't sure that was true. The other girls were inconsequential sheep. Not one of them seemed to have any interest in anything outside of what they were told to take an interest in. They served no other pur-pose than to make me feel more alone.

"Did someone make fun of you?" she asked, her brow furrow-ing with concern. I pictured my campmates as a coven of cackling witches, even though they were basically guilty of nothing but being blissfully oblivious to the evils of the real world that I inhabited. I couldn't blame them, but I wanted to.

I looked at Molly, her eyes filled with tears, glistening and shim-mering in the gently setting sun, and I wondered if this was what a moment before a first kiss felt like. I'd only had one big make-out ses-sion, with a kid I met at the county fair the previous summer, but the whole thing had been so heavily orchestrated that I hadn't had time to experience this kind of butterflies. I felt a rush of power over Molly. What if I told her everything I knew about the world, about God and His almighty apathy? About what it felt like to be lied to and used?

Instead I looked down at my hands and said, "I don't know why I did it."

Molly threw her arms around my shoulders and pulled me close, my face smashed awkwardly between her breasts. I turned my head to the side, closed my eyes, and inhaled. And then I felt myself start to cry. I felt like a faker, even as I realized I couldn't stop.

Molly put her hands on my shoulders and moved in until our foreheads were nearly touching, our bangs colliding. She wanted to tell me something important. "Do you feel Jesus here right now? Can you feel His grace?"

If grace felt like I was getting away with something, then, yeah, I could feel it. I felt relief. I turned my eyes up to meet hers and nodded solemnly. "I can. I really can. Thank you, Jesus."

When the plane back from Texas landed at the airport in Cleveland, I was nervous. All the way home on the flight alone, I'd thought about what I'd done. What had I wanted to accomplish by trashing the cabin? Just to see what would happen? I'd assumed that everyone would blame the boys (weren't they used to it?). But I hadn't thought it through enough to consider the consequences.

I had been alone in the cabin unexpectedly. I'd sneaked back after breakfast to retrieve some money, and when I realized that I'd been gone for several minutes and no one had come looking, I suddenly felt compelled to dare myself to do something I couldn't undo. If I'd come to this place to connect with God, maybe it was time we were alone together. I picked up Nicole's plaid suitcase, which looked as if it belonged to an old woman, and unzipped the front pocket that held her toiletries. In a rush I unleashed random stuff from every bag in the room except for Molly's, then saved my own bag for last. In front of God, I dumped the entire contents of my duffel bag in the middle of the floor, then threw the stiff pillow off my bunk for a final flourish. I never considered that this was the dead giveaway this reign of terror had been executed by me, the victim of the worst of it. What were the odds that Molly had kept it to herself? She'd have had to call my parents, and I was probably headed to juvie just as soon as they could pack a bag.

When I landed in Cleveland, Dad was waiting for me at the gate, his eyes soft and calm, his hands in his jean pockets. He was wearing a baseball cap labeled SOCIETY BANK. He seemed happy to see me, not pissed. He smiled and opened his arms.

I gave him a half hug and looked over his shoulder. "I thought Mom was coming," I said, nervous about why he might be alone.

"She would have come, she would have, but something came up and so you've got your old man. I thought we'd hit a drive-through, get you some real food after all that granola," he said, taking my bags and throwing an arm around my shoulder.

The whole way home in the car he seemed distracted. His favorite mixtape, labeled *Happy Sunshine Music* (up-tempo Beatles and Stones) played as usual, but he didn't tap his thumbs to "Got to Get You Into My Life," or whistle the notes through his teeth the way he often did when he drove. His hands rested at ten and two o'clock on the steering wheel. We made small talk for a while, but something else was on his mind. Maybe since I'd been gone, they'd decided to try to send me to some kind of private school. At the same time, he was acting so nice, I thought maybe something had happened to our dog. Just before we pulled up the driveway, I felt like I had to say something. I turned down the volume on "Good Day, Sunshine."

"Dad, is something wrong? Is Dusty okay?"

Dad put the car in park by the apple tree as usual and let the engine idle for a moment before slowly twisting the key from the ignition. He stared straight ahead.

"Dusty's fine."

"Well, what then? Is somebody sick?"

"You've always been a perceptive kid, E, and I've been trying to figure out if it's the right thing to tell you what I don't think we could keep from you anyway. You're going to see for yourself soon enough, and I'd rather you hear it from your mother and me."

My stomach dropped from a steep cliff and kept falling. I'd fantasized about my parents' divorce for a while now, but somehow I'd always imagined I'd take it better, that it wouldn't feel like somebody had died.

"When you were gone, a couple of weeks ago, I suppose, Butch lured Greg into the woods and raped him."

Dad looked down at his hands. I exhaled slowly, wondering if I had heard him correctly. *Lured him? Rape?* But he was just a little kid. How could that even happen?

"I don't understand. Butch, from next door?"

"I know it's a shock. Believe me. Your mother and I . . . We're sick about it. It's a parent's worst nightmare. Your brother is going to need a lot of support, but what's important now is that it's out in the open and it won't ever happen again."

I wanted to know what had happened but I didn't want to know what had happened. Had there been police, would there be a trial?

Greg and Simon and Butch and his stepbrother had gone into the woods to test their handmade bows and arrows. They'd just spent the better part of the afternoon hand-carving them out of a fallen ash tree. Joel and Butch had one, my brothers had another. The fletching was not complete on the arrows yet, so the point of the exercise in the woods was to test the bowstrings, make sure they shot at least a few feet. For a while they shot at pop cans, until it was clear that the bows were ready for their arrows, and then it was starting to get dark. Butch didn't want to go, though, saying something about how Greg's bow was bothering him, the string could be adjusted and made more taut. Something about the air in the woods changed just then, felt off somehow, and Simon said, *Come on, Greg, it's getting late. Mom will have a cow.*

And Joel said he was gonna head back, too, but Butch said, *Go on, I'll walk Greg back in a minute, we just have to finish this one thing.* And Simon left them behind, went home by himself, not sure what scene he'd just abandoned, or why he felt guilty. When he walked in the door, Mom and Dad were already ticked off. *Where have you been, can't you see it's getting dark, and where is your brother?* Simon told them his brother had stayed behind, *You know how he is, he doesn't listen.* But then a long time passed, too long, and Dad started calling Greg's name from the front porch. Mom was about to walk to the neighbors' when Greg came through the door carrying his bow. In his pocket was a secret bag of Skittles, hush money.

Only before Greg could even get a word in, Dad had picked him up by the back of his shirt, *How dare you worry your mother, do you know that she'd nearly called the police?* This little kid, barely out of first grade, could only cower and take it as the bow was broken over his already broken body, before he was left to sit and think about what he'd done.

My parents didn't learn about the rape until weeks later, when Mom, motivated by hearing of an unrelated incident in our neighborhood, felt compelled to have the all-important "stranger danger" talk with her youngest. She took Greg onto her lap and told him that his body was his own and if he ever felt threatened, he should always come to his parents. She had not really been prepared to hear what Greg had to tell her. In her grief and panic, Mom told a trusted friend, who called the police.

It occurred to me immediately that if I had told anyone what I had known about Butch—what I thought I knew, anyway—about the time in the tree house that he held me down, the creepy hide and seek, the sneaking and snooping around, this all could have been prevented.

"Is he in jail?" I asked.

Dad opened his car door and popped the trunk. I followed him out of the car, wondering how I would face my brother, wondering if I wanted to hear any more.

"Who?"

"Butch."

Dad shuffled his feet in the gravel driveway, kicking up stones. "He was arrested last week. He's in a juvenile facility now. We still haven't decided how to pursue this legally. It's very sensitive. We'd like to spare your brother any more trauma. But the important thing to know is that Butch won't be coming back around here anymore and neither will his family. We'll make sure of that."

In my peripheral vision I could plainly make out the house where Butch lived with his mother and stepfather. The house, the yard, the woods where we'd spent a hundred afternoons. I wondered about his parents. How did they sleep knowing what their child was capable of? Did they know?

Dad turned to look at me and I could see tears in his eyes. I quickly looked away; weeping adults embarrassed me. The only other time I'd seen him tear up was when Lennon had been shot, seven years before.

"Your mother and I are so proud of you, okay? That's the main thing. You kids are our life. I'm glad you're home, kiddo." He looked so small suddenly, smaller than Butch, not at all the size of a person who could protect us from monsters in the woods.

When I went inside the house, everything was quiet. Mom and Greg were sitting at the dining room table working on some kind of food-oriented craft. Chocolate chip cookies, finger painting with chocolate pudding? Nobody made any sudden movements but Mom looked up from the table when we walked in and smiled. I felt the enormity of what I now knew about my brother. Had Mom known that Dad was going to tell me?

That night we watched an episode of *Growing Pains* where Mike Seaver rides a dirt bike against his parents' wishes while camping with his friend Boner. Why must every joke have a sexual connotation? Why was television always trying to make everyone uncomfortable? I took to staring at my little brother to see if he was different, if you could see it in his eyes. Gone were the goofy laugh and the jokes about his belly button and Mickey Mouse, or aliens from outer space. Gone was the unsolicited hugging, a lot of the sweetness. He was timid, unsure of himself. He flinched a lot, as if expecting to be hit if someone got too near. He only wanted to be with Mom, and he was always with her in the months that followed, trailing behind with a My Buddy doll, the doll for boys, often repeating the mantra "It's not good to keep secrets from parents."

The light had gone out in my brother. And just like that, and forever after, for me, God went up in flames.

Knowing that something is not your fault and feeling it are two very different things. When the unsayable happened to me, I knew that what Butch had done was bad and there was something wrong with him that he would want to touch a kid that way, that he held me down, and that he tried to poison me with his idea of "love." I knew all of this but still blamed myself for trusting him and so easily keeping the secret; after all, what he'd taken was already gone. Silence was the first self-destructive decision I ever made, looking back, but I couldn't know how it would endanger my brother. I had taken on the guilt and the burden of experience gladly for the chance to spare my parents more grief. I couldn't bear to see my mother cry any more than she was already crying, and who knew what violence Dad was capable of when some outsider was the one who was hurting us.

Before I got home from camp, Greg and Simon had watched from their bedroom window as my father spoke to Butch's parents in the yard that connected our houses. They stood in a circle and talked, and for a while it seemed tense but it did not escalate. My brothers had expected fisticuffs, screaming, murder, *something*, but apparently such punishments were reserved solely for us. Still, whatever was said proved effective in that Butch and everyone related to him disappeared in short order. For a long time the house sat empty, but within a year a new family moved in. We never introduced ourselves.

Butch turned eighteen in juvie and the kids at school said he went into the army. I tried to imagine him maimed by a grenade, or savagely bayoneted and left to die slowly in a rice paddy, but no fate seemed terrible enough. In lieu of a trial, there was counseling with social workers, group therapy for Mom, a male therapist for my brother. I saw a psychologist exactly two times, once more than necessary to beat a mound of pillows as hard as possible with a plastic bat. I felt sure this all-knowing woman could tell just by looking in my eyes that it had happened to me, too, that I knew Butch wasn't a good person. The psychologist did ask me how I felt about what had happened to my brother. "Just shocked," I managed, because it was true.

Greg was prescribed art therapy, counseling, hugs, and martial arts. One of his drawings then was a portrait of himself as a bleeding monster lording over our mother, beating her with a whip, a bow on the ground at his feet and an arrow pointed at her back. Absent from any of his angry art imagery was my father, who managed to escape the majority of the tough confrontations by radiating more sadness and defeat than anyone. While Greg and Mom became inseparable, our dad never mentioned what had happened again. I followed his lead.

After that, my teen angst was at an apex. In the most basic sense, I hated my parents. They punished us for no other reason than the Bible told them to, and neglected us because they were really busy praising the Lord. If there was an all-knowing God whose infinite wisdom I was supposed to accept on faith, then by the same logic God made the child molester, and made him for a reason. I mean, thanks, God, for the sun, the stars in the sky, all the fishes in the ocean, and for moving us next door to a psychopath. I'm sure Your Divine Plan will make sense any day now.

By the time I entered the ninth grade with my new cheerleading uniform, I was free of the burden of faith in Him—and that was the bravest, smartest gift I ever gave myself. I decided to throw out the baby with the holy water—I didn't just place the blame on our church for promoting its version of God, I blamed the very concept.

In Dad's record collection, I found the inspiration for my newfound agnosticism, especially in John Lennon, the most outspoken of the Beatles about his distrust of religion in his songwriting. He'd infamously kicked off a mass freak-out when, at a press conference in 1966, he observed that the band had grown more popular than Jesus. This comment inspired a boycott of all things Beatles-related in the American South, denouncement by the Vatican, and Mark David Chapman's eventual murder plot. On Lennon's first solo record, *Plastic Ono Band*, my favorite song was called "God," a treatise against everything in which he'd once believed. *God is a concept by which we measure our pain.* The Bible was only as meaningful as you made it. For every church that claimed it was the only way, there was another that disagreed.

For a while there was quiet, we gave peace a chance at home, but it wouldn't last long. Another wave of tragedy would plow us over soon enough. When all was said and done, God was just like any other teen idol—inspiring devotion but ultimately disappointing because His best material was in the past. The dream was over.

9

RAIN

WE ALL AGREED THAT SOMETHING WAS DIFFERENT ABOUT DAD.
He seemed a little tired. The sanctity of the annual family vacation
had been honored without fail in our house, with Dad planning elaborate outings at least two weeks every year. When I was fourteen, Ja-
maica would mark the first and last time we'd travel internationally.
Our father relished the idea of treating us to a week at an all-inclusive
resort in the Caribbean.

Today, each of us has different memories of this trip. Mine are
mostly related to working on my tan and drinking unlimited virgin
daiquiris while a nice local woman braided my hair. Mom's are centered on failing to pass the scuba swim test, and the way Dad put
her down because of it. Greg's clearest memory is of Dad heroically
heading up a rescue mission when the paddleboat Greg was manning
got caught in a current. And Simon remembers that Dad woke up one
morning and discovered he'd had an accident in his sleep.

Instead of engaging in all the various water sports and sightseeing, he held back more than usual and took a lot of pictures of us doing that stuff. He would have been in that boat with Greg if he hadn't been feeling so shitty. The main event was meant to be scaling Dunn's River Falls in Ocho Rios, which involved hiking to the top of the waterfall while holding hands with other tourists and our guides. The ascent took an hour and a half, and Dad seemed uncharacteristically exhausted by the climb. He had to stop a couple of times.

Maybe he suspected then that he was sick, that there was a good chance he had the same colon cancer that had cut through his family like a scythe. His mother and uncle had both died of it in their forties. His cousin had died from it at twenty-seven. His younger brother would be diagnosed just a few years later. Dad was thirty-nine.

It wasn't long after we returned home that he had to admit he wasn't well. The fact that he could no longer get through more than nine holes of golf without feeling winded was what finally made him go to the doctor. The med school intern who examined him discovered a tumor the size of a grapefruit in his gut. When our parents told us, his eyes soft and hers red and weary, they said it was serious but that the odds were in his favor. It might be scary for a while, but he would get better, and we shouldn't worry too much; he promised to be straight with us.

It scared me that initially I felt numb and indifferent to the news that our father had cancer. This was a bona fide big deal and I couldn't seem to conjure up the empathy I expected from myself. I'd spent a lot of the last couple of years distancing myself from him and his erratic moods, and now I was just supposed to snap out of it because he might or might not be dying? I was tired of feeling so much all the time as it was, and I was determined not to let his illness affect me. He'd figure it out; hopefully he'd get to keep his hair.

It was easier for me to worry for my brothers. Sons needed their dads even more than daughters did, I reasoned, and at eight and ten, they were too young to handle the trauma if he died. I had access to genuine wisdom (to be gleaned via the library, I imagined) that little kids didn't have, and I wanted to sound credible enough when I said I would always be there to tell them the truth, and stay. I took them each aside and vowed to be a more involved big sister. They could always come to me if there was anything about the adult world they didn't understand. If for any reason both of our parents should die, I'd find a way to keep the family together, I promised. I think both Simon and Greg were equally confused by this mostly empty, speculative gesture, and after our one little talk, none of us spoke about cancer again.

Despite the nausea, fatigue, and smoking ban associated with his illness, Dad maintained an air of positivity, and put on a brave face every Tuesday for treatment. At the hospital he was a popular patient; all the nurses knew him and rooted for his recovery. He continued to go into the office every day, even after chemo, even though he could sometimes barely stand. Mom would try to get him to stay home, stop being a martyr, but he wouldn't have it. If he let his guard down now, maybe they'd notice he wasn't as necessary as they'd been led to believe. He insisted on working right up to his surgeries, but he slept a lot more and got really thin. Most alarmingly, he'd taken to writing us letters with a tone of finality that made me uncomfortable.

Dear Erin,

Do not be afraid of death for it is just another part of life. Someday we'll be together again.

I love you.

Always keep your intelligence. Think about it before you act and you'll do alright.

I hope someday you realize what a great friend you have in your mother. She really wouldn't steer you wrong.

You are beautiful.

I've always enjoyed being with you. I only wish that you'd realize that there truly is a God and Jesus is the way.

You've always made me happy.

I love you,
Dad

I never admitted to anyone that I was afraid, that I put the folded-up note Dad had written on a piece of scrap paper into the jewelry box he'd given me that played the "Dying Swan" theme from *Swan Lake*, and prayed for him. While my brothers took him up on every invitation to spend more time together, I found ways to distance myself even further. I deliberately focused on anything else, especially the myriad social melodramas inherent to teenagers. I was all about making memories where my friends were concerned, but when it came to my family, I couldn't imagine the source of my nostalgia. Mostly, I just wanted a boyfriend so I could have someone to depend on and express myself to fully.

Mom was stricken by Dad's illness and the new responsibilities it brought. She was the mother, the on-call nurse, the assistant, the house manager, the therapist to Greg, the ambulance, the bank, the cook, the runner of errands, the wife, the boss. It was a lot to manage, and she sometimes walked around with a wild look in her eyes. Her exhaustion had a new weight. When she hit that wall, no matter where we were, she'd have to stop and close her eyes. "Just give me twenty minutes," she'd bark, holding her hand above her head like a stop sign. A tension hung in the air—any minute now a new horror could befall us and then there'd be another thing to contend with. Her young children had been traumatized, the family cat had recently gotten shot by a redneck (she survived, but was a lot worse for the wear), Greg was so accident prone that Mom started to put lipstick on to take him to the ER so social workers wouldn't think she was trash who neglected her kid. What could be next, alien abduction?

Since the diagnosis, we'd taken to having breakfast at the home-style diner Belle's on the weekends—an optimistic stab at public togetherness and putting on a brave face. No one mentioned aloud that these outings were increasingly taking the place of church service attendance, but that was the truth. At first we skipped the Sundays when Dad was recovering from surgery, but eventually the whole house stayed quiet past seven a.m., which meant we'd be blessed with no church and more sleep. I had heard Mom complain to Dad about the lack of support she felt from the congregation now that we really needed it. People said they would pray for us, then handed out platitudes about all things being part of God's plan and offer proof of His grace in stories about a much sicker mother-in-law who'd miraculously recovered. After Dad's first surgery, a single Pyrex casserole dish had been delivered to the house. Just about everyone had a personal anecdote, but as Mom's loneliness compounded, she wondered what good it did. She was just beginning to lose her religion. I wondered what was taking so long.

One morning at the restaurant, our mother made a scene at the table. I was attempting to enjoy a decadent waffle weighted down by strawberry pie filling. I heard Dad say something about life insurance, about Mom having enough money to take care of things after he was gone. "I'm actually worth more to you dead than alive." Mom shot right up in her chair and slammed her hand flat on the surface of the table, producing a sound that made folks in the room take notice, their coffee cups suspended in midair. "Don't you say things like that to me, Jack. Nobody here is going anywhere." Her voice cracked and fresh tears sprang to her eyes.

Dad seemed a little sheepish, but I thought it must have pleased him, too—his wife needing him, his family too good to lose. I had hoped that cancer or chemo would give us a reprieve from his temper, act as a sedative somehow, mellow him out. It did seem to, for a while—I don't think he had the energy. But as the months passed, it was as if another tumor of anger was growing underneath. It needed to be excised.

———————

One rainy Saturday that spring, I arranged to take a trial ballet class with my friend Michelle at a dance studio in Cleveland, about a forty-five-minute drive away. The class would serve as an audition to determine at what level I might be placed. I'd been studying ballet since age seven and loved dance intensely, but the tiny local music school where I'd taken lessons for years had abruptly closed just as I would have graduated to pointe shoes. Two years had passed and I was looking forward to seeing if I still had it in me.

The biggest obstacle to enrollment would be the commute. I'd have a hard time convincing either of my parents to add an extra three hours of time-suck to their lives. It wasn't like I was training for the Olympics, but they both knew how important dance was to me. Dad had kept me in season tickets to the Cleveland Ballet for as long as I could remember. I thought maybe we could work out a compromise. If I needed a backup plan, Michelle was about to turn sixteen and would have access to the family Ford Escort. Her birthday was only a couple of months away, and we figured we knew enough people who could give us rides.

Dad agreed to drop us off at the class while he ran errands downtown. As he pulled out of the parking lot, he told us he'd be waiting for us when we were done. At the barre, working through the combinations of *tendus* and *dégagés*, I felt the relief of the body remembering. When we moved to the center of the floor for *piqué* turns and *grand jetés*, I instinctively lifted my rib cage in *relevé* to the familiar nocturne by Chopin. I thought I'd heard two instructors discussing my strong turnout and high arches, and damned if I didn't like my look in the mirror. If ballet ended up the only thing in life that I was any good at, then that was fine with me.

After class, we crossed through the small sitting area where girls waited for their rides. I could see Dad's Honda through the big picture windows. I'd been so caught up in the dancing I hadn't noticed that ninety minutes had gone by. The sky, darkened by rain, made it look even later than it was. Michelle and I quickly threw our jeans on and exchanged our slippers for rain boots, but I still needed to fill out some forms and talk to the dance teacher to go over my options. The instructor was just beginning to launch into her assessment when I heard the unmistakable sounds of an angry car horn. I knew it was Dad's. Michelle and I looked at each other. She was getting ready to go outside to talk him down so I could finish giving them my contact info. The teachers stopped their conversation, looked outside to the parking lot, and asked, "Who is that honking?"

I pretended to join them in their confusion—*Jesus Christ, calm down, guy*—but suddenly my father stormed through the door, knocking the wind out of the tiny chimes that dangled there from pink satin ribbons. He looked like a character out of Willy Wonka, a grown man the color of an Oompa Loompa throwing a tantrum like Veruca Salt.

"WHAT ARE YOU DOING, GODDAMMIT? DO YOU KNOW HOW LONG I'VE BEEN WAITING IN THE GODDAMN CAR, HUH? *HUH?* IF YOU DON'T GET YOUR ASS OUTSIDE RIGHT NOW, YOU'RE NEVER GOING TO DANCE AGAIN."

"But, Dad, I was just—" In my peripheral vision I saw some of the other girls cowering in a group along the wall. Michelle looked away.

His face was an alarming shade of red. "I'M NOT GONNA TELL YOU AGAIN."

Mortified, I turned around to put the pen back down on the desk. The instructor's hand was shaking and she looked like she might weep. Everyone in the room was staring at something on the floor.

"It's okay, sweetheart," she whispered, and handed me a trembling flyer. "Talk it over with your parents and come back anytime."

I grabbed the paper out of her hand and ran outside, praying no one would call the police. Michelle followed and we both slid into the back seat. Michelle squeezed my hand and we exchanged a look reserved for parental freak-outs—it was always better not to say anything that might incite him further. We sat in silence all the way home while I stewed in the knowledge that I was embarrassed of my father, and possibly worse; possibly, I hated him. Dad turned up the volume on the oldies station, and tapped his thumbs on the steering wheel. The Beach Boys' "Good Vibrations" was a grating backdrop to a waking nightmare.

Later, at dinner, it was as if nothing unusual had happened. I seethed through the meal, a common enough occurrence. *So much for Juilliard.* There would be no acknowledgment or discussion of what had happened at the ballet studio, not in front of Dad, anyway. Privately, my mother sympathized and apologized for his behavior but confirmed there was nothing she could do about it, at least not until we were on the other side of this latest family crisis.

Crises, I thought.

During our cancer year, if I wasn't sleeping over at Michelle's, I was awake in the dark, huddled in front of our small four-station television in the living room, the volume down as low as possible. Because the living room was situated just under my parents' bedroom with an air vent, my habit was to pull the rocking chair right up to the screen so I could watch adult dramas surreptitiously after everyone else had gone to sleep. One of my favorites was *thirtysomething*, a show that follows a group of hurtling-toward-middle-age friends in Philadelphia as they try to raise their young families and find meaning in their relationships and work. Like my dad, the two main characters, Michael and Elliot, both work in advertising, and their wives, Hope and Nancy, both stay home with the kids. It wasn't quite like us, but enough that I could project.

Then, in one of the episodes, Nancy finds out she has ovarian cancer. The lingering back pain she'd been experiencing is not due to anxiety over her newly published children's book but to a tumor. Suddenly she must have surgery and begin a course of chemotherapy. When she tells her ten-year-old son, Ethan, about the diagnosis—after he tells her, "There's something wrong with you"—he wants to know if she is going to die. Nancy says that she doesn't think so, but the truth is she doesn't know. Ethan is stoic to the news.

Until that moment I hadn't cried about Dad's cancer and what it could mean, but now I couldn't stop.

I'd tried to imagine a future without a father. Would it make me grow up too fast? Would I fall into a depression and take up smoking, or turn to drugs to numb the pain? Would it add to my mystique at school, make me more sympathetic? How would it feel, to no longer be beholden to fulfilling his expectations, or to know that he would never fulfill mine?

I liked it when he went on business trips, and not just because I knew he'd bring me a souvenir when he returned. Whenever he had to go somewhere, it gave me a chance to forget his cruelty, to miss him again.

Flashes of us came to me: His face when he was excited about something, his smile the first thing you'd see in a crowded room. His eyes when he was all there and totally engaged. How high I'd felt on the receiving end of his praise. Then: the terrible thunder of his escalating anger, the rattle of the belt buckle, the crack of the leather against skin, and the subsequent wail of the victim, the car horn blaring his tantrum. Sometimes I wished he weren't my father, sometimes I wished him away.

Dad's business trips gave me a chance to relax, to use the phone whenever I wanted, and to talk back to my mother with impunity. I had access to the Dr Pepper, Oreos, and Klondike bars that were otherwise off-limits to us kids. I sneaked whatever I could and hoped that Mom would forget she hadn't eaten them herself. Sitting in his chair, I'd watch the shows he liked and pretend to understand the appeal of *The Three Stooges* or a Bond film. It wasn't the same without his snicker there to punctuate every stupid joke. Or the warmer, softer laugh reserved for one of my witticisms.

I rocked in the chair, my face buried hard in a pillow to muffle my sobbing. No matter how closed off I felt, I didn't want him to die.

Did I?

10

JULIA

MY FATHER LIKED TO TELL THE STORIES of the formation of the Beatles, the certain coincidences that drew them together. Paul McCartney lost his mother, Mary, to complications from surgery to treat cancer when he was just fourteen (Mary was forty-seven). He was already playing music at that age, and would meet John Lennon only one year after she'd died, just in time for the sudden death in 1958 of John's mother, Julia. Lennon was seventeen (Julia was forty-four). Lennon and McCartney were mama's boys—good, blameless lads who knew the feeling of not having the chance to make their mothers proud because they died too soon.

My father, it turned out, knew exactly how they felt.

I learned early on that Julia had gifted John his first guitar, that he never got over her death, that he saw her face everywhere, and wrote several songs about her, including his solo work "Mother," replete with its primal screams and plaintive wails of *Mama, don't go, Daddy, come home*.

Julia was Lennon's first real muse. (In an Oedipal homage, "Mother" was also John's nickname for Yoko once they became inseparable.) Paul wrote "Let It Be" as a psalm not to the Virgin Mary but to his actual mother, who appeared to him in a dream to give him that message. That same year John wrote "Julia," a tribute to his first true love. The year was 1968—the same year my father lost his own mother.

Dad listened to Lennon's "Mother" quite a bit on vinyl. It was a song that was always in my life, as it was released four years before I was born. Even as a child I knew that Lennon was in pain when he sang *Mother, you had me, but I never had you*. The song opens with funereal church bells, then lyrically expresses the longing a child feels for a parent who abandons him and the frightening loss of control that such a thing invokes. The way Lennon recorded it ensures you can hear every blood vessel rising to the surface of his face, threatening to burst as he shrieks like an infant enraged. During the refrain, you can hear the spit hit the microphone. *He'll never get over it*, I thought, of Lennon, whenever I heard the song playing. Now I don't think anyone ever gets over the loss of a parent.

I did not connect Dad's Beatles obsession with John's and Paul's early loss of their mothers until after he died. Mom told me the sad, true story of my grandmother Ruth's death after Dad's memorial service, as we drove to the airport in the blinding sun. Dad had told her the story only once, early in their relationship, and never brought it up again. It was his way of saying, *You think you're fucked up, well, listen to this*. His mother's death was an event so powerful it broke him off at the neck. He stayed that way forever, locked in his head.

The polite silence in the house where my father grew up was just as palpable as the occasional stripes of violence that cut through the regulated calm. His father, John, a decorated pilot, was gone a lot, which left the caregiving of my dad and his two brothers to their mother, who, by all accounts, was a natural. Ruth was fair-minded and kind, exceptionally beautiful and even a little glamorous, classy, and strong and adventurous, having met her husband while learning to fly during World War II.

John was faithfully devoted to his wife, but he had a short temper. When he was home his presence tended to set the tone. *Wait till your father gets home* was uttered often (though as a threat Ruth never intended to carry through on). John was the type to hit first, ask questions never, and the boom of his voice scared her enough that she'd opt to keep the burden of her sons' bad behavior to herself. Still, little things would set him off. One of the boys swearing in front of his mother might get a backhanded slap to the face; another he would push against the wall by the neck with his left hand, his right one drawn back.

When Ruth got sick she was forty-seven. Her eldest son, Dick, had already left home; Dad was eighteen, away at college; and her youngest, Ray, was fourteen. John didn't know how to tell his boys their mother had cancer, so he opted not to say anything at all. Instead, Ruth was hospitalized with "pneumonia," and before anyone could figure out a treatment protocol, it was clear she wasn't going to recover. Jack was in his freshman dorm room when he got the call from Ray. "Come home," his brother said. "Mom's in the hospital and it doesn't look good." *Doesn't look good?* Jack had just seen her two months before, and she'd been happy then, looked healthy then.

Jack borrowed a friend's car and drove three hours straight to the hospital. When he finally arrived he saw his father and brothers somberly waiting in the hall outside her room. But when John saw his middle son with long, shaggy hair, a mustache, and bell-bottoms, he lost his temper and ordered him to leave and not come back until he looked presentable.

Jack's shock propelled him out of the hospital. He was at a barber in town, not far away, when Ray called the shop. *"Come now,"* he said, as if he'd been expecting some resistance or hesitation. Jack *wanted* to sit with her, let her know he was there and wouldn't leave until she was feeling better. If that would make her happy, he would keep his hair as short as a marine's.

Ever since Jack was small, his mother had been the only person in the family who really understood him, who could calm him down, defuse the anger that burned inside. She encouraged his creativity and his love for music. She didn't judge him for not wanting to enlist in the army. Merciful and full of grace, Ruth was a Lutheran saint. He tried to remember the few times a year he'd gone to a service with her. She'd never pressed.

He should have paid better attention to the sermons, he thought now, vowing to go again with her as soon as she was feeling better.

But by the time Jack paid the barber five dollars for a shave and a cut, his mother was dead.

11

I'M LOOKING THROUGH YOU

I HAD SEX WITH STEVIE WATERS IN MY OWN BED on a school night in 1991. Maybe you heard? It was around three o'clock in the morning. I was sixteen. Stevie had parked down the street and crept in through the window of my bedroom, which was on the ground floor. The sex was taking forever and I may have had the sound up a little too high on *Surfer Rosa*. Anyway, I wasn't a virgin. Though this would soon be news to both my parents.

My mom came downstairs to use the only bathroom in the house and heard us. Suddenly she switched on the overhead light above my bed, instantly creating the ominous yellow pallor of a police interrogation room. Stevie tried feebly to hide under my sheets, but suddenly my mother lunged at him and then recoiled, realizing with horror that he was stark naked underneath. She was determined to get him to leave. Her voice got really low, like the growl underneath a dog's bark, and she used that tone for every word she uttered for the next several minutes.

"You have ten seconds to get out of here . . . and never come back."

Stevie fumbled with his clothes and addressed my mother with an actual "Yes, ma'am." I would have laughed but I was too stunned. (Did I mention that I had a waterbed?)

Stevie was the big man on a small campus, a senior, a mama's boy, and the cockiest person ever to attend our high school. He was dating Heather Monroe, probably the most beautiful girl in the school, which gave him a kind of universal celebrity. Despite his public union with Heather, privately Stevie had a reputation as a very successful player, and it was widely believed he could seduce anyone in the game, even Christian virgins. He sat behind me in Speech class and one day had leaned forward and whispered to the back of my head, "You're a real stuck-up bitch, Hosier." That was all it took for me to fall for him.

The fact that most of my friends were guys in those days was a point of pride for me. I had aspirations to be like Dorothy Parker at the Round Table, like Nico in the Velvet Underground. I'd adopted Charlie, my main best friend, as my brother since we'd met in the fourth grade. He was small like me, wore glasses, and neither of us had any interest in relay races or jumping midair off the swing set. He preferred instead to sit under a tree quietly drawing. Charlie could draw better than anyone in our class. The day I first approached him at recess he had been leaning up against his backpack, reading a paperback copy of *Jaws*. No ten-year-old I knew had been reading anything but the Bible outside of our schoolwork, much less a horror paperback whose cover depicted a nude woman swimming above a stalking great white, its teeth a thousand glistening knives.

Charlie had a real sadness. The year we met, he had lost his sister to cancer, and his parents had just gotten divorced. He was living with his mom and missing his dad, David, an artist who lived alone a couple of towns over. Charlie's relationship with his dad was enviable, and beginning freshman year, he began to include me in their plans.

We'd spend weekends or holidays at David's house in the woods. He'd cook us meals, play Dylan records, and espouse the virtues of atheism, all the while smoking the French cigarettes John Lennon preferred. David treated us like equals and told us the truth about things. While my dad took me to see Wings for my first concert, David had taken Charlie to see the Pixies. I wanted nothing more than for my parents to finally divorce so Mom could marry Charlie's dad and Charlie and I could be siblings for real.

Charlie was disgusted by this idea. To invoke *My So-Called Life*: he already felt he was like Brian Krakow to my Angela Chase. He couldn't understand why I bothered with asshole jocks when I was getting all the quality intimacy I craved from him. Since freshman year we'd communicated faithfully every day via letters passed during third and sixth periods. Those letters contained every secret the two of us had ever had. Things we felt guilty about, shameful things we wished for, scary dark things, confessions.

While I would never try to convince Charlie that skateboarding could be as worthy an endeavor as playing the guitar or going to film school, I never questioned why I was attracted to the guys in high school who played sports, had muscles, drove fast. I just assumed everyone was.

What did I really *see* in Stevie Waters?

It wasn't that he was especially good-looking. He was wiry and small and his face was oddly ferret-like, pointy and sharp. He chewed gum constantly, sarcastically, as if the rules of decorum didn't apply to him. Teachers either feared him or, in the rare case, seemed smitten. He didn't have a good personality. (The most common descriptor attributed to him: "What a dick.") He was so manipulative, such a fast talker, that you wanted him to win, even at your own expense. A part of me even rooted for Stevie as he began to work me over. I'd wait for him in dark corners after school, giving in to the terror of his ultimate rejection. I wanted him to hurt me. I wanted for something *to* hurt.

Stevie was the first real Asshole I ever gave myself over to casually, but he wouldn't be the last. The idea that he had chosen me when we had so little in common was more than enough reason for me to try to win with him. I felt real pain in knowing that my efforts would be futile, that he had no secret beauty underneath the swagger, but it wasn't enough to turn me off. Some girls had a power over men and could reduce them to mush with a flash of their eyes or their tits. I wasn't like that. I wasn't about being the prettiest; I was about being the most determined.

Later that year, in the parking lot of our high school, a boy from a rival football team, Corey Fisher—just another kid from a broken home in a hick town raised on sugar cereal and regular beatings—would finally have enough of Stevie's smart mouth. What happened would become legend among those who were there.

A circle formed around the two of them and Stevie knew that the crowd wanted a show, that they were excited that his opponent had several inches and forty pounds on him. Before you could place your bets, Stevie sprang up like a pogo stick and head-butted Corey right between the eyes. The move wasn't exactly stealthy, and only made Corey angrier. After recovering quickly, he looked ready to murder. The kid had a move where he used his left hand to point at the place on Stevie's face where he was going to connect, and then followed through with his right, a process that took only a second. Even now, all these years later, I get a thrill out of imagining the look of surprise that crossed Stevie's face when he realized what was happening and what would happen next. No one was going to step in to defend him from someone who was about to make his face explode.

Wham.

Stevie had been practicing his haymaker when the promised punch made contact. Corey dodged Stevie's defensive swipe and hit him again, this time harder, sharper, and from below. A succession of blows made the middle of Stevie's face a sudden sauce of blood and snot, the cartilage of his nose pushed high and to the right. Tears sprang bright in his eyes, betraying uncontrollable fear as he flailed his arms, while Corey held a fistful of his hair to steady his face for more. Stevie's attempts to fight back were almost cute, the crowd would later note, he had so little to contribute. Only once Corey was about to introduce his knee to Stevie's teeth, and cartoon birds were tweeting their little death song above Stevie's head, did his teammates step in to break them up.

Forever after this beating, this public takedown, this sacrifice to school spirit, Stevie Waters would henceforth be known simply as "Steve," his powers sorely depleted.

———————

But that night in my bedroom, Steve was still Stevie. Fumbling with his belt, he looked at me sideways as my mom awkwardly turned her back for a few seconds. I mouthed a silent *I'm sorry*, which I'm not sure he saw, and then he was gone. (I thought it was strange that he would have to go through the door and not the window.) My mother looked older than I'd ever seen her as she slumped at the foot of my bed, while I silently fretted about my secret lover. Would he ever want to see me again?

"I am so, so disappointed in you," she said. My mother, ever ashamed.

"Calm down. It's not a big deal." I readjusted the sheets around myself and flipped my hair across my shoulders. I hated how small my body still was, how childlike.

"Not a *big deal*. Not a big deal? Erin, sometimes I look at you and I have no idea what goes on in your head. Your father . . ." Her voice trailed off.

"So don't tell him. It's none of his business."

She looked at me the way Piper Laurie looked at Sissy Spacek during the "dirty pillows" scene in *Carrie*. *I should have given you to God when you were born.* "That's not how this works and you know it. This is his house and I don't keep things from your father."

I genuinely couldn't understand why she wouldn't side with me on this. Keeping things from Dad was the only sure way to keep the peace. She asked me if we had used protection. I said we had. It was true. Back then we just assumed every sexually active teenager's destiny included AIDS if we didn't.

"He's a big deal at school, Mom," I said, hoping she'd get it. Didn't she want me to be happy? "I'm not doing anything abnormal." I hugged a red pillow to my chest and stared at Paul McCartney's head shot from the White Album. When Dad had given me all four portraits from his own album the previous year, I couldn't believe it.

"You're too young. We've never even met this person. And this is not how we raised you." She was right. But I wasn't in a listening place.

"Can we talk about this tomorrow? I'm really tired from all the sex." I couldn't seem to stop myself from disrespecting her and rubbing it in. She was more like an older sister who always narced than an authority figure I revered, as she would often defer to me in the same timid way she did with Dad. The only thing about my mother's disciplinary style I feared was her ability to incite my father, and I had recently found power in my open contempt for her and all she represented, namely complacency.

And then she looked like she might start to cry, and I felt sorry for her. I felt sorry for both of us.

"I'm sorry, Mom. I'm really sorry. And I know I'm in trouble and that you're disappointed in me and that I shouldn't have let him in the house. But I'm asking you, woman to woman . . . daughter to mother: let's not worry Dad over what happened here tonight. I don't see how it's a lie if we just keep it between us for now."

She looked at me with not a little pity and got up from her spot at the foot of my bed, the full wave of her sudden retreat making its way through the water mattress to me a moment later.

"I'm going back to bed. We'll talk about this tomorrow. I'm certainly not going to wake him up, but if he asks me I'm going to have to tell him. You are not to use the telephone or go anywhere but school or practice until further notice." She turned off the overhead light and closed my bedroom door.

Fuck. This was going to be bad. Everybody in the house was already on edge, but especially Dad. Almost as soon as he had been feeling more like himself at work, he was laid off during a regime change at the agency. It took a few months for him to find a new job, and his anxiety levels were higher than ever.

I fumbled under my sheets and in the crack of the bed's platform for my underwear—something, anything to cover myself and somehow desexualize my situation. I braced myself for the first wave of mortification I was certain to experience now that I was left to stew in my shame. I managed to find my bottoms, only recently purchased from Victoria's Secret, the new mall phenomenon that had made available the black silk that Stevie insisted I wear. (He said cotton wasn't doing me any favors.) My search was marred by the unmistakable sound of a man just waking at three o'clock in the morning to the news that his only daughter has been turning tricks downstairs in the room off the kitchen. I heard my mother first.

"Jack . . . I said keep your voice down." And then: "It can wait until morning."

"Are you kidding me? ARE YOU KIDDING ME?"

And then there was no mistaking the *thump, thump, thump, thump, thump, thump, thump* of his bare feet down the stairs at such a rate that he had to be taking two at a time.

Where, oh God, where was my T-shirt? There wasn't time. I gripped the sheets and comforter hard and pulled them up to my neck so that no inch of me below my face could be seen. I just kept thinking, *I am naked. I am naked. I am naked.* And then he was standing before me. Wearing only his underwear—white briefs (tighty-whities) with the trapdoor. He was the color of anger, flushed purple. His arms were raised, one finger pointing alternately at the ceiling, then at me. He was rocking back and forth on his feet, and looked ready to charge. I was horrified as I realized that he had intended to strike me straightaway but that our mutual state of undress was making him even more flustered.

"YOU ARE A WHORE. DO YOU UNDERSTAND ME? A WHORE."

"I'm really sorry about this."

"SORRY?" He made the word rhyme with *whore-y.* "YOU'RE SORRY . . . YOU'RE GONNA BE *SORRY,* YOU'RE GONNA BE *SORRY* WHEN I GET THROUGH WITH YOU. WHAT KIND OF A SUCKER DO YOU TAKE ME FOR, HUH? JESUS CHRIST . . . DID YOU THINK I WOULDN'T FIND OUT? I CAN'T BELIEVE THIS, ERIN, HOW COULD YOU DO THIS? I OUGHTA THROW YOU OUT ON THE STREET . . . ON THE STREET!"

I was definitely a whore.

"Can I get some clothes first?" I really wished one of us were wearing clothes.

"DON'T YOU TEST ME, YOUNG LADY." He wound back his fist and gritted his teeth.

"I'm being serious." Under the sheets I grabbed hold of what I hoped was a T-shirt, gripped it hard and tried not to move.

"I CAN'T BELIEVE YOU, ERIN. DO YOU KNOW WHAT YOU'VE DONE? I CAN'T EVEN LOOK AT YOU . . . UNDER MY ROOF. YOU REALLY HAVE A LOT OF NERVE. IT'S DISGUSTING. IF I EVER . . . IF YOU *EVER* . . . YOU ARE SO OUT OF HERE, DO YOU HEAR ME?

I knew better than to push it. I kept my eyes averted and bit down on my lip to keep it from trembling. If he wasn't bluffing, I could stay with Michelle. Or maybe stow away at Charlie's dad's place, though Charlie would not appreciate my predicament.

My father's hands were gripping his hair, still thick despite the courses of chemotherapy the year before. It had never even thinned. He'd been cancer-free for almost a year.

"I can't stand to look at you," he said. And then he was gone.

———————

My father had never been able to talk to me about sex. When Mom was pregnant with Simon, I was four and I asked him how Mom would get the baby out of her stomach. He looked at me for a second, as if this were the most obvious thing in the world, and said, exasperated,

"Think about it." I knew enough to know that there was pushing involved, so until my mother enlightened me, I assumed that babies came out of her butt.

Mom had always been more comfortable with those frank conversations. In fourth grade Rachel Kleiner became the first girl in my class to go through puberty and get her period. Rachel was also the lone Jewish kid in our entire town, and I unfortunately associated the onset of her menses with her Judaism, believing for far too long that Jews were the chosen people in more ways than one. Mom assured me that though it was unlikely that I would ever develop breasts anywhere near the size of Rachel's at ten, I would be right on schedule when it came to becoming a woman. So when I got my period a year and a half later, I was prepared.

When I was eleven there was a rumor going around our school that intercourse was achieved when the man peed *inside* the woman's vagina, a horrifying concept, if only for the cleanup it would require. I had so many questions, mainly what would be expected of me when the time came. Mom sat me down for "the talk." What she told me was indeed disgusting—that babies were made when a husband put his penis in the wife's vagina and they moved together— ("On purpose?" "Yes, on purpose.")—but that they also did this when they didn't want to make a baby, when they just wanted to express their love. It was part of marriage and adulthood and I wouldn't have to worry about it for years and years, but when I was ready, it was God's gift to me.

Later that year, post-Butch, I tried to contextualize what had happened with him with what I had been told about on-purpose lovemaking. I told my mother one night before bed that I worried I wouldn't be able to wait until I got married to give sex a whirl. Looking back, I was testing her response—would she be able to tell what I was getting at, that I had already had some experience? Instead she looked annoyed. "You are too young to know what you're saying," she said, shutting down any further Q&A.

After this conversation, Mom gave me a contemporary Christian guide to sexuality for teens. Ironically, this book all but diagrammed the joys of onanism as a way to abstain from premarital intercourse. Talk about a gift from God! After that, no matter what the question, I would seek out the answer there, finding, as I did, a welcome home in the bosom of books.

As a kid, I felt compelled to research what it meant to be an adult. The best way to do that was through books and music. Words were the way in. I read shampoo bottles, *TV Guide*, catalogues, popular novels, and religious texts—everything except great literature, because, duh, that's what school was for. It didn't even matter if I didn't enjoy what I was reading. Once I started, I didn't stop until I'd finished the whole thing. I craved the satisfaction that came from coming to the end, and from feeling I was as smart, or smarter, than the people around me.

Dad seemed particularly proud that the things I sought to read for pleasure were selections he might have made himself. Once I read Stephen King's *Carrie*, I was encouraged to read *The Shining*, *Pet Sematary*, and *It*. Though these were horror novels, he trusted that I could handle their themes because he could. When I got into Bob Marley at fourteen, I became very interested in the roots of Rastafarianism. When I told Dad that I was thinking of writing a report on the religion for a class, he went right out to a niche bookstore in the city and picked up figurehead Haile Selassie's autobiography, along with some other light reading on the subject. Mass murder, animal attacks, child-killing clowns, international politics, and *Rolling Stone* were all deemed acceptable reading material for me.

But even though he encouraged me to read about those things, he drew the line at human sexuality.

For instance: At age thirteen I'd seen an episode of *Donahue* after school that focused on the ethical merits of circumcision for American baby boys. At dinner that night, I casually asked my parents if they'd chosen to circumcise my brothers. Unfortunately, that's exactly how I phrased it.

"That's none of your effing business!" Dad actually jumped in his chair and spat a little when he said this.

"Jack!" Mom was surprised, too, but also smiling. (He'd said "eff-ing.") "Inquiring minds want to know . . ."

Later, Mom explained that circumcision was a private matter and I didn't really need to know, but since I'd asked she'd tell me. I hadn't even known the question had been strictly related to genitalia. In my mind I had been mimicking the political tone of the debaters on the show; I thought circumcision had something to do with the separation of religious tradition and secular practice. Or Christians copying Jews.

I'd had unrestricted access to the Rolling Stones catalogue, and had been singing along to the Beatles' "Why Don't We Do It in the Road?" long before I ever had an inkling of what "It" might entail, but sex in books was strictly forbidden. (Dad must have forgotten about the eleven-year-old character Beverly Marsh in *It*, who is sexually abused by her father and acts out by having a consensual orgy with six male friends of the same age.) Of course, that didn't stop my introduction to smut by way of V. C. Andrews's gothically incestuous *Flowers in the Attic*, which was *the* passed-around paperback of the slumber party set. I would never have dared share my knowledge of such books, including the oeuvre of Judy Blume, with either of my parents.

Blume's *Are You There God? It's Me, Margaret* is about a girl's changing body, required reading for all pubescent girls. At age four-teen, the same age Blume's daughter was when Blume dedicated her book *Forever* to her, I put that book, too, on my reading list. Dad often purchased these books for me—and I'd try to withhold what I *thought* they might contain so that he wouldn't censor my choices.

Published in 1975, *Forever* is a positive look at one young woman's first experiences with love and sex in high school. I say "positive" to differentiate it from the many messages teenagers often received about extramarital sex: mainly that it might lead to unwanted pregnancy, the transmission of venereal diseases, disfigurement from said infections including sterility, potentially fatal HIV/AIDS, a "ruined" vagina from too much "use" (something I'd heard on *Geraldo* in the late eighties), generalized discomfort and pain, and of course the suicidal tendencies and nervous conditions that result from any one of the aforementioned . . . or from rejection by a man who had no intention of marrying you.

The plot of *Forever* is simple. High school seniors Katherine and Michael meet at a fondue party. They are attracted to each other and begin to date. Being the inhabitants of teenage bodies, they make out, and being a virgin, Katherine is nervous and excited about embarking on her first ever carnal adventure. She and Michael are in love and he gives her a necklace after they do it, but will their love survive even the summer before they go off to separate colleges?

The first big sex scene in the book is perhaps unrealistic in that, with Michael, Katherine not only achieves orgasm during her first time engaging in intercrural sex (aka outercourse) after "moving together again and again," but does so before he does. I call bullshit on a seventeen-year-old male's abilities in this regard, but I'll allow this win for Katherine. Still, Michael has nicknamed his penis Ralph, and while this is unfortunate it certainly does nothing to mature the characterization of the average teenage boy whose Ralph is being touched by his girlfriend for the very first time. Finally, Ralph is relieved of his duties by way of a hand job (also known, among my friends back then, as an "old fashioned"), a version of "safer sex," without risk of pregnancy. Michael and Katherine love each other and they're being cautious and responsible while learning to express that through the primal act of lovemaking.

That said, Mike is also a creep. Early on in the novel he is described as being a "ginger" (redhead) with a mole on his face—two of the most ominous physical attributes in American literature. He grabs first and asks questions later, and accuses Katherine of being a tease when she's having her period. When she demurs he tells her he loves her sincerely and they fall asleep in each other's arms. But later he asks for another old fashioned right after he acknowledges that Artie, his best friend, is possibly suicidal. Finally, he gives Katherine shit about using a condom when It finally happens (though she insists). Throughout, he behaves like a douchebag, consistent with a person who attributes human characteristics to his genitalia.

Judy knew what she was doing: forever is a very long time. The lesson of the book is that your first love need not be your last just because you humped a couple of times, and that as we grow and change and evolve through life we often find someone cooler to hump, as Katherine does when she meets the college senior Theo, her fellow counselor at tennis camp. Michael has the nerve to chastise Katherine (and compare her to a vegetable!) when her grandfather dies and she's not in the mood to make love, but the patient and world-weary Theo suggests Katherine wait until her grief subsides before they even kiss. I mean, talk about a character a parent can approve of.

But not my father.

One afternoon he knocked on my door and presented me with a bag from the used bookstore we frequented. Inside was the *Forever* paperback, along with a nonfiction book on sharks, a used copy of *The Fellowship of the Ring* (we'd read *The Hobbit*), and *The Hitchhiker's Guide to the Galaxy*. I thanked him profusely and settled in with the Blume just as soon as I was alone. I flipped through and encountered something odd. Someone had torn out entire pages of text.

On one page near the front of the book, Michael and Katherine are getting comfortable on a couch, and on the next, Katherine's liberal grandmother is asking her if they'd slept together. Later, Michael and Katherine are sitting in a truck talking, and then . . . it's the next chapter.

Within the hour I had retrieved the ripped-out pages from our kitchen garbage can, and inhaled the book. If my father had actually read it, he might have related more to Michael—pushy, impatient, jealous—than to the emotionally mature Theo, who exists to illustrate that Katherine, and young readers like her, have a choice.

Unfortunately, in my real life, I didn't find out that "Michael" wasn't my cup of tea until "Ralph" made his debut, at which time I was already screwed. And therein lies the irony when a father tries to censor Judy Blume.

By lunchtime the day after Stevie and I were caught, everybody in the junior and senior classes was abuzz about what had happened. Charlie skipped out of third period English, depriving me of his daily letter, no doubt annoyed by my choice. Michelle merely shook her head when she saw me: I'd really done it this time. My only ally seemed to be Chris Wolf, creator of the skateboarding fanzine I took pictures for and my inside man on the football team. We'd met at camp when we were twelve and had fallen in and out of love ever since. No one woman could ever keep his attention for long, and his fondness for variety and access to an endless pool of contenders—even moms!—made him hard to pin down. But he was a loyal friend. Chris and I had both dipped our toes in the culture of high school football—he as an actual player, me as a cheerleader—while still maintaining our indie cred among the progressives.

After lunch he pulled me over to his locker and gave me his varsity jacket.

"Hosier, wear this and don't take it off for the rest of the season. Nobody'll mess with ya. I'm sorry to have to be the one to tell you this, but your boy Stevie is not on your side, do you hear what I'm saying?" We began to walk to Environmental Biology and parted the seas of ponytailed volleyball players. I couldn't tell if they were looking at me more than usual.

"What did you hear?"

"He told first string this morning during laps that you let him put it in your butt."

"What? That's not true." *Oh my God.* I felt the blood drain from my face. Chris's eyes searched mine as he wordlessly prepped me to steel myself.

"True or not, he said some other things as well, explicit things. Matt and I told him to shut it, but Coach was kind of laughing. You're gonna have to watch yourself with some of the Badgerettes—I think his girlfriend probably knows by now. But look, try to ride it out. You didn't do anything I haven't done." His mother had walked in on him in a similarly compromising position the previous summer. "How long you grounded?"

"I'm not sure yet, my parents aren't speaking to me."

"Whoa, that's rad. I wish my mother would try that." Chris's mom was an obstetrics nurse and she was forever telling horror stories from the delivery room in the hope that they might act as birth control on teenagers. Once, she felt compelled to loudly enunciate the three syllables of the word *clitoris* as she told me about a genital wart she'd found on one. Chris's dad spent a lot of time in the basement of their house, quietly tending to his model trains.

"Once a month she confiscates my Dwarves tape on the grounds that the cover art is offensive, and I have to buy that shit all over again."

"*Blood Guts and Pussy?*"

"That's the one." Everything I knew about punk music, skate culture, and all things gross I learned from Chris. Conversely, he never took the Lord's name in vain, and if I did he'd very seriously ask me to stop.

We took our seats at a long table in the bio lab. I was grateful to have Chris in my corner. (I did wear his varsity jacket for the rest of the season and it provided a kind of shield, even from my parents. Everybody respected that kid. When he was on the field, he growled at the other players and told them he'd kill their whole families. But inside he was all heart.)

"Excuse me, Erin." I looked up and saw the untrustworthy face of a nameless sophomore girl, evidently somebody's younger sister. She was in the company of an equally blond and giggly sidekick. "There's something in the upstairs ladies' room that you should probably see."

"Oh, thanks, I'll get right on that," I said with as much mock seriousness as possible.

Chris stood up. "You ladies wanna see my dick?" he asked. The girls feigned shock as he began to unzip his pants to open his boxers.

"Mr. Wolf! Your body belongs to you—let's keep it that way." Our teacher, Mr. Taylor, was also the football coach, and used to Chris's exhibitionist tendencies.

As he instructed us to open our textbooks for review, Mr. Taylor fumbled in his desk drawer, pulled out the bathroom pass, and silently set it on his desk. A few moments later he made eye contact with me and gestured to the pass. Even he seemed to know what awaited in the upstairs ladies' restroom.

I pushed open the door marked GIRLS. This wasn't my favorite bathroom in the building, as it tended to be frequented by teachers. School bathrooms always smelled like blood and paste. I checked the speckled linoleum floor under the door of each stall and hoped for the best. The place was empty. But on the mirror that stretched as long as the row of sinks, I immediately saw a lipstick message. It was written in a waxy, feminine scrawl, overly loopy—not the handwriting of anyone I'd ever be friends with—in purple frosted lipstick: *Erin Hosier is a SLUT*, the *SLUT* underlined three times for emphasis.

I regarded myself in that mirror with my name—surname spelled correctly, which was unusual—and thought of Scarlett O'Hara and *Heathers* and Yoko and Madonna. How was it that this was here and I hadn't even seen Stevie all day? Where was his punishment? I considered smashing the glass. I resented that I had been summoned here to clean up my own mess, yet I would never have destroyed school property. That struck me as somehow too hysterical, too predictable.

I approached the sinks and began to reach for a brown paper towel, then stopped. Someone had taken time and lipstick to scrawl this message, and it was impressive in size. It was meant as a warning and a fact, and though it predated my knowledge of the riot grrrl movement by a year, I saw that it was important not to censor the message. After all, my own father had recently come to the same conclusion. Leaving it didn't mean I wasn't hurt. I *was* hurt. But leaving it meant something more important: it meant I could endure it.

For the second consecutive morning, my father managed not to make eye contact with me over breakfast. My brothers watched and snickered, luxuriating in the knowledge that I had done something so horrible that it had rendered our father totally speechless. He was still too angry to even acknowledge my existence, and my mother didn't feel she could dole out discipline alone. I was in limbo on Punishment Island.

"Mom," I said, confronting her after Dad's car left the driveway, "don't you think it's kind of weird that Dad is refusing to speak to me?"

She shot me a look that told me not to start and addressed Simon and Greg. "Boys—get ready for the bus."

"*Mom*. Don't you think it's a little extreme?"

She frowned even harder. "I don't know what to think, Erin. Maybe you should have thought about your father before you did what you did."

"Are you suggesting that in the Freudian sense?" I had no idea what that meant, but it sounded like something a smart-ass would say.

"I don't know what that means." She didn't, either.

"Never mind. I can't take it back. Should I make plans to move out? Prepare myself to be removed from the will? Will I be going to boarding school?"

"Don't be so melodramatic. Maybe if you spent less time having a pity party and more time working on your algebra you wouldn't be in this situation."

I abhorred being accused of self-pity, which I thought of as having empathy for oneself. (Many years later in therapy I'd learn that empathy for oneself is an appropriate emotion.) In any case, I would never work on my algebra.

"All I'm doing is asking you to please talk to Dad. I don't think it's normal for him to be this mad."

"This is between you and him. It's not for me to interfere. I can't fight your battles for you."

"Clearly," I said, then hissed, "Why start now?" I flashed my patented death stare, designed to induce guilt, fear, and feelings of insecurity about her parenting, and stormed out of the kitchen to wait for my ride to school.

———————————

I'd lost my virginity the previous summer to my first boyfriend, James. We'd waited eight months into our romance to do it. We wanted to be sure it would be perfect and that we were doing it for the right reasons (i.e., true love). We both had some serious reservations about the consequences of sex, primarily that it would fast-track us to hell. James still went to catechism class and felt we should commit to a kind of pre-engagement before we went all the way. I knew he wanted to play professional baseball one day, but I secretly harbored doubts that I could be the wife of a professional athlete. My interests were all in New York City, a place with a reputation so hedonistic that uttering its name in mixed company often felt akin to baring my breasts. Surely city girls had sex by fifteen.

I wanted to start my life as someone who was brave in the face of adulthood. I consciously wanted my childhood to be over. I wanted to have sex in spite of the fact that I had a hunch I wouldn't marry James. We'd already been giving each other every kind of "job" in the human sexual repertoire for months, and I wanted to know what it would feel like to have something *inside*. For us to be *one*. Furthermore, I wanted to change. I wanted to have the proof of experience. I was feeling everything for the first time—love and lust and the fear of abandonment and of death—and I knew these things were archetypal as they were happening. I was determined to know what I was talking about, good or bad.

It finally happened in the back of James's mom's metallic-blue Firebird, the one with the I LOVE JESUS bumper sticker. Fitting, since we were parked on a hill behind St. Helen Catholic Church. The bucket seats made things awkward. We were both somehow half in the front seat, half in the back. The radio was tuned to the local R&B station, but the sex lasted only as long as a couple of commercials, so there was never an actual song to remind me of the experience, only an ex–pro football player's ad for his Toyota dealership and its low, low prices. *"When I make a promise I keep it."*

The hymen is no joke. I assume it's the closest a girl's body gets to feeling the sensations of labor and delivery (albeit on the tiniest of scales). There was a definite pop, then a slicing pain. There was a scream (mine) and a grunt (his). Then he collapsed, sweating all over me, still stuck. I allowed myself two moments to take it in—this was what sex was, and I had done it—then I wanted it out.

"Did you come?" he asked, sweat dripping like tears from his forehead onto mine.

"It just really hurts." I sucked air through my teeth as I pushed him up and off, wincing at the feeling.

"What's the matter?" James tried to kiss me. "I'm sorry if it was too quick. I just . . . I just couldn't control myself. That was amazing."

"Oh, shit." I noticed that I was bleeding. There was so much blood I could smell it.

"Shit, my mom's car! Get up, get up, get up!"

To make a long humiliation short, I bled all over the back seat. It was a cheaper model—the seats were blue fabric. We drove to my house, sneaked some Tide out of the family bathroom, and Lady Macbeth spent fifteen minutes scrubbing the remnants of her own virginity out of her soon-to-be-ex-boyfriend's car, a Kotex aggressively lodged between her legs.

We didn't break up that night. We stayed together long enough to erase the memory of the bad first time. He really wanted it to feel good for me. But one night a month later he called to tell me he'd kissed someone else, and he was "experiencing feelings of confusion." Also, he didn't know if he could ever come around to the idea of my wanting to leave Ohio. For three weeks after the breakup, I felt as if

I'd never recover. I called James every night when I knew he'd be back from basketball practice and begged him to reconsider. After the first week his mom stopped passing him the phone, always citing his loyalty to homework. "Don't you have homework to do, Erin?" I couldn't understand where our devoted love had gone, but I had no intention of pining forever.

———————

The double standard for sexually active girls was well known to me, but it was the kind of thing I planned not to internalize. I'd been reading back issues of *Ms.* while babysitting at Cat's house, the town ceramicist. She had bookshelves full of literature, poetry, and sex manuals for hippies. By the time I'd worked my way through a college course's worth of feminist prose (and some Philip Roth for contrast), I had pledged my allegiance to womankind and personal autonomy. My body, my choice. I'd anticipated some residual slut shame from "the culture," but I'd never planned on having to deal with it so directly from my father. My teenage sex life had always been the conversational domain of my teenage friends and my teenage friends alone. So I resented that my having had sex suddenly seemed to threaten my place in my family, if not the world.

Two nights after the episode, I tried to break the ice. "Hey, Dad, how was your day?" I asked as casually as I could after the news with Tom Brokaw, cornering him in the living room as he stood over the wood-burning stove, peering down at the fire below, poking around at a log like it might try to poke back.

I wasn't sure he'd heard me. He was always quiet after the news, which seemed to depress him. "It was long," he said, not looking up from whatever he saw in the fire. He had answered, though. That was something.

"Look, I know I'm in a lot of trouble. I know I did something really bad, and believe me, I'm paying for it. I mean, I think there's something wrong with me. Not physically or anything, just . . . sometimes

I do things without thinking them through. But at the same time, I think them through more than I think you guys give me credit for. I mean, I'm smarter than you think."

He looked at me for the first time in the forty-eight hours since I'd broken his heart. He seemed nervous and maybe a little relieved. "Oh, yeah?" he said.

"Yeah. And it's hard enough being this age and trying to figure things out and having to do it in front of everyone."

"Erin, you're barely sixteen years old. I know you think you know what you're talking about, but you don't. I don't really know what to say to you about this. I'm so . . . . disappointed. You can't imagine what it feels like for me."

"Yeah, well, that makes two of us."

"You're grounded."

"I know."

"Indefinitely."

"I figured."

"Are we supposed to take you to the doctor or something? Oh God." He looked down again.

"No, Dad, you don't have to worry about that. I can take care of myself."

"Your mom and I think you should maybe go talk to somebody. A counselor."

"Okay, sure. Whatever you guys want." This was going surprisingly well. I didn't want to push my luck. "I'm going to go work on my English paper now. Just wanted to check in."

He nodded. I turned away.

There was no going back from all that I knew about sex, but there was no approval like male approval. I was hooked on the high of being desired by boys, even as I was attracting them for all the wrong reasons. I was using them for practice; I wanted to be able to take on men when the time came. My father would never apologize for calling me a whore, but humility wasn't really his thing. Maybe in this case he didn't even owe me an apology; maybe I was supposed to learn that every action had its consequence and nothing about our relationship was ever going to be easy.

––––––––––

Indeed, that message rang clear all around me, and not just at church. Even in a Christmas-themed episode of *The Cosby Show* less than two years prior. As a rule, Cosby made for easy family viewing, but a scene in one episode made me very aware that my father was in the room, and not in a good way.

At the beginning of season six, prodigal daughter Denise, who has been on an extended trip to Africa, returns unannounced to her parents' house with a new husband, Martin (whom she's married just two weeks after meeting), and his adorable daughter, Olivia (to whom she has just become insta-stepmom). In this episode, Dr. Huxtable and his new son-in-law are bonding over apple juice in the kitchen when Huxtable laments that he never got to give his daughter away at her wedding. He then wants to know if Denise was a virgin when she got married, and Martin confirms that she was.

He delivers the line this way: "On our wedding night, I discovered that, of the two of us, only one of us had had prior experience, and as you know, I'm the one with the daughter."

Then Cosby does a dance of joy while wearing a jaunty sweater. Later, Martin arranges for a do-over wedding ceremony in the living room so his wife's father can turn her over properly. Other things happen in this episode—Olivia gets to meet Santa Claus!—but the image of Denise Huxtable's father talking to her husband about her sex life is the one I remembered.

Years later, just after my father died, I found a journal he'd been keeping around this time. It was an assigned exercise from my parents' couples therapist, something they'd started trying unbeknownst to me. There, for that October day in 1991 when he forgave me, was a short entry in his perfect executive cursive. It said only *Erin's not a virgin anymore.*

12

GIRL

SINCE EARLY CHILDHOOD, I'd heard all the Beatles albums and singles in no particular sequence, but in junior high I started to listen to the albums all the way through, the songs arranged as intended. My first favorite was *Sgt. Pepper's Lonely Hearts Club Band*, which Michelle and I would play whenever we were in slumber party mode or participating in the ritual of personal grooming. I will always associate the image of us daring our feathered bangs to transform into little Towers of Pisa with enormous cans of Aqua Net with "With a Little Help from My Friends" playing in the background. It played so often that we wore out the CD, until "Good Morning Good Morning" skipped in earnest on the repeated lyric.

During high school, I listened to *Rubber Soul* the most. Its release in 1965 preceded *Sgt. Pepper's* by a year and a half, but the songs felt more mature to me. The album perfectly encapsulates the quintessential teenage experiences of romantic turmoil and broken bonds, the questioning of authority, and early drug experimentation. Its lyrics are more nuanced and personal than those in the Beatles' five previous studio albums, the sound in general more progressive. (George Harrison uses the sitar for the first time.) Possibly the most melancholy of the catalogue, its themes are jealousy, distrust, anger, revenge, and regret. "Norwegian Wood" tells the story of a guy who waits around for a girl who dares to leave him alone while she goes to the office the morning after they have sex. It ends with him burning down her house. John had become disenfranchised with being the first Beatle to marry three years prior, and later confessed in interviews that "Norwegian Wood" was inspired by his own vast experience with infidelity. In "Run for Your Life," the clear message is *If I find out you're cheating on me, I'm going to kill you*. Throughout the album, there's lots of chasing of disaffected women who could not give a shit. I definitely fancied myself that kind of bird.

The band was growing up, too. In 1965, Ringo married his girlfriend, Maureen Cox, and George would marry Pattie Boyd the following year. Paul was seriously involved with his girlfriend of two years, Jane Asher, a beautiful strawberry blond actress, and wrote a few songs inspired by their arguments: "You Won't See Me," about the frustration of rejection, and "Wait," about a couple who doesn't trust each other when he's away on tour. "I'm Looking Through You" perfectly summarizes the moment you look at your friend and realize you don't know him anymore. It's the sound of love dying. For the first time in the Beatles repertoire, some of the songs were written under the influence of marijuana. Like seemingly everything about the band, their first time getting high was the stuff of legend. Bob Dylan was their gateway to a higher plane, sharing his stash with the Beatles and their manager, Brian Epstein, at the Hotel Delmonico in 1964. When Dylan handed a joint to Ringo Starr, who was at the time unfamiliar with the concept of "puff, puff, pass," he simply smoked the whole thing himself. Paul's first stoned impulse was to immediately write down all his trippy observations and big ideas. He woke up the next morning to find a piece of paper in his pocket with the words, "There are seven levels!"

The band was first introduced to LSD that same year when George and Pattie and John and his wife, Cynthia, went to a dinner party at the home of their dentist, John Riley. Hoping to literally and figuratively turn on his guests, Riley laced everyone's after-dinner coffee with LSD-infused sugar cubes. As soon as the group realized that something was wrong, they fled to a club, where they really started to feel the effects—George called it "a very concentrated version of the best feeling I'd ever had in my whole life." The experience was positive for John, too, and a few months later, he and George introduced Ringo to the drug at the infamous pool party in Beverly Hills attended by the actor Peter Fonda. At one point George was having a hard time, and Fonda was dispatched to talk him through his bad trip by telling him that he'd died three times when he was a boy, having accidentally shot himself in the stomach. The conversation inspired the song "She Said, She Said," on *Revolver*. Paul would wait until 1967 to follow in his bandmates' cosmic footsteps.

I decided to be a contrarian and drop acid before I ever truly got stoned on anything else. It was the summer before senior year and the stuff was easy to procure—all you needed was one friend with an older sibling in college, a stoner cousin, or, according to local rumor, access to one of the Amish boys who had been corrupted by their Yankee colleagues at a local farmers market and now sold the stuff for a modest profit.

That first time I was outside at dusk with a couple of my friends. Chris had given me a bitter square of paper to melt on my tongue, and forty minutes later we were floating slowly through a field full of milkweed plants, their pods open and expelling downy white fluff in the pink light of sunset. I watched a pin-striped monarch caterpillar inch along a leaf as if in slow motion. Later, it was cool to see the stars in the sky rain down on us as we lay in the grass, but later still, when the optics wore off and four hours of teeth grinding commenced, I was reduced to a journaling idiot ("Truth is green!" I wrote with some urgency in my diary). After staring at my face in the mirror (despite specifically being told not to) and obsessively plucking my eyebrows,

I felt terrible about myself, which would be, for me, the lasting legacy of hallucinogens.

Perhaps the most notable song on *Rubber Soul* is "In My Life," widely considered by music scholars to be one of the greatest songs of all time. John Lennon was twenty-five when he wrote its lyrics, Paul McCartney just twenty-three when he wrote the melody (this is one of only two Beatles compositions where there is any disagreement among the band about who was largely responsible for each). It's a song that wholly embraces nostalgia, as a present-day John looks back on his life and relationships. The song's final verse addresses his current love as a way of saying that though all the people and places have been meaningful, when it comes to life and love, he prefers the present tense.

Rubber Soul is the album that I associate with coming into young adulthood, as the Beatles were already halfway through their tenure as a band but just coming into their own as songwriters. I was young but feeling old enough to look back. I was creating a past that I couldn't forget.

That's the thing about growing up—once you know a thing, you can never go back to not knowing it.

13

HEY JUDE

IT WAS THE SPRING OF SENIOR YEAR, so we were almost done. Charlie, Bryan, and I barreled down State Route 44 in Bryan's 1978 Buick LeSabre, all the windows down and the tape deck blasting Nirvana's *Nevermind* as loud as it could go. Charlie rode shotgun and was fully engaged in his Kurt Cobain imitation, even down to the Sonic Youth *Goo* T-shirt he was wearing. His stringy blond hair was bob-length, his voice was a growl as he spat the words to "Lithium." Bryan swigged Mountain Dew like there was liquor in it (there wasn't, yet). I was in the back seat leaning forward, my head banging in tandem with theirs. It was 7:22 in the morning, and we were on our way to school.

Charlie was ranting as we pulled into Bryan's preordained spot in the modestly sized high school parking lot.

"I hate the Grateful Dead. The Grateful Dead isn't a *rock* band, they're not even a *band*! They're a bunch of fat old men making money off stoned hippies who should know better. That's why I hate everyone! All they do is go to these shows and take drugs and look at the pretty lights. It never occurs to them that there's never any good music being played."

Charlie was serious about the stuff he hated. Rock music was about expressing rage, not creating a soundtrack to play hacky sack to.

"There are at least six bands on my block that play better music than these guys who've been touring for the last fifty goddamn years. And those colored teddy bears on that car, all cute and happy, they make me want to fucking kill someone."

"Jesus, dude. It's morning still. Let's try to make it out of the parking lot before we talk about killing hippies," Bryan said. He was the son of a Vietnam-vet-turned-pacifist.

"I just feel so hostile right now. I feel this really good evil trip coming on, and I don't want to go to Government and fail this test. And I can't wait to not go to this school anymore."

There was definitely an us-versus-them theme going on between "the progressives," as we were sometimes called, and almost everybody else at Berkshire High. Charlie and I had both gained a reputation for being agitators. We wrote a weekly column for the school newspaper, where we criticized the local politics of the aggressive bourgeois rednecks who ruled the community, and also dashed off comedic essays on the significance of obscure pop culture events just to amuse ourselves.

We invoked our First Amendment right on a weekly basis, pushing articles through that, in retrospect, were pretty shocking (such as a piece for girls about how to obtain a legal abortion without having to receive a parent's permission, the law in Ohio). We'd started a movement to stop the tradition of the daily morning prayer that took place right after the Pledge of Allegiance, pointing out that ours was a public school. (It was ultimately demoted to a "moment of silence.") Because of this, I received a postcard in the mail from a concerned citizen—one of the parents who sponsored a Bible study that met on campus—announcing that he would pray for my soul. Dad was amused by the whole thing. I think he was proud that I felt confident enough to question authority to the point of notoriety. He didn't mind my rebellion unless I was breaking *his* rules.

I shared Charlie's disgust with the bands of our forefathers and the looming quiz on the Bill of Rights, but I was more distracted by the fact that my father had punched my brother in the face less than an hour before. I didn't bring it up. It didn't seem like the right thing to just blurt out.

———————

That morning, when our parents announced we'd be gathering for a family meeting later, we knew this could only mean the D-word. In some ways it was a relief. It would finally be over—the constant heaviness of Mom's disappointment and resentment, her exhaustion, and Dad's shaky, unpredictable rages. They'd been fighting more than usual. Dad had been increasingly jealous of her new friends and the time she spent away from home. He'd convinced himself that she'd been having an affair with her piano teacher. We could hear his hissed accusations through the bathroom door. They fought in there so much that we'd begun peeing in the woods.

We were all in our various corners of the house, grumpily going through the motions of our a.m. routines: Mom and I in the kitchen, Greg finishing up in the bathroom, Simon and Dad huddled near the stove in the living room. It was an idiotic fight—something testosterone-fueled and not really about anything substantive. Simon had said something in the wrong tone of voice, something that threatened Dad's authority, something about how he was old enough to decide how and when he'd find a way to school—so what if he didn't want to take the bus? Then suddenly one of them shoved the other and we heard the scuffle, the blunt crack of fist against skin, my brother wailing.

Both of Simon's hands covered one of his eyes. Dad looked sheepish for a second and then started to protest: "I'm the parent and you're the child. You don't tell me—" He sounded angry but unsure of his rights.

I watched our mother leap into action. "That's it! That's it! You are out of control, Jack, you're sick! *Get out of this house! Get out of this house right now!*" Mom screamed like she had never screamed before.

It was glorious.

Dad left. The entire incident was over in two minutes. Simon stormed out of the house just in time for the bus. "You can get a ride with me!" I'd yelled, but he was already on his own.

By the time Simon got to his eighth-grade homeroom (on the same campus as the high school, but in a different wing), a red swelling had formed and colored his eye, and as far as I could tell he didn't try to hide it. By lunchtime, rumor had it that a teacher had reported the condition of my brother's face to Child Protective Services, and by sixth period a social worker had been dispatched to interview us. We were both pulled out of our respective classes and detained, separately, in the vice principal's office.

"I think my father is way out of line and has been for a while," I said matter-of-factly to the young, mousy, less-than-intimidating woman sent to intervene on our behalf, feeling ready for my close-up.

"What makes you say that?" she asked.

"Listen, my parents' marriage has been a sinking ship for years now. I'm an eighteen-year-old feminist, and trust me, that guy's got issues with women." The social worker smiled, then remembered herself.

"What do you think should happen to your father now?" she asked.

"He could use some counseling," I said, "and maybe a Realtor."

The fallout was surprisingly light. An incident report was created and filed, a casual warning that if things should get so out of hand again that it was noticeable to the community, there could be real consequences. For now the consequences would be two consecutive overnights in a Days Inn.

The next family summit took place in the yard; it felt safer that way, with God and the neighbors as witnesses. Dad assured everyone that while he and Mom were separating, he'd still stay close by and see us all the time. Greg stared at them wild-eyed, bewildered, then at me, and yelled, "Isn't anyone going to even *try* to think about someone besides themselves?" Mom started to cry. Simon looked uncomfortable, his hands too deep in his pockets as he stared down at the grass. Dad looked sad, like he was hoping Mom would answer Greg's question, but no one said anything.

"Okay, then," I said. "Can we go now?" Greg stormed off to the house with Mom at his heels. Simon picked up his bike and headed down the road, and I went to call Michelle. But Dad didn't go anywhere, and wouldn't anytime soon, stubbornly staking his claim to his side of the master bedroom until he found a suitable rental.

So it came as a shock to no one but Dad when Mom moved into a tent outside. It was her silent protest at his noncompliance with the separation. Our parents had been in a kind of emotional standoff for months. Mom refused any of Dad's attempts to argue or to reconcile. She could be found in the house as usual once Dad had gone to work and most days when we got home from school. But after dinner, she retreated to the green nylon shelter under the apple tree, illuminated by the light of a Coleman flashlight.

One evening I ventured out to the glowing orb, softly lit like a lightning bug against the backdrop of pine trees framing the meadow. Spring peepers and crickets roared as I approached the tent's entrance.

"Mom, can I come in?"

"Of course, Erin. Come sit with me."

When I opened the flap to peer inside, the space of this cocoon was filled wall to wall with a full-size inflatable mattress layered with sheets, a sleeping bag, pillows, and an extra wool blanket. I kicked off my shoes and crawled through the opening to position myself cross-legged facing her on top of the mattress. Stacked all around the edges of the bed were small towers of books like totem poles. There were no behavior modification manuals or Bibles in this space. They'd been replaced by college textbooks in English literature, psychology, music theory, and French 101. One tower held titles like *The Courage to Heal* and *Women Who Run with the Wolves*, poetry by Margaret Atwood,

Maya Angelou, and Sylvia Plath. Tucked in behind them were spiral notebooks, pens, a jug of water, and an extra flashlight. She was like a super-nerdy twelve-year-old who'd decided to run away but couldn't decide what to leave behind.

"Wow, Mom, Maya Angelou. Are you . . . bettering yourself?"

"Why do you have to be such a smart-ass? I'm reading, yes, and I'm writing, and I'm learning that I have my own ideas about things, and that I'm changing. I think you're really going to like college—even just taking a few classes has really opened things up for me."

"I'm only going to college to get out of here," I said. "That, and to buy four years of time before I have to get a real job."

I picked up a poetry book by Sharon Olds called *The Father* and leafed through it.

"Why are you sleeping out here?" I asked. "It's really weird."

Mom took a deep breath and exhaled long and slow. "I just need some time to myself, to think. It's so peaceful out here. Don't you love the sound of the crickets?"

"Yes, but I can hear their annoying song from inside my bedroom. You've abandoned and banished us to that miserable house. I know you're unhappy. We're unhappy. Why don't you just leave Dad?"

Mom looked down at her hands. "I'm sorry, Erin. It's just not that simple. Marriage is complicated."

"What's so complicated? He's a dick!"

Mom steeled herself against my directness. I thought I was the stronger of the two of us and that she was just afraid to be alone.

"Erin, your dad has been through a lot. The cancer really took a toll, and then getting laid off—it's been a rough couple of years for him."

"Yeah, it's been a rough couple of years for all of us," I said.

There had been a lot building up to this explosion. The last few years had ushered in an onslaught of unlucky phenomena and our subsequent falling-out with our church. She could no longer talk about her problems with people who gave stock answers or only re-cited scripture.

Mom shook her head. "I know that. But your father thought he might not live to see you grow up. And he worries about being a good provider—that's a big thing for men. Those months when he was out of work were really stressful."

I couldn't really tell the difference between his out-of-work-stress bad moods and his work-stress bad moods. Advertising was volatile, but so was high school.

"I think change takes time, and I just can't be with him right now. Maybe one day you'll understand, but I hope not."

Mom's tent of one's own wasn't long for the world. One morning when Dad had gone to work and the rest of us were getting ready for school, Mom was fixing breakfast in the house while a storm was brewing outside. She wasn't typically bothered by the rain in the shelter of her tent, and had planned on resuming her time with her journals and homework after her morning routine in the house. But this morning was different; she had a bad feeling.

The sky turned green, then bruise purple. The wind whistled and twisted dramatically and made me instinctively hum the song from *The Wizard of Oz*, when Miss Gulch rides a bike in the sky. Mom ran outside and back in with armloads of books, stacking them against the wall of the kitchen. When she'd finished, she herded us all into the dank cellar of our farmhouse (a place Mom and Dad visited only if they needed to check the fuel tank, clean the furnace, or mitigate water damage). We huddled under the mildewy stairs while a tornado raged above.

The storm came and went quickly, lasting only long enough for me to finish making a list of things I wanted to take with me when I moved out. While the rest of my family fretted over possible broken glass and jostled lawn furniture aboveground, I plotted the dorm room color schemes of my future. When the winds died down and we could actually hear the quiet, Mom walked out to the backyard to see. Tree branches of all sizes were scattered around the open field. Green leaves shellacked the windows and the neighbors' cheap plastic lawn chairs, which had blown against our back porch. And a large oak tree had split at its base and landed directly on top of Mom's tent, which had just an hour before been a scarlet beacon against the yard. Now it was bleeding out.

Ultimately Dad was court-ordered to attend anger management classes and ended up moving into a rented house just up the road, as he'd promised he would. The house was white with a white picket fence, which struck me as ironic and sad. Being the family patriarch was what Dad knew how to do above all else, but without a roost to rule he quickly seemed to shy away from being a parent in favor of being a pal. Gone was the family villain who doled out the discipline, and in his place emerged a co-conspirator, just another obstinate child who lived to torment our mother.

After Dad moved out, I turned my attention to getting into college so I could get out, too. I hadn't exactly applied myself academically. My test scores were average and my grades straight C's, and I had never managed to complete the basic algebra course required in order to get into college in the state of Ohio. Still, it never occurred to me that I wouldn't have a shot at getting into Oberlin or Kent State University, a local kid's official collegiate backup plan. (The school's unofficial motto was "Can't read, can't write, Kent State.") I was pretty confident in the essay portions of my applications, so I was appalled when I received rejection letters from both schools. Didn't they know who I was? Kent replied that I'd be put on a waiting list until I completed the conditional math class.

Dad suggested I write a letter appealing the admissions decision, that sometimes a well-written plea could trump lackluster test scores. The letter was shamelessly manipulative, meant to invoke maximum sympathy on account of my no-good, divorce-happy parents and the toll their often-violent arguments had taken on me and my brothers. Within two weeks I received an acceptance letter. As long as I agreed to take and pass Algebra 101 at some point during my tenure, I could enroll at the main campus.

I was getting out.

With Dad out of the house, our lives became kind of a free-for-all. We kids had broken every rule that had been beaten into our developing bodies, and life seemed better for it. God's failure to keep our parents together meant no more church. God's negligence meant we could curse Him openly, watch R-rated movies with our friends, and drink pop with abandon while watching TV after eight p.m. Without Dad around to lay down the law, Mom rolled over pretty quickly. Even if she'd had the energy, her threats of discipline would have fallen on deaf ears, so she didn't bother trying to enforce a curfew. She relaxed her emphasis on nutrition and, citing her children's ingratitude as reason enough not to care anymore, lifted the ban on sugary cereals.

The house I'd grown up in bore little resemblance to the one I was leaving behind. Mom was working as a teller in a local bank, her first job since quitting her retail gig at Casual Corner to get married twenty years before. At night she would continue working on a bachelor's degree at a regional branch of Kent State. I made my own money waitressing and stayed out of trouble. For me, the prospect of leaving meant freedom from the tyranny of family—of fighting parents and the angry young men my brothers were becoming, of sick people. I couldn't see the downside of divorce.

14

IN MY LIFE

I WAS NAMED "MOST UNIQUE" in my yearbook's superlatives section. Probably not a compliment, but I took it as one. I thought it would have been better phrased "Weirdest," as the word "most" was redundant. I was photographed posed on a high oak tree branch that looked over the football field. Under the "Senior Salutes" section, where parents purchased a little space to inscribe custom messages of support over our grayscale baby pictures, mine read:

> *You have always been a woman of words, seeking a position of power. We pray that as you press toward your goal, you will never lose sight of what's important, and that you will know that you are loved. Keep the faith, baby.*
>
> *All our love, Mom and Dad*

A cross-section of what friends and acquaintances wrote in my yearbook revealed a couple of common themes:

Erin, have a great life. I don't hate you, I just enjoy disagreeing with you. Don't stop fighting for yours and others' rights. P.S. DON'T HAVE KIDS.

—*John*

I never really appreciated your gift for arguing until our confrontation with you know who. You really came through. I will always love you and never forget you even though we may not meet again. I hope that your dedication to causes will someday enhance mankind and that you'll be successful in educating our ignorant brethren. "Fight the power."

Isha lama lakem, with love and sisterhood, Tanya

Never stop shouting.

—*Jamie*

Face it, Hosier: We'll grow old and never see each other again. We'll pull out our purple and gold mementos and reread the zines and glance at pictures and wonder what happened to each other. Maybe we should get in touch, we'll think, but we probably won't. All I'll be is a sliver in your past of blurry memories. "I once knew a guy named Chris, wonder where he's at, probably a factory somewhere." Girl, you know it's true, and to think we were going to get married.

—*Chris*

The first weekend after high school graduation I went camping with Chris. It wasn't unusual for me to camp out with him and his best friend, Lewis, who were both heavily into two things—skateboarding and reenacting history, specifically the Revolutionary, Civil, and French and Indian Wars. They'd been doing this since they were kids and took it really seriously, sleeping in the woods all year long, eighteenth-century style. That meant making the fire with a piece of flint and some shredded tree bark, eating hardtack, mending their handmade uniforms with a needle and thread, and sleeping outside in the dead of winter next to a fire, in the arms of their mates under a ton of wool blankets.

Chris. I was going to miss him most of all. Several good friends, including Charlie, were also going to Kent, but Chris wasn't interested. He'd already started his own small landscaping business, and planned to stay in town, maybe forever. As soon as summer began and we were no longer in school, I realized he was the person I would miss seeing all the time when I moved away in the fall.

Camping out with friends killed the awful association I had with the woods and Butch. I told Chris about the ways the experience had impacted my choices with Stevie and the one that followed, an older high school dropout who picked me up from school in a classic Mustang. Chris knew about the obsessive friendship I'd had with another guy with a dark disposition, and the guy who helped break up my close friendship with a childhood friend, and all the selfish ways I'd behaved in the name of never being alone. He understood the instinct to test boundaries and never judged me for it.

By the time I was a fifteen or sixteen, abuse, assault, and rape were regularly discussed topics among my friend group. So many of us had had some kind of direct experience, or were close with someone who had been sexually abused, either recently or when they were little kids. Either we were gravitating to each other unconsciously, or sexual abuse was an epidemic. Even then we kind of joked about it. Sample snippet of conversation:

"Oh, you remember that guy—Tim? He was the one who fingered me without asking and refused to stop?"

"Oh, him. At least he apologized after. Lori just found out she's pregnant from that guy from Cleveland who raped her at the house party."

It came up when we got high and talked around a campfire, or drank light beer in Michelle's room when her parents weren't home. Or when a friend dropped acid and was stuck in a loop of remembering getting messed with by an older cousin. (Come to think of it, drinking or drugs were usually involved when we talked about this stuff.) Chris's experience was with an ex-girlfriend who had been preyed upon by her grandfather for years. Chris was preoccupied by the idea of avenging her and letting Grandpa know that someone else knew what he had done, but he was worried if he was to confront the man in person, it could take a violent turn. But more than that, it would blow up his girlfriend's life, and she wasn't ready for that kind of exposure. We talked about it all with each other, but we rarely disclosed to our parents what had happened to us. We wanted to protect them and spare ourselves the grief of having to explain.

This time it was just the two of us out in the woods behind his house, wearing our twentieth-century jeans. He made a venison stew with carrots and potatoes over the fire he taught me how to build. We talked about our friends, about our plans for the future. I told him about my parents separating, about Mom and the tent, about Dad and his new rented house, about the long list of reasons why I felt so compelled to leave home, never to return. Chris reminded me I was going to be living only a forty-five-minute-drive away, and that maybe I wasn't as done with my family as I liked to think.

"You know, it's okay to admit that you're sad about your parents breaking up," he said. "Just because you think it's for the best doesn't mean it doesn't affect you."

He was right. "I don't feel sad for them, though. Just for Simon and Greg. Greg's pretty upset about it." I hadn't thought I might be entitled to any kind of grief, only validation for having the foresight to steel myself for the end. Divorce felt like something that should only devastate a child, and I could clearly see why. Suddenly my parents were scattering, and I was on my way out, leaving my brothers to fend for themselves. They didn't call them latchkey kids in our town because nobody really locked their doors, but the sentiment was the same: no one was home.

Greg reminded me of John Lennon's son Julian, who at least partly inspired Paul McCartney to write "Hey Jude" in response to John's divorce from his first wife, Cynthia. I vowed to make a teachable moment out of the song for him—things might feel epically confusing now, but someday soon it would all make sense.

Chris and I stayed up talking, eventually falling asleep on our backs next to each other in the tent. When the sun broke through a crack in the tarp in the morning, I woke up with his arms around me, and it felt like relief and total safety. Chris had always been my friend; I'd always trusted him. Our friendship had a policy of no judgments because we were on equal footing. What strange timing to realize this was who I should have been with all along. I went back to sleep with a sudden knowledge that we belonged to each other. That whole summer, we were inseparable.

By today's standards, our love was so Nicholas Sparks. Our first time was under the stars in a little clearing next to the cornfields of Millers' Farm on Aquilla Road, on a blanket he carried around in his truck for such a purpose. We couldn't wait to be together, and when it was over he said my name. Kissing Chris was like writing a song with your best friend. There wasn't ever anything I couldn't tell him. When I maimed my hair with bleach and required an unanticipated short haircut, he shaved his head in solidarity. He never shamed me for not riding a bike, he just taught me how to ride a skateboard instead.

Both of my parents liked Chris. He was respectful, affable, and polite, and genuinely trustworthy. I think my mom had a crush on him, and my father liked his work ethic and the fact that Chris looked him in the eye every time they spoke. Dad was on his best behavior around him. It was easier for him to relate to my boyfriend than to me. With Chris, there was a clean slate—he could be the cool, laid-back dad half of him always wanted to be.

Months after the revelation that I was sexually active, my father seemed to regret not having taken a more progressive stance in the moment. After becoming light-headed and fainting in school earlier that semester, I'd ended up in the ER. When a nurse erroneously told my parents that the incident was likely due to pregnancy (instead of the dehydration it was), Dad didn't freak out. Instead, he told me not to worry and that everything would be okay. He looked a little choked up, but not at all angry. In that moment, he was all I'd ever needed him to be—steady—like Chris was every day.

When it was finally time to go off to college, Mom helped me stuff two laundry bags full of clothes and bedding, towels, and a few things from the kitchen. Packing up my room, I gingerly tugged at the iconic portraits of the individual John, Paul, George, and Ringo—the photo inserts from the White Album—that Dad had been happy to allow me to hang on the walls of my bedroom since I was thirteen. The white borders of the prints were pretty trashed, marred by multiple pinholes and the tobacco-yellow stain from the remnants of glossy Scotch tape. George's face had a purple cast from being bleached by the sun. *I really should have framed them*, I thought. They were precious and I'd handled them too casually. I placed them in a folder to take with me.

When Dad had moved out and up the road, he'd taken his stereo equipment with him. Mom would soon replace the hole on the shelf that had once housed the turntable and the speakers with a larger television, and for the first time ever, we would have basic cable. I decided to leave my CD player to Simon, along with a bunch of mixtapes and copies of albums I hoped would blow his still impressionable mind. The canon was massive—there was so much for him to catch up on, and I hoped he'd pick up where I'd left off in surpassing our father in his knowledge. With two fewer people in the house, I wanted to replace the sound of our arguments with music.

My parents maintained a united front by insisting on driving me to campus together to move me into the dorm. The air was thick with nervous tension as we packed up the car, the mood polite, somber, and expectant. Dad had left home; I was leaving home. Now it would be Mom on her own with my brothers, both of them in middle school and mad as hell. As strange as it was, it was also the same as ever—*What's one more hours-long round-trip car ride together?* I imagined Mom was thinking. Simon and Greg closed in to say goodbye.

When we were all set to go, we couldn't get in the car until the whole family fulfilled Mom's urgent need for photographic proof of this momentous day. This was our way: we would tiptoe around, confused and in pain, and then we would take some really up-tempo group shots. We'd been known to build pyramids in pictures, or pose as if for high-concept senior class portraits, holding our chins in our hands, laughing maniacally. That day, we posed beneath the apple tree, in front of the rhododendron bush, lined up on the porch steps, tallest to shortest. Dad and me; my brothers and me; Mom and me; Dad alone. After this, there would be no more photos taken of my parents side by side, and no more taken of our entire family. Not together.

END SIDE ONE

SIDE TWO

ERIN

15

SHE'S LEAVING HOME

IN 1915, KENT STATE WAS KNOWN by the moniker Kent State Normal College, a delineation that meant it offered four-year degrees. Change "Normal" to "Average" and that's what you got in 1994: the most unexceptional collegiate experience that the Midwest had to offer its roughly twenty-five thousand undergraduates. The university was mostly notable for the shootings that took place there in 1970 during the National Guard's raid on campus because of a student-led antiwar protest, and for inspiring Neil Young to write the song "Ohio" (as in, "Four dead in").

Since then, Kent's legacy had largely been defined, at least by my friends, by its music scene. Gerald Casale, founding member of Devo—KSU's addition to the punk pantheon—cited the events of May 4, 1970, as the inspiration to start the band two years later. Chrissie Hynde of the Pretenders did go back to Ohio, and still keeps a place in nearby Akron. And in the early nineties we had Guided by Voices and the Breeders (both from Dayton), and our college town's own stellar postpunk bands (Harriet the Spy, the Party of Helicopters). This, meshed with Cleveland's innumerable small clubs and now-closed music venues, made Ohio a respectable place to be from, at least as vibrant as Minnesota.

Not many people went to Kent to become great. We settled for "away from home." It was a great place to study if you wanted to be a nurse, an architect, or a fashion merchandiser, but those programs required nose-to-the-grindstone commitment, and I had no idea what I wanted to be. Charlie had been accepted to the film school, the very last year one could apply to the program. My mother was an English major who had to write too many long papers on books that I could always read for pleasure, even if I never would.

My roommate, Sally, was on track for medical school. She had somehow managed to get her hands on prescription pads and became the best source of Valium and Ritalin in our dorm. We lived in a tiny antiseptic room painted the color of old chewing gum, its walls like glossy barf (the opposite of antiseptic, actually). Sally livened things up by building a fort of tie-dyed sheets over the top bunk, where she preferred to crash out with her boyfriend, Edge, a skinhead in an industrial band. I contributed a My Bloody Valentine poster; Sally's posters were of Throbbing Gristle and Hüsker Dü. For a while it worked. But one day, toward the end of our first semester, she brought home a ferret Edge had "rescued" with the intention of keeping it as a pet. That lasted two odorous weeks before Sally and the ferret got caught and were forced to move out. I would have my own room for the rest of the year.

I inherited Lewis, Chris's best friend, to hang out with in his stead. We'd been classmates since we were twelve, but in college we became inseparable. Lewis was about six foot four and looked like George Harrison circa 1970. He rode a skateboard and wore his hair long to spite his parents, who were upwardly mobile and generally concerned with appearances. Lewis was a free thinker with a 4.0, always questioning the how and why of things. He never got high, but he always looked stoned due to chronic hay fever, and the stoners loved him because he made them look smarter.

Charlie and I lived in the same dorm on campus, but he would barely speak to me freshman year. He was too angry at what he interpreted as the ultimate rejection of him in favor of Chris, whom he considered to be a crass jock who stood for everything that Charlie despised—ambition, power, and an aptitude for competition. Charlie wrote in one of his final letters to me, "It bothers me that you can be so submissive," which made my cheeks burn with anger. That had never been my dynamic with Chris, who wasn't anything like Stevie or any of the guys I'd dated and been dumped by. In addition to looking like River Phoenix, he was the kindest person I'd ever met. He treated people with respect until they didn't deserve it anymore, and never lost his temper or acted irrationally. If he had any rage he took it out on the half-pipe he'd built in his parents' backyard. He always defused violence, even as he seemed to have a healthy understanding of its uses.

Chris came to visit me every weekend, and he was my primary link to home. As long as he came to me, I'd never have to go back. Eventually I would feel it was impossible to turn a country boy into the urban sophisticate I saw myself becoming, but even then I knew that love couldn't get any better than this. Chris was a romantic. He wrote my name in four-foot letters in the snow bank behind my dorm so I would see it on my way to class. He carved our initials into oak trees and called me *sweet girl* and *sweet pea*. He hand-stitched me an eighteenth-century waistcoat, blue wool with linen lining, as one soldier would for another. He covered each button in fabric and reinforced each stitch. On our last night together before I'd moved, he'd sliced his name in my right hip with an X-Acto knife, pressing deep enough to leave a forever scar.

———————

The scene on campus revolved around cliques of hipsters who loitered outside the student center in the quad between the dorms. There were the punks with their Mohawks and bright pink hair, their ubiquitous denim jackets with safety-pinned patches for bands like the Exploited and Anti-Flag; ravers and fashion students in vinyl dresses and six-inch rainbow-colored platform shoes; film students in black with their hand-rolled cigarettes; Black United Students in dreads and combat boots; skaters who wore giant wide-legged jeans, wallet chains, and Vans; art students with high-water pants and suspenders like 1950s greasers. The riot grrrls seemed to be split down the middle in either punker gear (the drummers) or baby doll dresses (the guitar players).

I was somewhere in between, and Lewis and I tried to mix it up with everyone. My fashion icon at the time was Courtney Love, who was clearly emulating Candy Darling, the transgender Warhol Superstar. I dutifully bleached my hair white and never left the house without a smear of crimson lipstick. I wore bathing costumes from the 1930s as dresses and paired them with little socks and vintage granny shoes.

It was the time of the fanzine, our version of a blog before the Internet would obviate the need for a cheap, stapled-together, photo-copied hodgepodge of collages and bad writing. Lewis and I included interviews with our favorite local bands. Our zine was *The Bob Ross Counterculture*, which featured interviews with our friends back home, pictures of skateboarders in midflight, and a one-of-a-kind coloring book centerfold, created in the spirit of a landscape painted by Bob "Happy Little Trees" Ross. It had a sunny disposition.

The student with the most famous zine on campus was Julian Sean, whose concept elevated the medium to the level of performance art. (It did help that he worked at Kinko's.) Every issue was a collection of sexually explicit prison letters from incarcerated men, procured when Julian took out a personal ad in the back of *Easyriders* impersonating a horny and open-minded biker chick. The question being perpetually answered by the prisoners: What would you do to me if you were here?

Julian and I had only one exchange freshman year. I was sitting alone between classes, idly reading a paperback in the newly renovated food court, when suddenly he appeared, bounding across the room, his eyes aglow from the reflection of the golden arches of McDonald's, seemingly fixed on me. We'd made eye contact in the student center before, but we'd never been formally introduced. I looked down at my Mary Janes, pretended to rifle through my bag for a notebook, and waited for him to pass. Instead, he helped himself to the seat next to mine and suddenly began animatedly talking.

"Who is your favorite Brontë sister?" he almost yelled at me, his body language frantic. I didn't understand the question.

"Oh, no . . ." I said, closing my book to show him the cover. "This isn't literature. This is for my sociology class."

"Answer the question!" he demanded, a slightly demonic look in his eye. I tried to conjure the Brontë sisters, but I couldn't remember which one had written *Wuthering Heights*, the only title I could recall.

"I don't know," I said. "Emily, I guess."

"Wrong! It's Anne!" he said, and stood up just as quickly as he'd sat down, practically kicking over the chair in the process. I realized this was some kind of joke but I didn't get it. I felt that I had failed the cool test. Julian slammed down a flyer in front of me, an advertisement for his latest event, a basement show in his apartment. "I have decided," he said, "that you can come if you want." And with that he was off.

Even though at first glance he was just another dark-haired guy in army fatigues and a Black Flag T-shirt, there was something different about him. When he looked at you, he stared, willing you to stare back. He could pick a fight without saying anything at all. If he went to see your band play, you noticed. If he invited you to one of his parties off campus, you went. He had a power over people, and the thought that I might be one of those people made me nervous. I liked to believe I wasn't the type to be intimidated by fame, but something about Julian's patented formula of physical ubiquity and social notoriety made me doubt that I had what it took to make such an impression on people. I was starstruck.

For some reason, I would never forget our first exchange, and fifteen years later Julian would become the most important person in my life.

Dad made a special visit to campus to take me to dinner the day after the news of Kurt Cobain's suicide broke, or at least I thought that was the reason.

Lewis and I had gone to see Nirvana on Halloween night in 1993. The show was at University of Akron (home of the Zips!) and it was both transcendent and an abortion. For one thing, this being Akron—known as the Rubber Capital of the World and adjacent to the Pro Football Hall of Fame—the crowd was full of the kind of testosterone-fueled meatheads that the band had come to abhor publicly. It was rumored that the entire Kent State football team was in attendance and they did not react well to the opening acts—the Boredoms, a Japanese experimental hard-core band, and the Meat Puppets, who mastered a sort of punk/country blend. Leonard Cohen's album *I'm Your Man* played on the PA between sets.

Finally, Nirvana came out in costume, with Cobain in full Barney (as in the purple dinosaur) regalia. The crowd went insane. Nirvana was only three songs in when somebody in the pit threw a shoe at Kurt, hitting him in the head, which briefly stopped the show. Kurt dropped his guitar and we thought that would be it, but instead he grabbed the Airwalk sneaker, unzipped his pants, and filled the shoe with the contents of his bladder, then seemed to consider throwing it back into the audience. He didn't, but he looked weary as he played, angry, and so over it. Less than six months later he would be dead.

The press was calling the reaction to his death comparable to that of the baby boomers to Lennon's murder. In some ways Dad was more shaken up over it than I was, worried, I think, that Kurt's depression and addiction might spread, giving rise to a sea of traumatized kids ready to jump out windows. He gave me condolences as if I had lost a close friend, which I found at once touching and annoying.

"When John died the whole world stopped for me—it was one of the bleakest days of my life," he said, looking me in the eye.

"It's so different, though. John Lennon didn't want to die."

"Well, no one *wants* to die."

"Some people do. Kurt Cobain shot himself." I didn't want him to try to soften it for me, or try to deny the ugliness of what had happened.

"I realize that. I'm saying that I understand the shock you must be feeling, that's all."

We both picked at our food in silence for a while before I wondered aloud how Simon was taking the news. He was a big Nirvana fan and had recently started playing guitar in his own band. Dad had gifted him a Rickenbacker 325 (Lennon's guitar of choice), and a few months afterward Simon was headlining the local cornfield ragers, covering "Rape Me" while wearing one of my baby doll dresses.

"That's actually what I wanted to talk to you about tonight," Dad said. "Your mom and I are concerned about your brother."

I wasn't surprised to hear it. Simon's life had changed completely within six months—everyone's had. Mom was trying to work full-time and do the single-parent-of-two-teenage-boys thing, while Dad got to hang back and be the cool one. Renting a place so close by, he now had the more liberal household. In the rental house, Dad smoked cigarettes inside. His place meant pizza and junk food, and his door was always open if either of my brothers wanted to come by and hang out, even in his absence. In short order, they had begun to defy Mom's house rules, and Dad wasn't doing much to dissuade them from taking sides.

I'd recently received a letter from Simon, who had sounded a little lonely, but I'd attributed it to his missing his big sister (since he'd told me he did). Simon could be so distant and then suddenly melt my selfish teenage heart by saying something emotional and sincere.

"What are you concerned about?"

"He's been giving your mom a hard time. She says he's sneaking out at night to hang out with the wrong crowd. He stole money out of her purse recently, and she thinks it was to buy drugs."

This shocked me. "Drugs? He's in eighth grade. What drugs?"

"I'm not sure if this is the extent of it, but she found some pot," he said. He kept putting the emphasis on my mother, as if he had no observational skills of his own. "She's concerned that he's headed down a wrong path," he continued, "so we're all going to meet with a counselor at the health center next week and she's going to talk to us about confronting him. We'd really like you to be there."

In Ohio in the early nineties, crisis intervention was in vogue, and consultations with members of the mental health community had become routine among the Hosiers. Greg had been to various support groups over the years at the local behavioral health clinic. Mom had gone for her own therapy after leaving the church. Dad had court-appointed anger management sessions, which seemed to be working. He appeared to be far more in control of his negative impulses, and I hadn't seen him lose his temper since that horrible day the year before. I wanted to believe change was possible, and if Simon was already acting out, maybe it couldn't hurt to talk about it. Still, the idea of an ambush made me nervous.

Dad laid it on thicker. "We're still a family, E, even if we're not all living under one roof. We need to come together to support each other."

_____

Two weeks later Lewis and I both found ourselves in Dr. Nancy's exceedingly floral-patterned office space for part two of Project Intervention. Part one had taken place the week before, when we'd all met surreptitiously with the turtleneck-clad juvenile counselor, whose role it was to facilitate a teachable moment about treatment options for wayward teens. Lewis was there because Dad thought Simon was looking for role models and looked up to me and my friends. Plus, I needed a ride. Unfortunately for Lewis, he was the only person there who wasn't a blood relative.

At this second meeting, we sat in a circle, Dr. Nancy in the middle with Mom in the chair to her left, then me, then Lewis, then Greg, the hot seat meant for Simon, then Dad to Dr. Nancy's right.

When Simon came in the door he was already seething and seemed only a little bit surprised to see us in the round, most likely having been tipped off by the unmistakable chamomile stench of a suite of therapist offices. He paused to look at us all incredulously before slumping down hard in his appointed chair, momentarily accepting his fate. He folded his arms across his body and leaned forward so his dirty-blond hair hung like a curtain to his shoulders, the tips of it dyed lime green. I knew I couldn't look at him or I'd laugh or cry or do something to make it about me, so I looked down at the soles of my Chucks and concentrated on the places where the rubber tread had come unglued.

Nancy began by introducing herself as a neutral party, a person who was there not to judge but to listen. She was there because Simon's family (and . . . Lewis) had become increasingly concerned about him and wanted him to know that he had a support system he could count on. This wasn't about blame, it was about acknowledging that our family had broken apart and we needed help coming back together. We had each prepared a letter to share our observations and concern and we would read them aloud, after which Simon would have a chance to respond.

My brother kept his head down as his feet hit an invisible drum pedal on the carpet. He shook his head and mumble-hissed, "*Whatever*" under his breath. Nancy held a folder of brochures in her lap; we held crinkly pieces of yellow legal paper.

"Simon, your mother would like to speak first. Let's listen to what she has to say."

Already weepy, Mom unfolded her letter on her lap and in a trembling voice offered forth the evidence she had about the stolen money and the marijuana smoking in the house.

"What money? I didn't take any money! You just hate my friends!" Simon screamed, opening up his arms as if to make himself a bigger target. "You've been nothing but a hateful bitch ever since Dad moved out, and I can't wait till I can move in with him."

Mom winced and looked down at her lap, already defeated. *Bitch*.

It was a word now openly being thrown her way, right to her face, and not for the first time. Nobody spoke up to defend her, at least not in the moment. We were either too stunned by how quickly his anger had escalated or afraid that defending Mom against insults somehow interfered with Simon's right to live his truth. Dad leaned forward and clasped his hands in front of his knees and smiled faintly as if to acknowledge the tension in the room.

"Simon," he said gently. "We're all here for you, buddy." Dad didn't attempt to look at a piece of paper before he spoke. He was the creative director of this meeting and he was about to sell my brother on the truth. "If you're getting high, let's discuss it."

Buddy? Discuss it? I was spellbound by his tone. Just a couple of years earlier this same person had threatened (again) to kick me out on the street if he ever found out that I'd been *bringing drugs into the house*. One minute I was quietly doing homework in my room and the next he had stormed in without knocking, pointed his finger in my face, and spat, "If I find out you're doing drugs, in or outside this house, that's it for you. Do you understand me?"

"I've never smoked pot in my life," I said, telling the truth and genuinely baffled by his accusation.

"You'd better hope not. Because if I catch you—" Here he clenched his fist and cocked his head to the side, then paused dramatically so I'd get the full effect of his huffing and puffing. "You. Are. Out. Of. Here."

I wanted to look him right in the eye to come back with "*Can't wait,*" but instead I said, "I can't speak for some of my friends, but I don't *smoke,*" emphasizing the word to remind him of his own bad habit, even now that he had been cancer free long enough to be considered cured.

Here in the therapist's office, I couldn't help thinking that his compassionate tone of voice had more to do with impressing our mother and Nancy than anything else. He hated what the divorce was doing to his kid, but he was anxious to show his ex that he was a kinder, gentler version of the husband she'd abandoned. I could see his game; he wanted to come home.

Nancy interjected, "Dad, you'll get a chance to speak, but right now it's Erin's turn in the circle."

I found it difficult to look at my brother, so I looked at my father.

Locking my eyes on him, I said, "I know what it's like to be accused of something you didn't do, Simon, so I'm not here to do that." Suddenly I regretted everything I'd just said and was about to say. I cringed for all of us.

"I miss you and I'm worried about you. The people you're hanging out with . . ."

"Are your friends!" he hissed, peering at me with disgust. "That's why you're here, because I have something you want!"

Is that true?

"That's not true, Simon. It's just that fourteen is . . . it's young to be smoking pot."

"You're such a hypocrite." He scoffed.

"No, I'm not. I was eighteen before I ever tried it." I turned to Nancy. "I admit sometimes I do smoke pot when I listen to music."

"Sometimes? That's funny. How much music would you say you listen to?" Simon scowled. (*Touché.*) "Because you're high every time I see you." He jumped out of his chair and broke the circle. I expected him to bolt for the door, but instead he walked to the room's only window and looked out. I could tell he was crying when he wiped his nose with the back of his hand.

He was absolutely right. I did listen to a lot of music then, probably more than I ever have since, and I was unreasonably proud of the fact that I had resisted smoking pot for as long as I had. *I don't need drugs to feel high*, I'd told myself every time I'd passed a bowl without hitting it in high school. More than anything I had just been stubborn—I wanted to deny my father the satisfaction of being right about me.

But senior year, when a group of us were taking a day trip to visit our future university, someone handed me a joint and instead of passing, I puffed. "It's nothing special, brick weed," Charlie said, by way of explanation. I inhaled. "Hold it in," he said, clasping at his lungs and sucking in his breath. As often as I'd been around marijuana smoke, I had never experienced any kind of contact high so I expected to be underwhelmed. I'd heard people say it sometimes took a few tries before the drug made its presence known.

But marijuana agreed with me right away. This high was both awake and mellow, enlightened and grounded. I liked the physical sensations of what was happening. Instantly it was as if I'd been walking in the desert, doused in sunshine. My eyeballs were hot, the roof of my mouth dry, a tangible before-and-after effect. I was so thirsty, and filled with gratitude that there was a plentiful supply of orange Gatorade right here in the car, all for me, *all for me*. I could plainly hear the way the Sonic Youth song that was playing had been mixed. I could hear every layer separately, at once. Jesus Christ, what wasn't to love about smoking pot?

"I'm not trying to defend my own behavior. I'm here for you," I said, adapting a line we'd rehearsed for a moment such as this.

My brother snorted through tears and shook his head at the window. Nancy nodded her head in encouragement.

Lewis spoke next. "Simon, I think you'd really like Minor Threat," he said suddenly, gesturing to his T-shirt, which depicted the DC punk band whose members embraced the sober pacifist movement known as straight edge. "I don't want to be friends with people who don't have their wits about them, and I know you could be a great guitar player if you weren't stoned."

Simon guffawed, turning around to glare and push his hands even deeper in his pockets "*You*. Who are *you*? You're just some guy my sister knows. This is such bullshit."

It was bullshit. It was bullshit because marijuana had been and would continue to be a familiar crutch for every member of the family but our mother, who'd quit smoking a little while after I was born. She found its high felt more like a low.

We were only ten uncomfortable minutes into this forced exercise, and it had already gone south. Lewis looked embarrassed and Nancy blessedly took back the reins and explained that this session could be over as soon as my brother accepted the gift of some therapy sessions at one of two esteemed facilities for juvenile counseling. It didn't take any longer for him to relent.

"It's not like I have a fucking choice."

"We're not here to condemn you, Simon. We love you so much," Mom said as she rose from her chair and walked over to the window where he stood, staring out. He shook his head and made a sound like he was going to say something but decided against it. Everyone was silent, waiting for it to be over.

"If I agree to go to counseling, can I go home?" he asked, not turning around.

"Of course you're coming home," Mom said. Nancy added that she thought Simon would really like the person she had in mind to pair him up with—a "really cool guy" who worked exclusively with teenagers. He could give it a try, and if he didn't feel a little better just talking to that counselor, there were others. Simon finally turned around to face our mother. His eyes were red and puffy. He wiped his face with his sleeve.

"I want to live with Dad."

This had not been on the table. Mom looked at Dad, surprised.

Greg sat up straight to interject, "If he goes, I get to go!"

"Simon—" Dad said, his voice warm and gentle. "You live at home with your mother. As long as you're both in school, that's what we agreed."

I'd never even considered that divorce would include a formal custody agreement. In my haste to be free, I hadn't given much thought to the years of fallout ahead for both my brothers. I'd assumed our parents' breakup could only improve the situation for them, but I saw now that even after how bad things had gotten at home, Dad's being out of the house won him the popular vote and shifted all the blame to my mother.

Lewis leaned forward in his chair. His voice barely above a whisper, he addressed Nancy. "Should I maybe . . . wait outside?"

After years of ineffectual corporal punishment, this supposedly healthy exercise in keeping one's kid out of trouble actually felt absurd. Looking at my brother, whose pain and embarrassment were palpable, I was ashamed of myself for participating, for allowing Lewis to be a party to it, for heaping this all on a fourteen-year-old. As we filed out of the room—Mom hanging back to talk to Nancy, as it had been decided that Simon could go home that day, at least, with our dad—I tried to catch my brother's eye to say a semiprivate goodbye.

"Hey," I said, moving in for a hug. "I'm always here if you need me." Simon took a deliberate step back, his expression a steely *how could you*.

"No, you're *not*." And with that he was gone.

What had been gained by ambushing Simon with the message that he was the only one who needed fixing when we were all broken?

16

I'M A LOSER

DAD STARTED COMING FOR WEEKEND DINNERS at the fancy inn in my college town, the kind of place you'd go on a date to eat something exotic like fillet of salmon. Those dinners were the first times we'd ever really talked to each other as "adults." We talked about politics and art and advertising and music. Sometimes he seemed like the most interesting person in the world. Yet for all Dad's knowledge, he'd traveled very few places outside the United States. He couldn't speak any foreign languages, didn't have any black friends save the ones in his record collection.

I was smitten again with him, yet he disillusioned me in new ways. I'd seen him slip NBA tickets to Simon's interventionist, a token of his gratitude. Always needed to be the hero around new people, that guy. In the car on the way back from the restaurant one evening, Dad announced, "I miss your mother. Dating other women isn't as fun as I thought it would be. No one else is as pretty, either."

He had a block when it came to Mom—he seemed not to remember how terrible they were together, how damaging their fights, how he often put her down in an effort to get her to see how indispensable he was to her, how physically shattered our house had been, how since he'd been gone she'd been rebuilding it herself. He suddenly looked smaller to me, a little like Dustin Hoffman. I felt sorry for him. But then . . .

"And that's not all. It's weird out there for me—I'm middle-aged, and suddenly I have to use condoms. I find myself going on dates with women only a few years older than you, and that seems to be the rule of the land. I feel like an old man."

"Dad, you *are* an old man, okay? And I am completely uninterested in getting a new sibling. Or step-girlfriend or whatever. *God.*" He was forty-eight, which wasn't ancient, but definitely seemed old for him to become a father yet again.

"I'm sorry, E. I know. But you're an adult now and it's just good to get a woman's opinion sometimes—you know about these things. I put up with more than two years of your mother not sleeping with me before I got out there again."

There it was, more than I ever cared to know about the sex lives, or lack thereof, of my parents. I looked at him with pity and told him I didn't know anything about the swinging singles scene of northeastern Ohio.

I had no idea if my father had ever loved a woman besides my mother, never knew if he'd cheated on her. I didn't know if he'd dated a lot in college, when he'd had his first kiss, how old he was when he lost his virginity. And yet he knew all those things about me.

"I'm really sorry about Mom," I said, trying to sound objective. "You guys had a really complicated thing for way longer than you should have. Now it's over, but you'll always be connected. And now you have the freedom to do whatever you want."

I wondered if this was how a friend would advise him. I would have preferred if he'd resisted the urge to be such a pal all the time, but he wasn't the only one who asked me for advice. Mom also needed a lot of reassurance about single men and their intentions. Even though she was nervous, I had a hunch my mom would fare better in her next relationship.

His face fell. It was time to change the subject. I knew he'd been lonely, but on these evenings when he visited I could see he was alone. Now I was the primary woman in his life. From pickup to drop-off, these visits were long goodbyes.

I wanted him to be proud of me for standing up and making noise about what I believed. I wanted to debate him on the issues. I wanted him to explain why he voted for Reagan in the eighties, to defend his sporadic conservatism, to tell me about his drug use and that it was all in the past. Neither of us could articulate what it was that we needed from our relationship, so instead we were polite.

———————————

I had introduced my mom to Charlie's dad, David, as soon as my parents' divorce was finally in the works, and to my delight they'd quietly started dating. After it became apparent that they were going to be spending all the major holidays together for the foreseeable future, Charlie called a truce. Two years into the collegiate experience, I found I was no closer to figuring out what I wanted out of it. My method of choosing what courses to take was to flip randomly through the semester catalogue and simply sign up for any class that sounded remotely interesting. (I once took a course called Urban Geography, not realizing it had nothing to do with finding one's way around a city.) I considered making art history my focus, but Charlie thought that was lame—"Why not just be an artist?"

I remember being really shocked by the suggestion—I didn't have any talent that I knew of; I couldn't draw or play the guitar, and I was too out of practice where ballet was concerned. To dedicate your life to creative endeavors was a huge responsibility, and my creative strengths were appearing in the moody pictures my dad took of me and appreciating the fact that the Pixies were a perfect band. I never wanted to admit that what came naturally to me was writing—I felt embarrassed by the notion that I might be able to make a living that way.

The only thing that otherwise inspired me was social activism and the fantasy of becoming an ER doctor who could deliver bad news with compassion. I wasn't optimistic about my chances of passing the medical boards when I couldn't pass remedial algebra, so I went with public health education. I really believed that if people just had all the information, they would make good life decisions, change, and get better. If I just had all the information, I could prevent bad things from happening. I could change the system from the inside.

As soon as we could, Lewis and I rented a two-bedroom house outside of town and started our lives as working adults. I was paying my own way through school (though my father, and later my mother, would help occasionally with loan payments), so I worked several odd jobs. Waitressing was a constant, later supplemented with part-time gigs related to fieldwork for my major. By junior year, I'd cut my classes by half so I could work more often to cover tuition. My primary minimum-wage job was with Harmony Place, a state-subsidized living facility for people with HIV and their families, where I worked as an onsite resident assistant for twelve apartments and manned a twenty-four-hour AIDS hotline. While interning at Planned Parenthood, I would become the guest speaker in the middle school health (or music) class, the lady who put the condom on the banana (or not, according to the mandate of the school).

It wasn't all altruistic—there was a stint at a local talent agency selling photo packages to the naive parents of would-be child models, and a job designing ads for local businesses to run in the *Daily Kent Stater*. My best girlfriend on campus, Denise, a graphic design major who shared my dream of getting out of Ohio, was working there and showed me the Photoshop ropes. I did whatever I could to build a résumé and pay the bills.

Chris moved into the rental house and lived with me and Lewis, and even enrolled in a couple of classes. It was his way of trying to prove that we could stay together, that our lives would mesh, even if he didn't get the point of a liberal arts degree. He already owned his own business and now had a significant commute. Even though we lived out of the same bedroom, we saw each other only a few conscious hours every week. As much as I loved the time we spent exhausted and entwined in the middle of the night, our increasingly separate paths wore away at my resolve to be with my best friend forever. I was spoiled by his devotion to me and to us—I couldn't really imagine a world where I wouldn't be somebody's favorite girl.

When Chris announced that he would move out after just one semester, I could feel myself disconnecting. Maybe this was my father's legacy, a man making me feel special and then taking it back. We tried to act like it was no big deal—we would simply carry on from forty-five minutes away, as we had been—but I knew it was unlikely we would make it. We were moving in opposite directions. I wanted to move away and reinvent myself, and he wanted to stay in town with me, put down roots, raise some chickens, and get a bunch of tattoos. From that point on Chris and I were living history. Soon enough I would mess up what we had, accidentally on purpose.

———————

I was still as restless and boy crazy as I had been in high school. With Chris living back in our hometown, I wasn't getting the constant hit of emotional drama I craved. I developed obsessive crushes on guys I'd see at the student center or at shows, guys in bands, artists, all young but on the cusp of something. One day I was walking down Main Street off campus when I spotted a young Elvis Presley lookalike washing dishes in a restaurant window. I walked right inside and applied for a bartending job, and got it. His name was Paul; he was an anthropology major and he drove a classic Camaro.

Once we'd formally met, I realized we'd had a class together the prior semester. Cult Films. He was one of my secret campus crushes. Though we'd never spoken and had never been introduced, I'd assigned him the name Brando because I spent too much time staring at the back of his neck when I should have been paying attention to *The Wild One*. Whenever he was around I felt drunk on the smell of him, shy, and distracted to the point of forgetfulness. I was forgetting that I already had a boyfriend and had no time for another. Though Paul remained completely aloof at work, the intensity of my attraction inspired a seed of ambition in me. I wanted to know if I could win him over, if I could meet the challenge of getting the guy I wanted. I willed him to see me, prophesizing our future life together through the sheer force of my fantasy.

Paul was decidedly not boyfriend material. He was a bad boy, kind of a fuckup whose primary concern was the location of the next party, and he only seemed to know I was alive when he was wasted. One night, after we closed down the bar, drunk on gin and tonics, we kissed in the dark outside my apartment building. His kissing style was lazy, uncommitted, his top lip a sneer, his bottom lip a lethargic pout; I felt like I was doing all the work. It was the opposite of the dynamic I shared with Chris, my best friend, who adored and accepted the real me, knew all my history and supported my every life choice, the best kisser all along. Yet after a few drunken make-out sessions with Paul, I knew I would need to break things off with Chris. It was a shitty way to rip off the Band-Aid—I was still years from graduation, but I suspected I needed to implode us if I was going to be able to easily leave Ohio. Also, I was selfish and wanted the high of another grand romance.

Paul wasn't interested in a relationship with any one person and told me so right at the outset of our hookups. "Don't break up with your boyfriend on my account," he said whenever I tried to share the details of my life. "I'm not cut out for exclusivity."

When we'd started up he had been casually seeing another girl, Lois (whom he described as "a feminist"). One typical night I met up with him and his friends at the Loft. I was wearing a GOD IS MY CO-PILOT T-shirt that depicted a crude image of a woman wearing a strap-on dildo, her male lover assuming the position. "That shirt is awesome!" Paul laughed, pointing it out to his buddy. "That would look so good on Lois"—referring to her giant rack. I shrank forward over my beer, hiding my 32As. How could I be so enamored with this guy who wasn't even that into me? It reminded me of Stevie and his endless parade of conquests in high school—the more he ignored me, the more it felt like I needed boobs to get attention.

The breakup with Chris was a process, slow, angst-ridden, and full of tearful discussions in hushed tones that served only to reinforce how much we loved each other. At first I was honest, confessing to kissing someone else (though I wouldn't admit to its ongoing nature). I blamed it on my growing restlessness and need to pull back. All around me my friends were breaking off their hometown relationships. "It's the right thing to do," I told him, "a preemptive strike."

"But we don't know what happens in the future," he reminded me. "Maybe you'll want to stay; maybe I'll want to go."

"It will just be harder to prolong the inevitable," I countered. "This way we can have time to process the change." We wanted different things. I especially wanted different things.

For what turned out to be only our first final breakup ritual, we went camping in the same woods where it all began, familiarity and symbolism everywhere. Chris built a makeshift sweat lodge to make our separation more ceremonial, one of the grand gestures that had always defined our relationship. I credited two men with being responsible for my unflappable confidence when it came to negotiating my place in the world—my father and my boyfriend. Chris had always been there where Dad came up short. He was the one who'd ultimately taught me how to drive, patiently walking me through his flawless parallel parking technique when my dad couldn't get through a single lesson without total exasperation. As the second man in my life, Chris undid much of the damage of the first. Looking at his face as he told me there'd never be anyone else, eyes bright with tears through a cloud of steam, I knew I'd set the bar unattainably high for all my future romances. No one else would have known me when.

Even though I was now free to be with whomever, whenever, I was determined to make a boyfriend out of the most unwilling candidate. Paul and I were hooking up regularly enough that all his friends at least recognized me (triumph!), even though they didn't know my name. I tried to ensure that we spent a minimum of three nights together every week. I inserted myself into his life, made nice with his meathead roommates, listened to ambient music I didn't love by English DJs.

We had little in common besides our willingness to have sex with each other. For one, there was a python in an aquarium in his bedroom, and in the living room an enormous fish tank that housed a mean-spirited grouper rumored to attack fingers. And he housed a three-foot-long caiman crocodile in a homemade habitat he'd constructed in the window of his enormous storefront apartment. Every week he'd feed it live white mice or raw steak hanging off of a stick. The croc would thrash and hiss, his powerful tail smacking the water and invoking terror in all who witnessed it. I was charmed by the fact that Paul didn't like me anywhere near where the killing machine was living. *He cares so much, he wouldn't want me to get maimed by a wild animal.*

Eventually I figured out that the way to Paul's heart was to match him drink for drink. He loved to be drunk more than anyone I'd ever met, so hours spent without the company of alcohol were rare. I was often so hungover that I'd sleep through my morning classes. We rarely laughed. Our alone time was a series of games and tests he set up to eradicate boredom. My job was to keep him occupied and overstimulated.

He was always challenging me to do something crazy, bonus points for physical exertion outside my comfort zone (not difficult considering physical exertion for me meant brisk walking around campus). Despite my fear, I was forever trying to be cool and prove myself worthy of his respect. Once Paul made me follow him as he climbed an abandoned water tower in the middle of the night, taunting me to not be a pussy and just trust him. The tower swayed in the wind and flecks of rust fell onto my head, dislodged by his footsteps on the ladder ahead of me.

"It's great, Erin, you'll see—it's not too much farther. Totally going to be worth it."

When we got to the top we could barely fit on the rickety platform. Clinging to him, I looked down and felt nauseated with fear.

"Look up," Paul said. "Look at all the stars." Ugh, fucking stars—what was the big deal about stars; we could see them just as well while standing on earth. It seemed like it took hours to climb up this thing, and now we were just going to have to get back down. This would become a metaphor for our relationship.

Paul would speed down back roads while I rode on the roof of the car, my legs gripping his body through the sunroof, a high-stakes version of sitting on my dad's shoulders. The idea of a man challenging me to be brave felt like home. We "borrowed" people's canoes on the edge of Brady Lake, then rowed out to its moonlit center to slip into black water, abandoning our clothes and my fear. But I couldn't help noticing that everything we did together happened under the cover of darkness. The only time I saw him in the daylight was the next morning, when he'd leave his apartment for class.

The more he resisted calling me his girlfriend, the more I was determined to make it so. Though he never reached for my hand during the few times we were alone together, unencumbered by the posse of friends who always seemed to surround him, I convinced myself that if I stuck with it long enough he would discover that I was The One and not just a hookup. I thought I saw little signs. For one thing, he always opened the passenger door for me when he picked me up at night. Surely that meant something chivalrous, a little tenderness in the rough. One day about nine months into our relationship, I felt comfortable enough to tell him how much I appreciated that little gesture, that I found it uncommonly sweet. He looked at me quizzically for a few seconds before realizing what I was talking about. "Erin,

I open that door first because it's the only way to unlock the driver's side, which is broken."

Oh.

———————

One morning after class, following another drunken night together, there was a message from him waiting on my machine.

"Erin, it's Paul. Please call me as soon as you get this. I have to talk to you about something." Usually we stuck to the three-nights-a-week rule, so it was unprecedented that he would want to see me again so soon. My mind raced. Finally, finally, he'd had a realization. He loved me and he couldn't wait one more minute to tell me. Even though I had left his bed not three hours before, there was something important he had to say, something that couldn't wait. I was contemplating what tone of voice to adopt when I called him back when I heard the roar of his car engine outside my basement apartment window. He'd come over to tell me in person. I swiped on some lip balm and hoped I looked as good as I felt.

When he came inside he looked stricken, his face dead serious, which I'd never seen before. I braced myself for a declaration and moved forward for our inevitable embrace. "Wait," he said, pulling back. "I have to show you something."

With that he unbuttoned his pants to reveal a rash of angry red bumps all along his lower torso, moving down. He looked at me searchingly. From all the infectious disease slideshows I'd been privy to in my classes, did I have any idea what this could be? I didn't, but I expected it was sexually transmitted. How long had it been there? Not long, he said. He'd just noticed it that morning. With that the truth came out. He didn't think he'd gotten anything from me, but there was this girl in Cleveland he sometimes saw, and maybe she was shady, he wasn't sure. He was sorry not to have been up front about it, but there it was, he was sleeping with someone else.

I was shocked, but I saw this as an opportunity to rise above. I would be his nurse, even in the face of infidelity (he'd never promised me anything, after all, and I'd cheated on Chris with him). If nothing else, he seemed genuinely worried that I'd catch what he had. We went to Planned Parenthood and the rash's etiology turned out not to have been sexually transmitted but seemed more likely to have been acquired from the gym where Paul constantly worked out, thus rendering his confession moot and only confirming my lifelong disdain for formal exercise. As he recovered, I reveled in my selflessness, my ability to be cool in a crisis. Instead of being angry that he'd never explicitly told me that he'd been sleeping with someone else the whole time, I would take it in stride. May the best woman win.

In the aftermath of the ordeal he seemed humbled, more willing to see that I was there and to engage. We'd been through something together now, and I was convinced it was meaningful. Just because he couldn't emote didn't mean he didn't want me around. I had gotten to be the hero of my own melodrama once again (no matter how delusional), and that was enough to sustain me. The odds that we'd stay together once I left Ohio were extremely low.

I probably picked Paul in the first place because I sensed he wasn't capable of committing to anyone. The longing for the unattainable in a relationship reminded me of the relationship dynamic I shared with my father. I craved stability but relished inconsistency. Where Dad had opposing personality traits that always kept me guessing, I was drawn to Paul partly because he was too relaxed to ever get angry. I was always digging with both of them, like a reporter writing a profile interview for *Rolling Stone*. I had to uncover my dad's many sides so I could figure him out; there just *had* to be another side to Paul. His unwillingness to stop me from leaving would ultimately encourage me to go. And yet! I also fantasized constantly that once I was gone, he'd come to see how much he needed me, how worthy of pursuit I'd been all along.

I didn't technically graduate from college, though I had all the necessary credits and my grades were pretty good. After five years at Kent I'd successfully completed several internships and had more on-the-job experience than a lot of my peers. The sticking point for the university was that I'd never passed the remedial algebra class that had been conditional to my acceptance in the first place. I'd attempted to take the class a few times over the years, but always dropped it out of sheer frustration and defiance. If this math class, which had served only to make me feel intellectually inadequate, was really so important that not passing it would have the power to ruin my career prospects forever, then fuck it—I'd have to find another way to be a successful social worker/magazine editor/general creative in New York.

My friend Denise had already moved there, and had found us five hundred square feet to call our own (or at least rent).

"I guess I'll need to learn to get by in the world without problem solving," is how I phrased it to the deadly serious person from the registrar's office who called to tell me I would have to make up the class in the summer if I wanted to receive the diploma. "Because I'm moving to Brooklyn in two weeks, and I'm never coming back."

Even if it was all for show, I walked in the procession in cap and gown. Mom and Dad were both in the gym, sitting next to each other. At least I could give them the photo op, shake someone's hand as they slipped me the leather-bound placeholder. My parents knew about my missing math class, but they also knew I'd made up my mind. I was an adult after all; I was going to do what I'd maintained I always would. I had saved $650 in tip money from a stint at a sports bar called Slam Jams, enough to cover my portion of one more month's rent and some groceries. It wasn't much, and I liked that it wasn't. I would have to make it work.

Afterward we met up with Paul for lunch and yet again I created meaning where there was none, as he was just meeting my parents for the first time. I was so proud that he would be the one to drive the white van loaded with my stuff to the city, the one to help put the futon together (a boyfriend activity if there ever was one), even if he had never held my hand in public, even if he had never called me his girlfriend.

The day before I was to leave, Dad came by to see me off. He was much more emotional than Mom was about my move. For her it was pure excitement—she was happy that I was going to do what I'd set out to do. Mostly, I think she was relieved I wasn't engaged or pregnant, and not following her own more traditional path.

"You don't ever have to do anything you don't want to do, and you can always change your mind" had been her refrain ever since her own emancipation. She liked to point out different scenarios in which I'd be supported.

"You can always call off the wedding," she'd say of any future engagement, "even if it's the night before and everything's paid for." *Good to know.*

Whereas Mom had given me a set of luggage, Dad's going-away present was a manual camera of my own, the first I'd ever owned, an homage to the days when I'd follow him around, posing. He took a long time explaining the magic of aperture, the difference in lenses, and showing me how to load the film. I already knew all of this—we'd been over it before, but I felt my father stalling.

"You should always take pictures," he said. "For evidence."

He opened his wallet and tried to write me a fresh check. He'd already allowed me to list him as a backup on our lease in Brooklyn. "Don't do that," I said, waving it away. "Seriously. You've done enough by being our guarantor. I want you to know that I can take care of myself."

"Why do you think you're so ambitious?" he asked. "Do you think it's because you're the only daughter?"

"I guess that must be it," I said. "That, or I just take after you."

17

COME TOGETHER

THREE YEARS AFTER *MS.* MAGAZINE was shamed for misspelling the word "feminism" on its cover ("FEMINISIM"), I was an intern in the editorial department. Denise's connections had paid off, and the hiring editor was impressed with the fact that I'd been reading the magazine since I was a teenager. Like with KSU, I'd written a passionate letter in order to show my commitment to the organization's ideals, reciting its most iconic cover images from memory, going back to the inaugural "Wonder Woman for President" design. I wanted to be a woman who didn't need a fish or a bicycle.

In 1999 and 2000, the magazine was publishing bimonthly, and for purposes of unbiased reporting did not accept advertisers. Its offices were in the heart of Manhattan's financial district, on a high floor of an old bank building. The staff was made up entirely of women, and the six interns were the only staffers under thirty. Some were destined for academia or careers in journalism. One was a young mother who published a magazine for other young mothers. One produced porn in

Brooklyn. Another was a self-described "thick chick" whose platform centered on fat acceptance and positive body image. One was still a teenager, a recent high school grad. We were part of the movement's "third wave," born after the 1960s. Where our foremothers burned their bras and rejected the tyranny of high heels, we tended to eschew that decade's hippie-er politics, didn't mind a push-up, and sometimes preferred a fuck-me pump. Our worldview was a little more post-gender, queerer, more accepting of a diversity of opinions. We were flashier feminists.

At *Ms.*, the devil wore Eileen Fisher. This was something of a disappointment, because I actually counted live access to Prada among my reasons for wanting to live in New York City. My fantasy version of a magazine editor regularly wore high fashion to the office and had immaculate hair. In reality, with no advertisers to suck up to, no one bothered with lipstick and everyone wore comfortable shoes. Though I never expected *Ms.* to have *Vogue* levels of name recognition, it surprised me how many people who called the office thought they were contacting a publication having to do with multiple sclerosis. To me this was a public relations failure—surely we interns could impart our advice on how to target a younger demographic, the future of the movement.

At a magazine, the magic happens at weekly editorial meetings, where feature content is decided, stories are assigned to writers, and the big issues of the day are debated. At *Ms.*, interns were paid a stipend of respect and MetroCards, and part of the former was allowing us to attend staff editorial meetings. Sometimes cofounder and American icon Gloria Steinem would attend, once to talk through a piece about Hillary Clinton's projected run for senate. Gloria was always asking the interns their opinions and advocating for the magazine to stay relevant with young women by writing about issues that concerned them. It was apparent every day that we differed from the more seasoned editors on certain subjects—not on anything sacrosanct like abortion rights or equal pay, but on beauty politics (thumbs-up for lipstick), porn (thumbs-up to stripper unions and making a living off your own ass if you wanted to), and even our collective sense of humor (thumbs-up to rape jokes). When it came to story discussions, every once in a while an editor would ask an intern's opinion.

Quiet absorption of someone else's debate was not part of my skill set. Which is how I found myself loudly arguing with a senior editor over the merits of an exposé of high school cheerleading. The presiding opinion among the old school was that cheerleading, as a concept, was a very obvious result of oppressive patriarchal structures meant to keep young women in bouncy miniskirts with nothing but bloomers beneath.

I surveyed the room. Nobody else seemed scandalized by this point of view, which propelled me to immediate protest. "Sure, but have you ever seen the state championship competitions on TV?" I asked. "It's a sport in its own right—some of these athletes are training for the Olympics."

The features editor eyed me impatiently. "Don't even get me started on the Olympics. Synchronized swimming is not a sport. It's a lifestyle . . . choice. At best, it's exercise. I'm not sure. But I know that a 'sport' that exists solely for the support and encouragement of men, to the exclusion of other women—that's the very essence of male entitlement."

"Maybe young women are cheering for themselves," I said. Everyone stared, expecting me to continue. The intern closest to me smiled nervously and dropped her eyes to her notebook.

I wanted to tell them that it wasn't about the boys anymore—it was about artistry and grueling practice. Instead I could only say, "But there's tumbling!" fully realizing how this sounded but unable to stop myself. "And stunts that require a lot of skill and team building. Cheerleaders get more injuries than football players and that's why school boards don't want to insure them—because people whose perception of cheerleading hasn't caught up with the times don't want the girls to do anything too strenuous or dangerous."

I told the room that at my high school, I had launched a campaign to keep our squad from being "ground bound" our junior year. It had been the closest thing to a political movement at our school, winning the right to perform all the tricks we'd been working toward all summer. When no one seemed moved, I went with the obvious. "Men are cheerleaders, too, especially at the college level. Even George Bush—"

"*George Bush*," the editor said, exasperated.

I backed down, aware that I'd never get a job if I went around arguing with people I wanted to pay me someday. Just because the staff at the magazine were all feminists didn't mean they were all mentors. Media job hours were long and the deadlines constant. In order to maintain its competitive edge, *Ms.* had to remain relevant by sometimes leading with a baiting cover story about an issue that the editors didn't care about, but that might lead to a sound bite that sparked a conversation during a slow news week. When it came to creating content, it was every bitch for herself.

I spoke with my dad once a week on the phone, mostly about work, strategizing about my next move. After I'd outed myself as a cheerleading apologist, Dad advised me to listen more often than I talked. He was measured, reassuring. "You're not there to make friends, E. You're there to network, and that's different. Do your job—use it to meet people who can hire you later—then move on." I wasn't sure about the magazine world, but I knew I wanted to do something with publishing and continue working with writers. I liked talking with journalists and watching the editors transform their work. I wanted the kind of professional triumphs that I could share with my dad, who'd had a fancy career. I wanted to be the one who'd made it after all.

In addition to the full-time hours at the magazine, my freelance life became a series of $100 checks. I'd been living in the city a few weeks when I got a minimum-wage gig working nights and weekends at the concession stand at the Paris Theater, a posh single-screen arthouse cinema across from Central Park and next to Bergdorf Goodman. Because Miramax held a lot of premieres there, there was always a swarm of celebrities around. At first I would keep a diary of every famous person to whom I served Twizzlers: Jennifer Lopez, the Coen brothers, Eric Stoltz, Julianne Moore, Gena Rowlands. One night's premiere brought out Michael Douglas and Catherine Zeta-Jones (whose skin was like the milk in the saucer that Madonna licks up in the video for "Express Yourself"). Despite the twenty-three-degree temperature, Catherine refused to wear her mink stole to cover up her cleavage on her exit to the limo, lest she rob the waiting photographers of their shot.

Our lobby was so small that it could hold only about three major movie stars, maybe four if they were all women. More than once I got up close and personal with a few legends at the Paris. I had a front-row seat when Lauren fucking Bacall submitted to an interview with a journalist in the lobby. Nicole Kidman made nice with the ushers at an early screening of *Moulin Rouge!*, sharing that she was often too nervous to sit through her own performances and preferred the company of the staff, *naturally* (she used to work at a movie theater herself before she became a famous person). I once threw up in the stall next to Julia Roberts in our tiny theater bathroom. She had come to see *Life Is Beautiful* with her mother on a day when I was hungover. I heard a familiar voice through the door asking me if I was all right. "I'll be okay, thank you," I said quickly, an inexplicable southern accent affecting my voice like we were on the set of *Steel Magnolias*.

Across the street from the Paris, at the Plaza Hotel, Sarah Jessica Parker filmed the iconic episode of *Sex and the City*, in which Carrie says goodbye to Big in front of Pulitzer Fountain in homage to *The Way We Were*. Mark Wahlberg and an actress I recognized from daytime television made out furiously in front of the double-paned theater doors, their kissing style full of deep tonguing just in case no one was noticing. Actors always seemed to be putting on a show, even when they were off duty. Still, just being in the presence of movie stars made me feel impossibly cool, even if our association was through a thick wall of glass or triggered by their need for Milk Duds.

I found one part-time job via a famous writer I had met through the magazine. Her friend was a successful songwriter who needed a personal assistant. The songwriter's fame was just starting to fade when I came into her life—her record company had put her on an allowance, and my job was mainly to cover for her when she was going to be late to events, a chronic problem. She could be a taxing person to be around, but she got invited to a lot of interesting parties, and always smelled so nice, like wet flowers. I'd seen her get off the phone with someone with a sincere "I'm leaving right now to meet you," only to just then enter the shower, which in itself ensured that no one would be seeing her for at least seventy-two minutes, so long was her golden hair.

I took care of her cat when she traveled, picked up her meds, and let the cleaning woman in. The songwriter was a recovering addict, which was the subject of her latest album. She wrote about snorting up lines of pills and cleaning the shit out of her apartment, which she never actually cleaned. Once a week a woman from a service came to suck up the balls of cat hair and spun-sugar girl dust that had accumulated around the various boxes of albums and unopened fan mail. In three years there she'd never even unpacked. But she was rich and generous and paid twenty dollars an hour, and I liked going to parties attended by Sean Penn. Otherwise, no matter the front I put on for my dad about my glamorous life, I was broke and lonely and confused about the future.

I met the aunt of an old friend from school, who offered me work for her boutique umbrella business. I prepared her weekly invoices and helped her set up her booth at trade shows. I did odd jobs for her wealthy friends, dropped off their old clothes at Housing Works, alphabetized their libraries on Central Park West, transcribed interviews for journalists on a deadline, picked up groceries from Gristedes, and returned ill-fitting blouses to Ann Taylor. If you knew one rich person, you were exposed to lots of rich people, and those rich people all needed endless amounts of assistance. Could I exchange someone's shoes for a different size at Barneys? I could for twenty dollars. Could

I take the train to Chelsea Market and buy the special wheatgrass for the cat? I could do anything for twenty dollars.

At the Paris, despite our lowly station, all who worked there felt we were going to make it. Case in point: upon moving to the city, Denise had casually taken a lindy hop dance class, and a year later she was already on tour with a professional team of dancers. The other *Ms.* interns were getting jobs at Condé Nast. A painter I knew was premiering his first solo show at a gallery downtown, the burgeoning director already using her credit cards to pay for her first feature.

Desperate to make my mark, I cut my hair like Edie Sedgwick on the off chance I might be *discovered*. It happened one day when I was taking tickets at the John Cassavetes retrospective and a man actually asked if I had an agent. He introduced himself as an executive producer for *Law & Order* and thought I should audition for their casting director. But then he advised that I would need some head shots, and I knew from friends that those cost real money. I briefly studied with a friend's acting teacher, a guru of experimental theater who let me attend his workshops in exchange for reading my high school diary, so he could better understand the mind of a teenage girl. His classes met three evenings a week in a church basement, where actors would complete floor exercises like emulating an animal of our choosing and delivering our lines in the animal's voice. (I noticed most preferred howling animals, so I chose to growl.) In the end, that wasn't the kind of actor I wanted to be, and I didn't want to make a real commitment to auditioning all the time, and dental work, and the casting couch, and Los Angeles.

———

By the time I'd lived in the city for six months, I'd already been back to Ohio twice, finding it excruciating to be apart from Paul for too long. Both times I took an Amtrak to Cleveland, a twelve-hour haul for what would be an eight-hour drive, but the train was cheaper than renting a car. I was broke and full of my feelings and living for forty-eight torturous hours of reconciliation with my un-boyfriend. Each visit came with the promise of abandonment; even though I was the one coming and going, the excitement of not knowing whether I would ever see him again was always laced with the fear that he wouldn't want me to. When I'd moved, I'd hoped that I'd be driven to distraction, that my feelings for Paul would cool and I'd meet someone else to have an inexplicably intense affection for and connection with, but it wasn't like that—no one was as interesting as the one who wasn't there.

In theory, we were still together. He wasn't looking to see anyone else, he'd told me, and who knew what would happen once he gradu-ated the following year? I'd hoped that in my absence I would become essential. It only happened once I was leaving during one of these rare in-person visits that Paul mumbled the words I'd longed to hear since before we'd even met two years before. When he finally said *I love you*, it was more like an apology. I didn't care—it was worth it. Every anx-ious hour, every terribly lonely night crossing the bridge to Brooklyn smelling of popcorn grease, was worth the memory of lying in the dark of his bedroom, his face buried in my neck, the weight of his brooding heavy in the air, drunk on the power that I'd made him miss me.

That first fall, in September, Dad came for a visit for his birthday. He was big on taking vacations with my brothers, which they'd been doing every summer for years, the three of them walking book reports of information about the American Southwest and its desert camp-sites. I'd always begged off the trips to spend more time with my boy-friend. I was pleased that he would be coming to my town and looked forward to showing him around.

Dad stayed at the Waldorf Astoria in midtown Manhattan, an ex-ecutive dad hotel if there ever was one. It was funny meeting him there, seeing him emerge from the fray of the crowded lobby, his hair the same color as the gilding. I'd planned a Lennon-centric outing, which meant taking the C train up to the west side of Central Park to the Dakota, the historic apartment building where John and Yoko lived and John was killed. I took the camera he'd given me to take pictures there, and I'd meant to take the portraits that would define us forever, but I overexposed the film. Still, I can see us there in our scarves with our paper cups of seventy-five-cent coffee we'd gotten from a truck, elaborate sandwiches from the deli in my counterfeit Donna Karan tote bag, entering the park at West Seventy-Second Street to Strawberry Fields to sit on a bench by the Imagine memorial. We listened to the hippies strum their guitars for a small audience of bums drinking beer out of brown paper bags, and us. I asked him for the millionth time to tell me about seeing the Beatles in Cleveland in '66. *Tell me about the mania,* I said. *Tell me about how the crowd stormed the stage. Tell me about how the ticket cost just five dollars.*

The Beatles toured the U.S. three years in a row (from 1964 to 1966), but the city that would one day house the Rock & Roll Hall of Fame banned them from playing there in 1965, so rabid were the fans at Public Hall that first time around. When the band came back in '66, the venue was Cleveland Stadium, and Dad was there. But four songs into their set, during "Day Tripper," the crowd broke through security and stormed the stage. The Beatles were sequestered for half an hour before it was deemed safe for them to finish their set. By then you couldn't hear anything but screaming. Seeing them live was basically the worst way to experience the music, but at least Dad could say he'd been there.

He'd taken me to Cleveland Stadium to see Paul McCartney during his solo tour in 1990, my first stadium concert experience. By then McCartney was forty-eight, which of course seemed impossibly old at the time. He played a lot of hits—"Get Back" and "Eleanor Rigby" and "Hey Jude." We were on the ground, the tickets courtesy of Dad's agency, so close to the stage I could see the wispy ends of Paul's mullet blowing in the breeze. I got doused with beer by the drunkards behind us, and I was with my dad. It wasn't exactly cool, but it was rock 'n' roll to me.

As we ate our sandwiches in Central Park, we talked about my future and his past—about work and supporting oneself and what it meant to be an adult. My internship had ended and I had begun to apply for entry-level jobs in publishing, both in magazines and in books. I'd heard that the publishing houses ran at a much slower pace—no more staying at the office until ten p.m. in order to meet closing deadlines; you could take your reading home. I asked Dad if he hoped I'd end up in advertising like him, but he shook his head vigorously.

"There's no freedom in advertising and almost no creativity. You're dealing with clients who have bad taste and rarely know what they're talking about, but their wish is your command, see, so you have to make it work." I stared at the mosaic pattern of the stones spelling IMAGINE, erasing the second I and the N in my head, so that I saw IMAGE. Someone had placed Granny Smith apples around the circle.

"In the corporate world, you know you're replaceable because there will always be someone who will be willing to do your job for less. You constantly have to hustle, to solve the problems of the American dream, to come up with sparkling prose for the most ridiculous product. And for what? Not for art, just for money. Truly anyone can make a commercial."

At the time Dad was working as a marketing director for a chain of retail stores, a job he preferred to the carousel of the agency grind. He was the happiest I'd ever seen him.

"If you can, you should aim for a career where you get to be your own boss," he said. "Starting my own agency in my twenties was the most fun I've ever had at work. It didn't last, but it was worth it to try." We sat quietly for a while and watched New York walk past.

The rest of the weekend was filled with museum tours, meals with friends, and the first Broadway tickets I'd ever paid for myself—it was my turn to take him to the theater for his birthday. (His reaction to Judith Light's performance as a breast cancer survivor in *Wit*: "Her tits still look great.") I thought it better to gloss over such a disappointing takeaway; we had a kind of silent pact not to revisit anything painful like cancer, divorce, or the past. When we said goodbye on his last night in town, we agreed to make it an annual tradition.

For my first Christmas in the city, Simon had given me a can of Mace. Just the idea of New York City scared a lot of people back home. I never even took the can out of the package, convinced I'd surely do more harm than good just having it in my possession. Denise and I lived two blocks from the subway and the streets were always loaded with people. To me, living in one of the most densely populated cities in the world meant so many potential witnesses and made me feel much safer than I had in the tiny, whisper-quiet town where I'd grown up.

One night, exhausted after a late night out in Manhattan, I got lost on the way to an unfamiliar subway station. I was far from home, and it was after midnight—the commute could take more than an hour. I flagged down a cab in order to ask for directions, a strategy I'd had good luck with once before. An off-duty driver pulled over, and when I told him I was a little lost he offered to give me a ride home. I had no cash on me, and wouldn't have been able to afford the half hour trip, and told him so. He was kind and said he was headed back to Brooklyn anyway. "No charge," he said, shaking his head. "No charge for you."

"Here," he said, offering the front seat instead of the back, "This way we talk. I tell you about my country." I was too new to the concept of taxis for this to give me pause; if he was off duty, it seemed reasonable to sit up front like a normal passenger. It was only after he lit up a cigarette and offered me one that things felt a little off, as there were multiple signs in the car instructing one not to smoke. He told me how he had come two years before from Pakistan, where he had been an engineer. He could make twice his salary driving a cab in the States, and send it home to his wife and daughter. It was a lonely life. I kept steering the conversation back to his family, sensing that I'd indeed been reckless to believe there would be any free rides in life, even from a self-described married father who worried about the safety of young girls just trying to get home. The clove smell of his cigarette hung in the air despite the fact that the windows were rolled down.

"Will you have friendship with me?" the driver said expectantly, gesturing to his lap once we'd reached a stoplight in my neighbor-hood. "Sorry, no," I replied, and jumped out of the car, bolting down a one-way street toward my house.

I was frustrated with myself for being so naive and trusting as to go along for a ride with a stranger—of course he would offer himself up for a blowjob; I was learning that access and opportunity were every-thing for some. Spend twenty-five minutes with a man you've never met before and chances were he was already trolling for sex, even if he was married.

Not long after Denise and I had moved into our apartment, we started receiving unwanted late-night visits from a stranger. We'd been so psyched that the building seemed to lack the notorious pests that plagued the city—namely bedbugs, rats, and roaches—that we hadn't prepared for the human variety. At night I slept in our makeshift living room/kitchen, simply converting the futon from couch to bed. One weeknight, at about two a.m., after an hour or two of fitful sleeping, I was awakened by a soft knock at the front door, really just four or five steps from the bed. Startled by its quiet, non-urgent tone, I simply lay in bed for a while, holding my breath. Had I really heard that? Our apartment was in a corner of the building on the first floor, with no neighbors to the left or right—the sound really couldn't have been coming from any other door. But then the knock was followed by an eerie silence.

A few nights later I heard the same soft knocking in the middle of the night. This time I woke Denise, and we crept to the door to look through the peephole. It was an older man neither of us recognized, just standing there waiting, his profile creepily illuminated by the light of the building lobby. Finally he walked away. A week went by and no knocker, until one night I heard the doorbell. The bell in the doorbell was broken, so it made only a faint clicking noise that came from pushing the button manually, but I could hear it distinctly. I looked at the clock: 2:22 a.m. This time we called the police. Not 911, but the precinct office line—we didn't think it was an emergency, since the knocks hadn't seemed menacing. The cops disagreed, four of them rushing to the scene with guns drawn, casing the stairwell but coming up empty, and staying to take a full report. They advised us to watch our backs around the neighborhood and call again the moment the creeper returned.

"What does he want?" we asked one of the young officers.

"I'm guessing he wants one of you to let him in," he answered. "If he rapes you, he can say you knew him or you wouldn't have answered the door." Breaking and entering by invitation.

The following week, Denise thought she saw a man fitting the peephole description staring at her by the mailbox. We went to the building's super, Pedro, who grew quiet when we told him about the knocker. "Thank you for coming to me—I will take care of this," he said. Two nights later, Pedro called to tell us that he'd confronted the man he suspected was the culprit, someone who lived on the third floor. "He won't be bothering you ladies again," he said. The man was a drunk, and when he drank he was known to wander the halls. Pedro threatened to tell the man's wife he was trying to peep on two young women and that was the end of that. For our trouble, Pedro would wire our apartment so we could receive free cable. We considered these reparations acceptable, and never saw the man again.

———————

After Paul graduated from Kent that year, he came to visit for a few weeks and ended up staying for good (thankfully finding new homes for his reptiles before leaving campus). He hadn't had a game plan beyond possibly joining the family real estate business back home, so this development exceeded all my expectations. We moved into our own place, a third-floor walk-up in the Prospect Heights neighborhood of Brooklyn. It wasn't much—the shower merely spat on us pathetically as we stood underneath its head. We bought a couch, we bought a bed, we bought a George Foreman grill. Every night we ate chicken breasts and rice pilaf and basked in our ambitions, reveling in a kind of practiced domesticity while Paul waited tables at the Olive Garden in Times Square, but got on track to get his broker's license.

At the turn of the century, it seemed that we had just gotten to New York for the last of the gritty nightlife. Inside the 1/9 subway station at Fiftieth and Broadway was a bar frequented by punkers and writers called Siberia. Most people seemed to ignore its existence— the door was discreet, the windows blacked out—though you certainly couldn't miss the loudest music I've ever heard blaring at commuters late at night. Inside, the nine-by-twenty-three-foot space was split into two rooms, the front a makeshift performance area, the bar in the back featuring three-dollar bottles of beer that most people just threw on the floor when they were finished. The unisex toilet there made CBGB's infamous bathrooms seem luxurious by comparison, made worse by the fluorescent lighting that likely acted as ipecac to all who dared enter. Within a year Siberia would close down and reopen at street level ten blocks south, offering a larger but equally disgusting dive bar experience. We knew it couldn't last.

Also in its final years was Kokie's, a salsa bar in the Williamsburg neighborhood of Brooklyn notorious for selling ten-dollar bags of cocaine out of its men's room. The rules were unspoken: Purchase a miniature Budweiser at the bar in the front room. Buy the bags of terrible-grade coke in the closet from the imposing, expressionless gentleman. Go to the back room, where modest tables lined the wall of a makeshift dance floor. Line up to do bumps off keys behind a vinyl privacy curtain located in the corner while middle-aged dancers perfected the mambo. The bar had been quietly doing its thing for about ten years before a new police regime came in and forced it out of business.

Paul treated the city like it was just another college town, his instinct to park down by the river and climb on some rocks, ignoring open container laws and No Parking signs with abandon. His presence emboldened me to be less cautious. Though he knew how to find certain kinds of trouble, I felt safer just having a guy around.

Then, at a fancy book party with the singer-songwriter for whom I worked, I met a successful literary agent whose firm, a posh Midtown boutique agency, needed an assistant. We hit it off talking about our favorite contemporary writers (she suggested I read more Denis Johnson) and she invited me to interview for the job. The office was on a high floor of a building on Fifty-Seventh Street that overlooked the glass-enclosed rooftop pool of the New York Sports Club below. The space was so light-filled that a scrim was necessary most of the day, and even then, sunscreen. There was a wraparound art deco terrace whose design had since been outlawed; there was really nothing stopping anyone from toppling right over the waist-level railing. It was the most beautiful view I'd ever seen.

I liked the agents so much. When I interviewed with the founder of the agency, he asked me what my favorite bands were—if I was a Beatles person or an Elvis person—and what shows I'd seen in the city. Would I like to hear about the time he saw the Talking Heads at CBGB back when he was my age and thought he wanted to work in the music business? I wasn't sure what a literary agent actually did every day, but I knew I could answer the phone and pick compelling hold music. When I asked about vacation days, my new boss said he'd never actually thought about it—he presumed that if I spent more time out of town than I did at the office, that might be noticeable, but otherwise he would leave it to me. Everything about it felt right—the culture, the office, the reading part; it was a dream job. There were only four people in the whole company—I loved the idea of being the fifth. It felt familiar. A family of five.

As soon as I found out that I'd gotten the job, I called my father.

"Did you get it?"

"I got it."

"I had a feeling you would. Way to go! That's great!"

He was very excited by the news, his praise animated and full of congratulations. I could hear him grinning. It was everything I'd always wanted, to feel the glow of his unwavering support. Winning the approval of the guy I'd once so disappointed felt just as good as getting the job.

———————————

Exactly one year later, everything started off normally one Tuesday morning. Paul's realty office was just ten blocks from mine in midtown Manhattan, and that day we were both at work by eight thirty. I got my usual bagel from the deli on the corner, and the large fresh-squeezed orange juice that was beyond my budget but really worth it. I was looking forward to sitting on the balcony and chatting with my favorite agent, who was always the first one in. No sooner had we said hello than one of the agency's authors who lived downtown called to say she'd just watched an airplane fly into one of the Twin Towers. Out the windows we could see smoke billowing in the sky, and we began to hear the urgent wail of sirens. We turned on the local news on the television in the office, and for a brief few minutes, people were speculating the crash had been caused by a small commuter plane, some kind of horrible air traffic control accident.

"I'm going to cancel my lunch date," the agent said. As she did, we saw an enormous ball of fire explode out the side of the second tower, a second airplane, a jet. I dialed the number to my dad's office—he was the first person I thought to call. I got a recording instead of a dial tone: "All circuits are busy now. Please try your call again."

I tried again and again, and finally got through before the first tower fell.

"Dad, can you see what's happening?"

He was so calm, serious and concerned but with no panic in his voice. He was glad to hear from me, and had been trying to get through, too. He'd already assured Mom that I was likely a good mile away from the towers, and that I wasn't alone. I hadn't been able to reach Paul, either, and hoped he was on his way on foot. I didn't have a cell phone.

"Do you think this is it?" I asked, momentarily convinced we were at the commencement of the holy war, a Biblical prophecy coming true.

He let out a soft chuckle. "No, E, I don't think this is 'it.' I think it's terrorism and it's horrifying, but it's not God. It's people doing terrible things, and it's almost over." He seemed so sure. "It's okay. We're going to be okay."

I felt soothed by his reassurance.

After we said goodbye, the first tower went down. More colleagues, having now arrived, huddled around the television to watch the surreal horror of the Manhattan skyline collapsing into an atom bomb of ash. Now the Pentagon was on fire, and no one knew how much destruction was yet to come. The news feed kept replaying footage of desperate people hanging out of top-floor windows, waving their arms frantically amid black smoke before tumbling out. How many people had died in the destruction? I managed to get an email through to Paul: *Meet on the corner of 57th & Lex?* I hugged my colleagues before we all scattered in different directions, each needing to find our own way home.

Outside on the sidewalk, half the people clustered there were hunched over their flip phones, one finger in their ears to block out the noise as they attempted to make calls; the other half were turning to each other and saying, "I can't get a signal . . ." New Yorkers scanned the crowds for people they knew, or stood with their hands on their hips, staring into the middle distance in search of a plan. *Where should we go?* Some people paced, their hands covering their mouths. A hastily scribbled sign announcing where to go to give blood was duct-taped to the side of a coffee cart. The urgent clamor of the sirens had concentrated downtown, but the biggest emergency in the country could still be heard in every direction.

"A plane went down in Pennsylvania!" someone said. "Thousands are dead," said someone else. I watched one woman drive northward on southbound Lexington Avenue, her face a perfect replica of the Munch painting *The Scream*.

The weather was freakishly beautiful—clear and sunny skies, azure blue. When I finally found Paul in the crowd gathering on the corner, we went to the Irish pub down the block and stood in the packed room, watching the three televisions that hung over the bar, strategizing how to get home to Brooklyn. The subways had been shut down, so people were walking over the bridges out of Manhattan, but Paul was nursing a back injury and didn't think he could swing it. We decided we would take a bus downtown to Union Square and try to wait out the subway ban.

City buses were running first come, first served, for free. The wait was long and the buses were standing room only. I hesitated too long before getting on, worried that cramming in would make me panic and barf, and the woman behind me gasped that she needed to get to her daughter. "Make a decision!" she said, exasperated. I snapped out of it and pushed my way to the center. Paul was the last one on. The air on the bus was acrid with fear. We were all so close together, huddled around a transistor radio tuned to 1010 WINS, listening to the reports of the chaos and horror happening just blocks away. *Five blocks from the* Ms. *office*, I thought. Now those blocks were gone.

When we got off the bus at Union Square, plenty of people were having lunch on city sidewalk cafés, taking advantage of their freedom.

"People still need to eat," Paul said when we passed them.

"Not today," I said. "People died."

"But *we're* still alive. Come on," he said, "aren't you hungry? I my-self could go for a cheeseburger." He clutched his stomach dramatically. Hungry: really? This was the kind of bickering we'd been engaging in more often lately. I overempathized and he was from the school of *If it doesn't directly affect me, then it's not really any of my business.*

Around noon we got sandwiches from a deli and free bottles of water. We joined many people who were stranded and aimless and made the pilgrimage to one of several makeshift blood banks to do-nate, but they'd exceeded their capacity after only a couple of hours and sent us away. Eventually we ran into an acquaintance, for whom we set aside our dislike because it was a national emergency and he had a car and was going our way. The roads were officially closed to nonemergency vehicles, but people were still getting out. We drove into Williamsburg, then past the Navy Yard, where marines stood on rooftops poised with machine guns. There was a lot of chaos in the streets, people yelling and throwing up their hands in prayer, weeping openly. But there was also a stunned sense of normalcy and calm. Many people were laughing. The buildings had come raining down, and the country was under attack, but we'd merely been inconvenienced.

For the first time ever, I wanted to go home to Ohio. Two days later, I did. I wanted to spend time with my parents, especially Dad, whose birthday was a week away. An unfamiliar patriotism had taken hold of me—I was feeling defensive of New York City, the capital of everything great and hated about America. War seemed inevitable, and suddenly we were on alert for bombs and terrorists and envelopes of anthrax in the mail.

Yet the worse things got, the more thoughtful and contemplative my father became. It was as if the sixties had prepared him for this moment in history, and this too would pass. I stayed at his house for a few days. We watched the news together and I slept for hours by the vanity fireplace in his new condo, feeling safe and parented. Dad said it was just fine with him if I wanted to move home. There was no way I'd ever leave New York, but it was nice to hear.

For the second half of the week, Mom arranged to pick me up in a restaurant parking lot halfway between her house and Dad's. I don't think they'd seen each other in person for a long time. She'd been down all week, her nerves still frayed, worried for all of us. When Mom pulled in, Dad got out of the car to talk to her while I got in the other side. She was already crying softly when he leaned into the driver's side window. I knew he was pleased to be able to be there for her, to gently tell her that he knew everything was going to be okay. I was safe, and we were all together, and just like we'd weathered all these storms as a family, we'd survive this shitty time in history, too.

"I just feel so helpless," she said.

"I know," he said. "But you're not alone. We've got these healthy, strong kids, and we're all going to make it." He reached in and squeezed her hand. I saw her chin tremble.

"Thanks for saying that," she said.

"You know you can always count on me, Paige," he said, and smiled. "It's just a rough time."

This was Dad at his best. It wasn't just his reassurance and certainty that the world would not stop turning—it was the fact that enough time had passed that he and my mother were finally becoming friends for the first time. My parents had grown up together, hurt each other, left each other, and survived. It was different this time, now that Mom had her own identity. In the eight years since their breakup, she had moved up the ladder from receptionist to marketing exec for a small nonprofit. Just as Dad acted as a professional mentor for me, he also helped my mother. This was the dependable and strong father I'd always dreamed of, now finally stepping into the role, softened by age and experience, his paternal imprint a hand on our shoulders. As we pulled away from him in the parking lot, Mom and I marveled at how someone so historically capable of causing so much torment was also gifted at relieving it. It was the last image he would leave with both of us, him standing alone by the car at dusk, watching until we were out of sight, his hand frozen in a wave goodbye.

18

THE END

WHEN IT ENDED FOR DAD he was listening to *Abbey Road*. It was seven o'clock in the morning, an ungodly hour to be at a gym on a treadmill. This was a new routine, part of a health kick no doubt inspired by some insurance-related wellness initiative. He had a girlfriend, Maggie, and things were getting serious. In fact, LifeWorks, the unfortunately named gym, was attached to the hospital where Maggie worked as an oncology nurse. There he was: jogging in place when the arrhythmia occurred, headphones in his ears, attached to a portable compact disc player. I imagine he went facedown; there had been no other warning. He happened to be working out next to a cardio-thoracic surgeon. That person started CPR within one minute. EMTs were there in about three. Somebody got the paddles. He wasn't alone for a moment.

In the ER they worked on him for forty-five minutes before they got his heart beating again. Maybe that's an exaggeration, but that's what I was told. It wasn't like on TV, where it takes just a couple of minutes before someone in scrubs flatly says, *Time of death*. They kept trying until it worked because they knew he had a family, and that those people would have to see it for themselves, adjust to the news. *That's so nice of them*, I remember thinking. *They didn't have to do that.*

I was at the office. Less than twenty minutes before, I'd kissed Paul goodbye on the train. I had just been at my boss's desk catching up, having some coffee. It was a little after nine a.m. when the first call of the day lit up the phone on my desk. I answered the general office number, but I had a direct line, too. That's the one that rang.

I picked up. "This is Erin."

"Hey, it's Simon."

"Hey, Simon, how are you?"

"Okay. How are you?"

"I'm good."

There was a pause. "Well . . . I don't know. Dad had a heart attack. And I'm calling to tell you he's in the hospital."

"What?" I said, though I already understood. I'd simply said "what" to buy time until actual comprehension hit. "Where are you? Are you driving?"

"Yeah." He was whimpering now.

"Take a couple deep breaths, okay? It's gonna be okay." I knew Dad was dead. I knew Simon knew it, too.

"Do you need to pull over?" I asked. "Maybe you should pull the car over for a minute."

"Okay."

He was in shock, on the brink of losing it. He pulled over and took a deep breath. Maggie, Dad's girlfriend, had just called him from the hospital, and he was on the way to tell Greg. I asked where Mom was. He didn't know, she was out of town at a conference, Virginia, maybe. He gave me Maggie's number. His voice broke and he said, "Erin, this is bad."

"I know," I said. "I'm on my way." I called Paul, told him what had happened, and asked him to please come and get me. I was very robotic in my delivery of news. He'd been planning to drive back to Ohio later that day for an annual fishing trip with his own father. We'd simply go back to Brooklyn, I'd pack a bag, and we'd leave immediately.

When I hung up, my voicemail light was blinking. It was my mother relaying the news, crying outside a Hilton conference room in Virginia. "Your dad's had a heart attack," she said, her throat opening like a swallow's, then closing on the *ack*. I called her back. She, too, had spoken to Maggie. There had been a handwritten note in his wallet: *In case of emergency call Maggie Whitman.*

No one had said, *He's going to be okay.* I heard myself take on a voice that sounded reassuring and optimistic. In my head, I opened the What I Know About Cardiac Arrest file. See, this was why I'd studied public health—just for this very moment—it all made sense now, of course. I told my mother that I'd heard that ER docs give aspirin to people in the midst of heart attacks. Did she know if they'd administered the aspirin? And also, they always called for "epi" on medical shows; I was sure that had happened upon arrival. I'd read in *Time* magazine that they were doing something with stents. It would be terrible if they had to cut him open, of course, but people survived those bypass surgeries all the time.

"Erin, he's in a coma. He's still alive, but I don't think they're planning any surgeries." We agreed to meet at the hospital.

When had Dad and I last spoken? Had I ever returned his call from two nights ago? He had left a message; it was probably still saved on the machine. Our last conversation had been about our upcoming plans for Thanksgiving—he was going to host, the first time he'd ever done the cooking himself. It also would have been the first time I'd have gone to two separate turkey dinners: one with Mom and David on Tuesday, then Dad and Maggie's debut meal on the actual day. How would Dad make a turkey if he was in a coma?

I had expected if Dad were to die early it would be from a recurrence of cancer, maybe in his sixties, at least a decade on, when I was in my thirties, old enough to cope. I'd imagined sitting at a kitchen table with him when he told me the news that they'd found a tumor in his lymph nodes. He worried about it. He had been unable to quit smoking. He'd tried hypnosis, cold turkey, and the patch. Even once he was five years cancer free, or ten, he kept up with his doctor's appointments. A couple of years before, extra tests had been ordered. Some specialist hadn't "liked" a scan he'd just run; the results were inconclusive. I couldn't tell if Dad was holding back information. He'd taken me for a drive to town and we walked around the square and lurked outside the log cabin sugar house.

"There are certain things I need you to be prepared for, things I need you to take care of when I'm gone. Those things always seemed to scare your mother, but I know you can handle it."

He told me about a safety-deposit box, and even produced a key. "There's information about investments and accounts that will have to be managed. Some pictures of my parents, and some cash I've been saving for your wedding."

"What wedding would that be?" I asked with a laugh. He was so old-fashioned sometimes.

"Just know that it's there just in case."

Further tests had revealed Dad had been born without a spleen. Turns out you don't even need that thing. *False alarm.*

Cancer is a process, as bad as that is. If Dad had a recurrence, I would have had the chance to absorb the news, discuss it, plan that trip to Europe I'd always wanted to take with him. I wanted to go to the Louvre. I wanted to go to London, Strawberry Fields, and all that. All the names of all the places we'd never been ran across the bottom screen of my mind like a news crawl.

I walked down the hall and into an agent's office. She looked at me and her face began to crumple like she already knew.

"My father's had a heart attack," I said.

"Oh my God," she said, standing and picking up the phone on her desk in one motion. "Who should I call? Do you need me to make you a flight reservation?"

"Paul's coming. We'll drive and be there in less than eight hours."

She nodded. "You know, my father had a heart attack and he recovered. There's so much they can do now. It's really advanced."

I recognized that she needed to say these things, and even though I had just said these same things to my mother, I knew they didn't apply.

Paul emerged from the elevator and helped me collect my stuff. He looked so young, had just turned twenty-four, but here he was, living like an adult in our apartment, no longer a small-time weed dealer or a waiter at the Olive Garden. Now we were grown-up. I wore a Diane von Furstenberg wrap dress, and he wore the vintage silk Pucci tie I'd found in the no-name antique store; we were a version of adult I never thought we'd be. Things were just starting to get good; I'd finally gotten him to love me.

Suddenly I was very aware of everyone's age. The agent and my boss, both in their forties, came to see me off.

Don't worry, they said, *we'll take care of everything. Be careful driving. Let us know when you land.*

My boss, a powerful man, looked uncomfortable, unsure of what to say. His face was red, hands in his pockets, eyes cast down. He couldn't look at me. His father called once a week to talk about the stock market. He had four children of his own. My dad would have known what to say.

———————

Our railroad apartment in Prospect Heights was next door to a funeral parlor. When we'd moved into the place, I'd given little thought to how often we might come in contact with the bereaved. Every once in a while we could hear women weeping through the walls, or smell the cigarette smoke of anxious mourners when it wafted up to our open window, but today all was quiet. I confronted the contents of my closet: a whole row of little black dresses ideal for cocktail parties and business dinners. Surely it would be wrong to put out negative what-ifs into the universe by packing anything black or formal. No funeral attire; I was not going to jinx it. I would simply dress for a hospital: enough underwear for a week and my gray hoodie, the navy peacoat my father gave me.

Before we hit New Jersey I heard from my brother Greg, who was calling from Dad's house. Now Dad's heart was beating fine, Greg explained, but he was in a coma in intensive care and they were "looking at his brain." Even ten minutes out would have all but guaranteed brain death. But then why keep going? I tried to remember what I thought I knew about resuscitation. *Resurrection?*

Greg and Maggie were scouring through his things to look for official paperwork: a will, a do-not-resuscitate order, a notice of some kind, a letter that expressed his wishes, a sign.

"Oh, *sweetie*, I'm so sorry," I heard myself say to my brother on the telephone, as if I were his mother, as if his loss were somehow more profound than my own. It felt that way, or maybe I was trying to distance myself from too much pain, and already rewriting history.

Once we were in Pennsylvania, we listened to *Abbey Road*. I didn't know then that Dad had been listening to it that morning, too, only that it was his favorite. It was the last album the Beatles ever recorded. I laid my head on Paul's lap as he drove.

I remember fainting as a child, the feeling of slipping through to blackness, the coming to, looking up at the sky, my mother's face. This must have been the way Dad felt when he went out, running on Abbey Road, forgetting to breathe.

Five hours in we got pulled over for speeding. Paul tried to explain the circumstances: "Her father just had a heart attack this morning. We're on our way to the hospital in Ohio" had no effect on the cop. He probably heard that every day.

We made it a little after eight p.m. The hospital was not ten minutes from where Paul's parents lived, which made it feel oddly convenient. Greg met us in the lobby, which was all glass and soft lighting. We were in the serious part of the building, the after-hours entrance. The place felt closed for the evening. Greg looked thin and dour, holding an uninspired cup of coffee, a hospital cliché. He gave us limp hugs and tried to prepare us for the imminent family reunion.

In the ICU waiting room was Dad's every living relative in Cleveland. His closest friend, Bob Gardner, was on his way from Nevada. He and his wife, Greta, had known my parents since they floated down the river in inner tubes with them in the seventies. Thankfully they'd spent a lot of time together over the years. Weak smiles, frowning eye contact, whispering. A hospital vigil made up of people you only ever see on special occasions is a bad sign all around.

Every few minutes my shock and confusion would renew. I had the urge to turn to the nearest person and say, "Can you believe this? Can you believe this is actually happening?" Every moment was more surreal than the last. We were *alive*. We were alive and surrounded by the color mauve, which I'd read was supposed to inspire spiritual calm and decrease sexual desire, thus the chosen shade of many clinical settings like nursing homes and detention centers. All I could see was the color of fresh bruises.

On every wall of the room were signs shouting in offensive fonts.

ABSOLUTELY NO CELL PHONES!
If you must make a call, please use the courtesy phone near the coffee maker.
Cellular technology interferes with lifesaving equipment.

Already I was defensive. *Know what else interferes with lifesaving equipment? Sudden death.* I went with Paul to the designated ICU entrance, through the doors, past the nurses' station on the right. That smell: bacterial death by antiseptic, putrid and lemony. That sound: exhaling machines, the beeps and alarms of heart monitors, a nauseating suction, muffled weeping, conscious and unconscious moaning. Here was my father: unrecognizable, swaddled in a hospital bed, intubated, his ex-wife and his new girlfriend at his side.

"Erin's here . . ." Mom whispered to him as I approached. She embraced me. Paul held back nervously near the foot of the hospital bed; the pale yellow poly curtain draped his shoulder. A physical rush of terror coursed through me like an amphetamine. The machines were doing all the work. I leaned in to get a look at his face. His eyelids were fluttering, his pupils fixed on something unknowable toward the ceiling. He was not there. His hand was warm, though, and dry. I slipped my own into it as best I could and squeezed. I hoped he'd have some response that indicated *I'm only sleeping.*

Paul and I went out into the hall, and I told him to go home. On the car ride from New York, I'd tried to store up his affection. I didn't need him to rescue me, and I wanted him to be free of this heaviness. He'd had these plans for a year to go camping with his father, and that, too, seemed meaningful. "I don't feel right leaving you here," he said, in a tone of voice I'd never heard before. I realized he was afraid. This was the biggest thing that had ever happened to either of us. I wasn't sure if we were solid enough to withstand any extra neediness on my part. And I felt protective of Dad. He was the one who needed us, who needed me. I had to be there for him.

"Please go—you'll be helping me. This is going to be really intense and I'll need to be here all the time." The adrenaline had been pumping for hours, but now I was beginning to enter into a new phase. A kind of grandiosity had overtaken me. I was my father's daughter, the firstborn. I didn't want anyone or anything interfering with the work ahead. I told him that I loved him and that I'd call often with news. It was a relief to see him go.

Maggie hugged me hard. Being a nurse, she knew how to deliver a low, reassuring whisper of clear information. She had learned how to whittle down her weeping to a sniffle. I'd met her only once before, the last time I'd seen Dad, when we'd spent the day going to antique stores. We'd listened to the new Ryan Adams album in the car, the two of them holding hands in the front seat like they were reenacting a scene from *The Graduate*. I couldn't remember the last time I'd seen him so stupidly happy. He told me he loved her, and though she was still married to someone else, the two of them had a plan. As soon as she got both of her girls off to college, she would leave her husband and eventually the two of them would move to Utah and retire as state park naturalists. I looked at her now—blazing copper hair, thin like my mom, thin like me.

"I'll tell you everything I know," Maggie said, and motioned for me

to join her in another little room off the ward, a private suite for yell-
ers and criers. She explained what I'd been preparing myself for. "Erin,
he was under for a long time—too long. I've just never seen anyone
bounce back from this." I appreciated her candor.

"What should I do?" I asked her. "What can I do?"

"His vitals are stable. It's a waiting game now, but there's nothing
to decide tonight. Do you want to sit with him?" I did.

They left me alone with him. His body was there, but where had
he gone? I pictured him standing over us, to the side of the bed, like
the spirit in the movie who hasn't yet walked into the light. Spirit
Dad looked at me silently contemplating Comatose Dad and smiled
the smile of the proud father, the calm and reassuring presence. *You're
here*, he seemed to say. *You made it.* Aware of the insanity of it but unable to control myself, I turned and spoke to Spirit Dad, even as I held
Comatose Dad's hand. "Duh, where else would I be?"

I never wanted you to have to go through something like this.

"You went through it with your mom."

I don't think we ever talked about that. It was true. I don't remember ever having asked him what it was like for him when his mother
died. Had it been like this? A hospital goodbye?

"Dad, I need your advice on what to do in this situation."

C'mon, I never could tell you what to do. Nobody could.

"That doesn't mean I wasn't listening."

————————

After ten minutes, Maggie came in and said we should go home and
try to get some sleep, my mother, my brothers, and I. We could come
back in the morning for updates and meetings with doctors. We all
went to his condo, but we couldn't sleep except for twenty minutes
here or there. We were bright sources of energy, ready to do whatever
needed to be done. Together, we would wait for someone to tell us the
next thing to do. We would make the calls, and wait for Bob to arrive,
and get organized. I alphabetized the spice rack, first thing. A bache-

lor who didn't cook and had at least ten unopened jars of herbs and seasonings would need to know how to find the bay leaf. Mom found Dad's address book and made lists of people to call. Maggie disappeared into a storage closet under the stairs. Greg and Simon camped out in Dad's bedroom.

I wondered what Maggie had told her family about where she had been all day. Maybe pulling a double shift at the hospital, which was certainly true. She left soon after. The house was full of signs of his life with her. Dusty lavender roses were just beginning to droop in their crystal vase, which sat on the Mexican tile hearth of the fireplace.

I found a stockpile of cards meant for Maggie in a folder labeled ROMANTIC CARDS. A cartoon bear pouting under a thought bubble: *Wish I was kissing you* . . . Inside, an image of the bear sitting on a park bench holding a red balloon: . . . *Instead of just missing you!* It reminded me of my own cache of notes from him—any holiday was reason enough to receive another reminder signed, *Love, Dad*. Even St. Patrick's Day was an excuse to say *Irish You Were Here*.

On day two at the hospital, I decided I loved the nurses, with their space-age uniforms and silent platform loafers, angelically tiptoeing in with the bags of fluids and syringes. They were almost aggressively respectful. They changed the rules for us. We alone of the families could come and go as we pleased—as long as we kept it to three at a time, we could camp out. Later, I loved how they told me they'd never forget our family. How could they, really? We were on our best behavior. We were unrecognizable, even to ourselves. The drama was never us-against-them; it was inherent and it was moment-to-moment, and we were grateful for every second of their help.

The chief cardiologist, Dr. Hussain, who had been on call when they'd brought Dad in, asked to speak with us—the whole family—in the ICU waiting room. We gathered in a large semicircle around the small man while he calmly explained that sometimes the heart just stops beating, that an autopsy would likely reveal that he'd been living with heart disease for some time, atherosclerosis, clogged arteries. He had most likely never seen it coming and merely slipped into a different consciousness; we should take comfort in the fact that he didn't suffer. What was important to understand now was that given the extraordinary length of time he'd been clinically dead before the heart got going again, there was no hope of recovery. (On the EEG results, the line that indicated brain function looked like a wet spaghetti noodle thrown against the refrigerator.) Hussain recommended that, as soon as we were ready, we take him off life support.

He stepped forward. "Which one of you is his daughter?" I raised my hand. "I understand you live in New York City?"

"That's right," I said.

Hussain was my height, and he came close enough to whisper. "I lived there myself many years ago. I studied at Weill Cornell. Your father must have been very proud to have such a high-achieving daughter."

I just said, "Thank you."

Then he hugged me and patted my shoulder. "I'm very sorry we couldn't save him, dear. I can promise you we did everything possible."

Hussain moved down the line. He spent a moment with each person, looked them in the eye, touched them. When he approached my grandfather, a quiet, stoic man in his eighties, Hussain didn't hesitate but took the older man's ruddy, wrinkled face in his small brown hands and said, "In some ways it will be hardest for you. It's not supposed to be this way, is it? The son before the father."

We held our breath. Dad respected, loved, and feared his father, John. A man of very few words, John locked eyes with this strangely emotional surgeon and crumpled into quiet sobs.

It occurred to me that I'd been preparing for Dad's premature death all my life. But now so many people were headed for a world of hurt, so many people who didn't even know he was all the way gone, just hanging out until we could convince ourselves it was hopeless.

I considered trying to open myself up to God. I figured I had already been rendered crazy by the last twenty-four hours; it couldn't hurt to go with the flow. When Pastor Doug came to the ICU to pray, the first time we'd seen anyone from the church in probably ten years, I reacted as if he were Santa Claus. Pastor Doug was enormous, probably nearing three hundred pounds, and as soon as I saw him I threw my arms around the world of his stomach and pressed my head against his chest and let him hold me for a long time. I was twenty-six years old, and decidedly not a hugger, but I didn't have much control over my overwhelming gratitude on behalf of my dad. If this person wanted to stand over my brain-dead father and pray to Jesus, *who might already be walking with Your Son, Lord*, and hold our hands to form a circle of protection, of strength, then I was going to be a vessel for that. For those three days, I would be as accommodating and polite as a preacher's daughter.

We had unanimously decided that we would let him go after the third day. That way everyone who needed to see him would have a chance to say goodbye. There would have to be a memorial service, something would have to be done with his body. After another long day, our motley crew gathered again at Dad's, each of us again dispatched to our own corner of the house to assemble material for the memorial. Simon and Greg to the master closet in the bedroom, Mom to the filing cabinet in the office, Maggie to a trunk full of photographs in the guest room, and me to the record collection in the living room.

There was so much to do and see! Here was the last marijuana cigarette he'd ever smoked, likely just yesterday morning, its charred roach in a vintage green Depression-era glass ashtray on the Shaker table near the kitchen. His tastes had changed in recent years, had become countrified. There, a recently acquired pool table looked pristine but for a stack of unopened mail. Here was a coffee mug with Maggie's lipstick print in the sink. There were his leftovers in the fridge, the Chinese food containers holding untouched rice. He ate almost every meal out, a bad habit we all shared. Here were recent pictures of my brothers laughing and looking psyched to be on a boat, hanging on the fridge door under Rock & Roll Hall of Fame magnets. There was my press pass to the United Nations from a one-off freelance reporting stint.

Antique china, houseplants, and a new pool table didn't paint a picture of the person I'd known. The only way to conjure those memories was through his music. I got to work on a last mixtape for Dad. I made a list of essential songs, ninety minutes' worth: the Rolling Stones, Van Morrison, Rod Stewart, Bruce Springsteen, Neil Young, Bob Marley, Joni Mitchell. And last, the Beatles, the music that would forever bond us: "Here Comes the Sun," "A Day in the Life," "In My Life," "Let It Be," "This Boy," "The Long and Winding Road," "All You Need Is Love," "Something."

While I combed through vinyl, cassettes, and CDs, Maggie emerged with presents for all of us, things she knew he'd want us to have. Electronic swag for my brothers—a camera and DVD players, stuff he'd won in a golf tournament, some T-shirts, a windbreaker.

I was hunched in front of the record player when Maggie walked up behind me and wrapped my shoulders with a patchwork quilt from the 1920s, its hand-sewn squares delicately frayed. She described its provenance, how he'd deliberated over several from different eras before finally choosing this one just the weekend before, procured at a favorite antique store. I'd been eyeing these old quilts last time we were together, and lamenting the lack of "home" to be found in my apartment in Brooklyn. This quilt wasn't the fanciest or the most pristine, but it had the most character. Here we were in his house without him, rummaging through his stuff—not because we wanted anything, but because we wanted evidence that he would have wanted us to have it. And here was a gift with my name on it, designed solely to be comforting.

I pulled the blanket tight around my shoulders and finally let myself cry.

19

GOLDEN SLUMBERS

GRIEF IS HEARTBREAK MADE MANIFEST. It is a fever. It overcomes you; it's completely physical, all throb and ache.

After my father's death, our family's nightly conversation was: "Does your chest hurt?" *I wonder if this is how a heart attack might feel.* "How's your head?" *It hurts.* "Do you have a fever?" *About one hundred degrees, yes.*

Jolting awake was the only way I knew I was ever asleep. I would drift off only to be startled by the memory of why I was so tired. I felt I owed it to him to stay conscious.

There are two kinds of sleep for grief: no sleep/heart pounding, or dead sleep/heart pounding . . . like in the story "The Telltale Heart" by Edgar Allan Poe. You hear your heart in your throat. You put your chin to your chest and watch the primal drum thump right under your rib cage, a flutter you'd never noticed before. That rushing in your ears, is that music? It's the symphonic crash of blood through your arteries. It's always been there and yet you never listened so closely before.

It feels selfish to sleep. Yet the people around you really need you to try to get some rest. No one can rest unless they know that you're taking care of yourself first. (Who else would you take care of? The person you're grieving for is dead.) You can't rest because you fall asleep and forget, only to wake up again and remember. Better to stay awake for as long as possible so as to stave off the forgetting.

None of us had slept. My mother, brothers, and I were overwhelmed, exhausted, and dazed to the point of hallucination. On the second day, we took a break from the mixtape and the photo albums and sat around the kitchen table, drinking flat Coke out of a plastic two-liter bottle. A woman from Dad's office had brought over a sheet of lasagna large enough to feed a fire department.

Trays of cold cuts, rye bread and pickle spears, many squeezable condiments, fried chicken, ambrosia salad. Those aggressively delightful fruit-on-a-stick bouquets where the strawberries tasted like pineapple and everything else like melon.

While my brothers, my mother, and I stuck forks in our rubbery pasta and pretended to eat, Mom and I spoke in hushed tones about funeral arrangements.

We'd winced at the "packages" offered at the place my aunt suggested, which all had names like "Autumnal Slumber" or "Eternal Pasture." The well-meaning funeral director seemed more like a car salesman, youthful and eager to please. Were these the only choices for stationery? Wasn't there some way to customize the *Thanks for Your Condolence* cards, and the all-important guestbook? Why did the leather have to be this color? Everything was so disappointing. We had expected luxury. Artistry. Individuality. Resurrection. Closure. Instead we got a taffeta-strewn chapel and an audio component, for around $8,000. We'd deal with the ashes in the summer.

We knew, even before we found the letter neatly filed in an envelope in an office folder labeled IN THE EVENT OF MY DEATH, that we'd all be taking Dad's ashes out west to Lake Powell, bordered by Utah and Arizona, his favorite place to travel every summer with Bob and their lifelong friend, Dan. I'd guessed the letter was written around the time he'd been afraid the cancer might be back, years after my parents' divorce:

> *I'd like my ashes spread over Lake Powell. Bob will help you with this. Across the channel from Gunsight Butte is a point of land accessible by car that would make a nice place. There's a cassette tape marked "in the event of my death" with the tape collection. It's a compilation of songs that made an impact in my life. It would be nice to play as you are thinking of me. For the trip to Lake Powell, I'd like Erin, Simon, Greg and Paige to go. Take the money out of the life insurance policies. Invite Bob & Greta, and Dan & Laura, my closest and longest friends. Don't make a big thing out of it. It's not the end, and I'll be pleased that my remains are spread in the most beautiful spot on earth.*

As Mom and I recapped all we'd learned from the funeral director, Greg cut in.

"Hello," he said, eyes narrowed, his hand waving to get our attention. "Simon and I are sitting here, too, and we should get a say in whatever you guys are talking about."

His rising tone of voice meant that he was about to pick a fight. Mom tried to neutralize the situation, but the family dynamic of girls on one side, boys on the other all but ensured an ugly scene.

"I don't think Erin's trying to exclude you guys—"

"Why is she asking you what you think about this and not us? You're divorced!" Mom looked down at her hands.

"But she's our *mother* so I'm asking her advice," I said. "I've never tried to plan a funeral before." Our parents' divorce made me senior available next-of-kin—the person who signed the paperwork in the hospital and was officially responsible for the body. We needed to appoint an executor for the will, and I did not want that job. I was hoping Mom would step in—she seemed the natural choice, having handled the family finances all our lives.

"I knew this would happen! You think you can just swoop in from New York City and make all the decisions? That you're somehow Dad's favorite because you're the oldest?" Greg spat, cheeks ablaze.

"Dude, chill. We are on the same page," I said. Why was he lashing out at me? "I just want to do what Dad would have wanted, and I didn't know you disagreed."

"How do you know what Dad wanted? You barely knew him."

That stung. "I know what he told me," I said. "He was worried he was sick again last year and he told me he wanted to be cremated."

"Oh, yeah, you and Dad were just *so close*," Greg said. He was in my face now. "Daddy's little girl. Too bad you haven't been around for *years*."

"Where is this coming from? I was just here a couple months ago, and you don't know anything about my relationship with Dad."

"Oh, really, did you know that his girlfriend is still married?" (Yes. He'd told all of us.) "Did you know we played golf together every weekend we could since you moved to your precious New York City?" (I'd figured as much.)

"Did it ever occur to you that I might have had my own relationship with Dad, one that you don't know shit about?" I yelled.

Mom screamed, "STOP IT! STOP IT! STOP IT!" Whatever decorum we had achieved in the hospital in front of nurses and doctors had completely unraveled.

Even in tragedy we couldn't come together. This family crisis was no different from any other—all these years later and we were still the same. Side A: politely supportive; Side B: plainly resentful. A mere sentence could escalate into a war. My brothers: lashing out in the anger they came to openly identify as "the Hosier way," completely resigned to the chaos. Our mother (who sometimes felt more like our sister): weeping over our inability to get along. Me: defensive that I wasn't the one who started it. When it was over: all of us stomping off to stew in our own private hells. Afterward: like nothing had ever happened.

In the middle of the night between days two and three, I finally fell asleep on top of Dad's bed, wrapped in my new patchwork quilt. I squished my face into the blue Aztec-patterned pillows that smelled faintly of him. At five thirty my heartbeat woke me up, the blood whooshing through my arteries. I lay perfectly still for an hour just listening to the sound of the clock radio's numbers as they flipped faintly in the dark. At six thirty I jumped when his alarm sprang to life with the country sounds of WGAR, the saddest music ever played.

The third day was meant to be his last day, the day we were to let him go. It was the worst day. His body was bloated and purple, his lips swollen around the tube down his throat. His breathing had evolved into a series of rhythmic gasps. We were bewildered by what was happening around us, to us, through us—and we felt guilty that we were dragging things out, the idea of him in pain.

But we weren't ready! We needed time to adjust and ponder possible outcomes and new realities. Just the day before I'd seen Simon whisper in Dad's ear, "Wake up, please wake up."

That morning I'd clung to Mom's tiny body on the sidewalk in front of the hospital as soon as we'd arrived. *Wait.*

"Wait," I said out loud.

I looked at her in a panic, as if for the first time. "I'm not ready," I heard myself say. Mom held me and started to cry. "I know he's already gone, but I'm not ready to let him go."

Mom and I had dealt with death together once before. I had gone home for a visit and found our cat looking frail and sick. Kitty was old by then, almost fifteen, and had long ago lost her sweet disposition. She was not just thin but back to her kitten size, the way she'd looked when I'd sneaked her into the fold from a box of free kittens born on a friend's farm. Like all our cats over the years, Kitty was tough, preferring the great outdoors to the comforts of an indoor litter box, but lately she'd been living in the garage and avoiding food. I suddenly knew she wouldn't make it twenty-four hours. Mom was more hopeful. Kitty had lived so long in the country—she'd made it longer than all our other cats. Still, something was eerily different this time. The stillness around her unnerved us.

We made frequent trips to the garage, supplying her with a new blanket, trying to ply her with treats. She seemed to want to be alone. The next morning, when we checked, she looked worse than she had the night before, and she'd stopped grooming herself. Mom said we should call the vet. While I went to get the phone, Kitty took her first steps in hours, and moved toward Mom pathetically, meowing as if in pain. Mom called me, and within seconds we had our four hands on her. She'd used all her strength to make it into our arms. A great ripple seemed to move through her from her head to her tail, and then it happened again. I said, "Kitty, go to the light." Mom and I were both crying. Just like that she was gone. In her final moments on earth, she had tried so hard not to be alone.

We all had time alone with him. I didn't believe he could hear me or that anyone was listening, so I spoke freely.

"What will I do now?" I asked as I moved a tendril of his sandy gray hair off his forehead. I'd never touched my father's hair before. It struck me as an absurd gesture, but still, I felt compelled. In some ways, this man belonged to me. Now that his heart was beating perfectly strong in his chest I rested my head there. You only get to hear a few heartbeats up close during your life. Your mother's, your significant other's, your father's—this primal drumbeat, proof of life. I would never again have the opportunity to touch him, to know what his hair felt like through my fingers or the scratch of his cheek against mine. He was as good as gone.

"I forgot to ask you a million questions, like what you think I should do with my life?" I felt a pang of guilt as I said that out loud. There were other things about him that I wanted to know more than what he thought about me. How had he lost his mother and moved on? How had he lost our mother and moved on? How had he maintained his optimism and spirituality? How were things for him before he had us, and how were they afterward?

I wasn't yet ready to ask the tougher questions: *Why did you sometimes want to humiliate me? How could you hit us? Why didn't you protect us?*

A nurse rolled brand-new white tube socks on his feet straight from a package of four. Small feet, like a kid's. His sock-clad toe stuck out from under the hospital sheets. He'd recently gotten a ridiculous tattoo on his outer left calf, a tidy rendering of a Native American warrior brandishing a spear and with a large penis dangling between his legs, a petroglyph. Dad had waited until he was fifty-three to get his first tattoo, and this was what he'd decided to go with. I assumed it was an homage to his Southwestern travels, but I wondered what it was about this particular image that spoke to him.

When I was eighteen, I had shown him my own first (and last), a stupid blue star outlined in red on my right biceps, drawn freehand by a drunk person so that it resembled the work of a child wielding a magic marker, which was not my intention. I had done it on impulse to stick it to Chris, who'd been fretting for a year over choosing the perfect image for his own first ink. When I showed up sleeveless for a visit with Dad, my fresh tattoo slick with weatherproof salve, I expected him to be upset. Instead, his eyes lit up and he guffawed. Then he smiled and said, "That's a pretty cool mistake."

We gathered again in the mauve ICU waiting room. Our family doctor, who'd diagnosed Dad's cancer all those years before, walked us through what to expect. He and Maggie would go in and remove the tubes, the ventilator, and turn down all the beeping machines. Then an ICU nurse would administer the morphine that would ease Dad painlessly into death. He would likely go peacefully within five minutes.

A dozen of us stood around the bed in a circle—Mom to his left side, then me, Bob, his brothers, their children, his father, my brothers, and Maggie closing the circle. His head was propped up on a pillow and tilted to one side. He was breathing on his own. He looked better than he had in days, his color much less jaundiced, like a man merely passed out drunk. Bob joked that he'd seen him look a lot worse many times before. The main thing was that he was free. We all laid our hands on him. I think someone said a prayer. I heard Mom lean over and whisper in his ear, "Thank you for our children."

We cried a little. I stared at Dad's face and after a while he began to sigh. We'd been warned there might be snoring, but this sound was more like a melody, a song. It made sense to me. His breathing was so strong that he didn't die in five minutes, or ten, or anytime soon. We stood around the bed like that, all of us, for an hour, just watching him breathe.

"What you're witnessing," the doctor explained, "is the human body's instinct to live." Sometimes this happened and brain-dead people lived on fumes for hours and sometimes days.

Every thirty minutes the prettiest ICU nurse would come and administer morphine, her face apologetic and sensitive. She crept around us in her blue booties and gently shot him up, assuring us each time that he was feeling no pain. I looked forward to morphine, to going out in a similar fashion, unconscious but high, surrounded by the music of eternal love and eternal regret. Maybe he was already above us looking down, beaming with reassurance that he was okay on the other side. *It calls me on and on across the universe.*

After two hours passed, his breathing was still steady and rhythmic. He was simply in a deep sleep. Extended family began to disperse. Surely they were not meant to pay their respects as long as we were, and besides they had a lot of work to do for the memorial. We were so depleted, there was nowhere to go but the Denny's restaurant across the street. As my father lay dying, I was ordering Moons Over My Hammy. I managed to eat, but didn't taste it. Food was simply something to be dealt with now.

At Denny's the family talked about logistics. I would call the bank tomorrow and cancel the credit cards. To my great relief, Mom had said she would handle the settling of the estate. Was it too morbid for me to accompany the body to the crematorium? Someone gently reminded me that the funeral director had told us that though it's not illegal, he's seen exactly zero family members do that. I had clearly watched too much *Six Feet Under.*

My brothers and I went home to finish the mixtape, but Mom was there for his last breath, and Maggie, one on each side. Mom called us to say, "He's going fast now," and we rushed back to the hospital from his house. By the time we got there, he was gone. The nurses told us to take as much time with his body as we needed, but within reason, as we knew they had to take him. *As much time as we needed* meant five minutes.

I sat next to him on the hospital bed and marveled at how much better he looked, how healthy now that he was unencumbered by the life-extending machines. And yet, he was dead. I put my head on his chest one more time, and breathed in the sterility of the crisp white blankets that swaddled him. This was it, the unyielding finality of death, and the last moments of a relationship all encapsulated in a four-minute window of forever. I signed the forms to donate any organs they could salvage. He would have wanted that, we all agreed. His body was still warm. Now it was up to me, I thought; I'd never been more my father's daughter.

———————

That night, Paul came back. I'd fallen asleep on a futon in the room with the computer, and suddenly I was aware of someone lying behind me, encircling me in strong arms. I tried to turn to him to say something, but before I knew what was happening my body began to seize like it was hypothermic, and I lost control of my ability to calm myself.

"Oh, Erin. Jesus. Tell me what I can do. Let me take you out of here." He seemed impossibly far away, through a tunnel.

I couldn't stop trembling. So this was shock. I tried to focus on my breathing, tried to get a rhythm going. It took a couple of minutes of imagining I was hooked up to an IV filled with sedative sunshine for me to finally begin to melt.

"He's not going to make it," I said. "He died."

"I know. I'm so sorry. I'm here." The words I'd been waiting to hear didn't sound the way I'd imagined. Instead, I wanted to amp up the self-reliance more than ever before. It felt strange to lean too much on my boyfriend, or anyone. My body felt scraped out and so far away from everyone, especially Dad. Yet in my head he was everywhere.

I couldn't leave. There was so much to do.

———————

The next day, I drafted a eulogy while Mom composed an obituary for the newspaper. We wrote to stay focused. We pored over mysterious phone numbers on scraps of paper. Mom made the calls to old friends from the early seventies, people who hadn't spoken to Dad in years, all his old colleagues.

Stunned by shock, I'd forgotten how to dress. Since forever, how I looked was my thing. Most of my stay-home-from-school sick days were due to bad perms or the wrong colored tights; I never left the house without makeup. I would typically wear vintage dresses, usually adorned by some kind of whimsical detail like a brooch or oversized buttons. But I hadn't been to very many funerals in my life. I remembered that when Jane's husband had died a decade before, she'd worn head-to-toe white to the church, with an enormous hat that shadowed her face. I had that image in mind—inexplicably—when I bought an outfit for the funeral that was probably more appropriate for a job interview: white oxford shirt, black pleated pants, open-toed heels half a size too big, clothes to disappear in and never wear again. (In fact I never did.) *Do mourners wear lipstick? Is all white just for wives?*

Since high school, my hair had been changing color on a spectrum of platinum, to blond, to auburn, to bright red, to copper, to brown, and back again. That fall it was bleached blond, and I'd recently gotten it chopped into an edgy bob at a Japanese salon. But now the platinum color seemed cheap somehow, disrespectful. I didn't want to look artificial or punk at my father's memorial service; I wanted to look like somebody's beloved daughter. Paul's mom offered to call her hairdresser, who saw me that night and dyed my hair a tasteful auburn, an homage to Dad's favorite oncology nurse when he was going through chemo. Only later did I remember that red was Maggie's color, too.

Now that Dad was gone I wanted to know everything. He kept meticulous records, an organized house. So many secrets were lying out in the open. The attic was full of alphabetized boxes of files packed with evidence of his successes and failures—a pile of résumés through the lean years of layoffs and accounts lost and gained, seven years of tax receipts, copies of motivational speeches he'd written focused on marketers.

In a file labeled HEALTH there was a *Personal Wellness Profile* for the hospital gym where he'd been working out the morning he died. It was a "Questionnaire Plus," meant to be a comprehensive assessment of his ability to engage in exercise in seventy-five questions. Oh, shit. *Age*: almost fifty-four. *Family Health History*: he marked colorectal cancer, ovarian cancer, and cataracts, but not coronary heart disease, despite the fact that his brother had recently had a quadruple bypass before age fifty, and his father had survived a massive heart attack. He marked the box claiming "I'm as healthy as anybody I know."

In the *Eating Practices* section, he claimed he indulged in fast food only two to three times per month. *More like per weekend*, I thought. He did not weigh *only* ten pounds more than he had ten years previous, but he did admit to drinking three or more drinks in a sitting on the days he drank. Under *Drugs*, the question was "How often do you use drugs or medicines that affect your mood, help you relax, or help you sleep?" He had chosen "Rarely, a few times per year." Oh. (This was markedly at odds with the truth apparent in three heavily rotated coats in the house—each containing quarter-ounce bags of weed and rolling papers.) He smoked ten or more cigarettes a day and reported that he planned to quit smoking again within the next six months (despite the cartons of freshly purchased Marlboro Lights stashed in his sock drawer). In the bathroom medicine cabinet: a newly prescribed bottle of Viagra, a known bummer for the heart. But who could begrudge him? If it was good enough for Bob Dole . . . He'd been to the doctor twice already that year, presumably for prescriptions and a cancer screen. He reported that his cholesterol was in the range of 181–199 (really?) with normal blood pressure.

When it came to *Safety*, he admitted to sometimes driving after he'd been drinking. He admitted to never wearing sunglasses. (He liked the sun in his eyes.) He didn't always wear his seat belt. He didn't always wear a helmet. Under *Stress and Coping* he said he was "coping very well." Under *Feelings*, with 1 being "all of the time" and 6 being "none of the time," he marked 6 in response to "Have you felt downhearted and blue?" He'd also never felt worthless, inadequate, or unimportant. "Have you been a happy person?" was met with a 1: *all of the time*.

He'd been happy when he died.

His AOL account was riddled with porn spam. I absentmindedly spent hours erasing it, though no one around would have known how to find it, or probably cared. I scanned the sent file of his email, looking for my own name. There was an email I'd sent about an unfortunate vacation experience I'd recently had with Paul. We'd gone to Cape Cod to make the kind of romantic memories that might plant the seed for a forever love, but as usual my attempts at unmitigated joy were thwarted by a number of mishaps—overexposed film and Paul's unwillingness to abide signs that read KEEP OUT or YOUR CAR WILL GET STUCK IN THESE DUNES among them. Upon returning from vacation, I'd gotten an angry red rash that I assumed, because of its placement on my body, was obtained by squatting to pee as we tried to make our way out of the dunes we'd gotten stuck in with our car. After many agonizing days of no relief, I learned it wasn't poison ivy at all, but a simple reaction to shellfish, and a couple of doses of Benadryl were all I needed to quell the discomfort. I was in the habit of writing about my personal failures to him. He wrote back that he'd saved my account on his hard drive "for years of enjoyment" and signed it "Love you all the time."

All the time, happy. *All the time*, loved.

I re-sent the email to myself and shut down the monitor, staring at my reflection in the black, knowing for certain that time was up.

20

HERE COMES THE SUN

THE SIGNIFICANCE OF "HERE COMES THE SUN" in our family's life was profound. It was practically a family theme song, its legacy sealed years before I was born when my parents walked down the aisle to its hopeful, optimistic melody. On the *Abbey Road* album, it was never released as a single, so therefore never charted, but it's easily my first and best-loved Beatles song. I've been to few graduations, weddings, or funerals where it didn't feature. Even my evangelical grandparents could sing along to it, *doo-doo-doo-doo*. It sounds like a song that was composed in a flower garden after a long winter of discontent, which is exactly how it came to be, written by George Harrison at Eric Clapton's house in 1969.

George was the most spiritual Beatle (he even looked like Jesus Christ). Though all of them were interested in a higher consciousness, he was the first one to publicly go on an active quest, first traveling to India in 1966 to explore Hinduism, Hare Krishna, and meditation, and inspiring the band to open their minds to Eastern philosophies.

Like Paul, he was raised Roman Catholic, and he clearly rejected the assorted dogma surrounding that religion, if not the essential idea that God was real and eternal life worth seeking. Until the end of his life, George signed his name accompanied by two symbols on either side—the Sanskrit for *om* and a simple cross. Where John rejected the ritual and the deity, George embraced several, and used his post-Beatles catalogue to make a joyful noise—*All Things Must Pass* is an album of praise songs.

I like to imagine that Dad was ushered out of this life by the song, a kindred spirit on a hopeful note. There was never any doubt that song would close the memorial service.

It wasn't long enough for me. Even as it was beginning, I didn't want the service to end or for all the people to go and leave us alone. Hundreds of people came, old friends and colleagues, people I didn't know but who seemed to know me. The mixtape we'd finished the night before played too softly in the background. It was a funeral parlor, after all, not a rock concert. Everyone was so kind. So many of my old friends: Chris and Lewis were there, and Denise drove in from New York. Paul's father. All of the Gardners.

I felt conspicuous, yet strangely invisible. I'd come dressed for my day in court—I cursed myself for getting wrong what had always come naturally: looking like myself. If anyone noticed a change, no one mentioned it, only that I looked so much like my dad.

I sat next to Paul in the second row of chairs in the makeshift chapel. He held my hand tight. Simon and Greg, my mother, and Maggie were in my periphery. Deep breaths, Tic Tacs, a little stocking stuffer of Kleenex. Pastor Doug set the tone for the reflection, telling the room that anyone would be permitted to speak if the spirit moved them. He reminded me that we were there to celebrate the life of a human being, as flawed as he was excellent.

"Jack wasn't a perfect guy—none of us is. At a memorial, we don't focus on that aspect of a person; what matters is whether or not they took a look at their shortcomings and made moves to change them. I spent a lot of time with him when he was dealing with cancer—he was always eager to talk about the great unknown. He thought deeply about life and what came next. Over time, I saw him work on the aspects of himself he wanted to transform."

I appreciated hearing that a person didn't have to be perfect to be loved. The tributes were incredibly moving. I loved listening to peoples' memories and perceptions. One of the copywriters from his office spoke first. He was only a couple of years older than me, and had a sweet disposition and a nervous stutter.

"I'm ashamed to say it, but I'm twenty-nine years old, and I don't know how to tie a Windsor, and the tie I'm wearing today is one of two ties that Jack tied for me. I've just been sliding the same knot up and down for the last two years. He gave great advice, the best boss I've ever had."

Another man Dad had worked with on a pro bono fund-raising campaign called Project Love, a school-based mentoring program for teenagers, spoke about Dad's passion for the cause. "Jack talked a lot about the importance of kindness, how necessary it is to get to kids early. With his help last year we put a curriculum in one hundred and five area high schools. He always had a smile on his face that suggested a sincere caring. He always said, 'If only we could do more.' He wanted to make a better world."

Jane walked up to the podium next. She told of our mother's singing group and the way Dad had pulled some strings so they could record their songs in a real studio. Afterward he took them all out for a big dinner to celebrate their accomplishment, and paid for the entire day. Jane said she wasn't used to that kind of support from a man, and that his children were very lucky to have had a father who possessed such fruits of the spirit.

A few people praised him for his skills as a writer and ease in front of an audience. When it came to work, he was tenacious. If he didn't know something, he would just absorb a subject until he knew it better than anyone else.

He was perhaps not the great athlete I'd always assumed he was. On their annual trips, his friends sometimes thought of him as their own kid who needed reining in. He had a habit of weighing down his bags with interesting-looking rocks he collected in every new place. "Jack would eat all the food, never wash the dishes or put anything away, and sometimes got us in trouble. But he made up for it in other ways." The audience chuckled knowingly. He'd had another reputation outside of being our dad, but it didn't surprise me that he didn't tend to pick up after himself.

Bob told an anecdote about how they met. "Thirty years ago almost to the day, my boss came to me and asked me to drive to Cincinnati with some guy named Jack. I had a Volkswagen bus and was trying to become a middle-class hippie—I wasn't particularly excited about taking a four-hour drive to Cincinnati and back with a stranger, only to haul some stereo equipment. But eventually, about halfway through the drive, one of us turned to the other and said what hippies said to each other back then: 'Do you get high?' We had a great trip. What started there was a friendship that lasted thirty years. We grew up together, but Jack never lost that childlike spirit."

Bob had never lost his Christian faith, and credited my father for "leading me to Jesus." I hadn't heard Dad talk about church or Jesus or the status of his belief in either since before the divorce. It had never occurred to me that he would be instrumental in someone else's spiritual awakening. But Bob told the story of a man who showed him the way. "I want to be able to explain what kind of friend Jack was, and the thing that I keep coming back to is First Corinthians, if I just replace the word 'love' with 'friendship.' Friendship is patient, friendship is kind; a friend doesn't insist on his own way."

When it was my turn to make the closing remarks, I felt the pressure of the last five days. This was the life I was born to witness, and the speech I was born to write. I tried not to allow my eyes to rest on anyone in particular as I unfolded my handwritten notes.

I've struggled with faith my whole life, but I never struggle with my faith in love. What is love for? It can't be explained with science, and yet, what would our lives be without it? I still struggle with religion and the question of God, but since I believe in eternal love, who am I to question eternal life?

My father's first love was his mother, Ruth, who died too soon, when he was just a teenager. She was the light behind that famous smile, and the tears in his eyes when he was moved by something. I remember being in a car with him one day, and I was just leafing through a fashion magazine, and there was one of those perfume ads with a scented insert, for Chanel No. 5. And I said something offhand about the perfume's reputation, and the longevity of it, and he got real quiet and said, "Oh, my mother wore Chanel No. 5. I'll never forget the way she smelled." He just never got over her loss, it really influenced the way he expressed love for people.

And then he met a girl named Paige. They were just kids, really, when they got together and had us. And my dad was such a family man he loved nothing more than taking us all on a trip somewhere, playing the role of the tour guide, the big spender, the family photographer. But he was also one of those men who considered it a weakness to pull over and ask for directions or help, and sometimes we got lost and my parents had some memorable arguments. My dad sometimes had a hard time admitting when he was wrong, and a hard time saying he was sorry, but oh, he loved my mom. And I was lucky enough to witness that love over and over and over.

Once, when I was probably ten, we all went roller skating. I wasn't very graceful in skates, so I shuffled along, hand in hand with my dad, and after a while I got a little tired and we leaned up against a railing to rest, and watched all the people roll past. And suddenly he exclaimed, "Look at that woman over there!" and I was like "What? Where?" and he said, "Right over there! The most beautiful woman in the room!" And I followed his gaze, and there was my mom, directly across from us, skating by herself. "Your mother is always the most beautiful woman in the room," he said.

My parents were divorced after twenty-four years, but I want you to understand, speaking as their daughter, that I honor their decision. They were both able to change so much as individuals, and these last years my dad didn't have such a problem admitting when he was wrong, and he was able to say he was sorry. In short, he grew.

The last and perhaps eternal love of my dad's life is his beloved friend Maggie. Soon after they met two years ago, he suddenly became curiously giddy, almost obnoxiously so. He called me up one night and announced, "Erin, I'm in love!" He was so happy and I couldn't help but be happy for him, but I never anticipated that I would be able to witness the depth of that love firsthand. And some of you know that my dad had a thing for redheads and a thing for nurses. And Maggie is a redheaded nurse! When he was sick with cancer, he was always so moved by their kindness and mercy, and of course their morphine. But how could anyone have anticipated that Maggie would also become his nurse, as she did this Saturday, when she helped release his body from those awful beeping machines, hoses, and tubes? Not many people get to participate in something so profoundly meaningful.

This morning Maggie shared with me a few of their love letters to each other, and one was signed, "I am with you always. Love, Jack." Dad always told the ones that he loved that he loved them. He told his family, he told his girlfriend, he told his kids, he told his kids' friends. And it wasn't just on your birthday, or after the World Trade Center was attacked, or just once in a while. It was a constant, omnipresent barrage of love and appreciation. And I know everyone in this room gave it right back. He just made it easy to.

When my dad took his last breath, he took that breath lying on his back in a bed in the surgical intensive care unit at Southwest General Hospital. There were two people in that room sitting on either side of him, each holding one of his hands, each holding each other's free hand, each telling him they loved him. They were

the loves of his life, Maggie and Paige. Who's to say that his moth-
er, Ruth, wasn't in that room somewhere, too? Just to close that
circle: lover, friend, mother. Home.

So I'm trying to learn from this and I'm going to allow myself
to pray, even if I'm not sure what I'm doing. When I pray, I will
pray to Love and to Grace. And when I need to talk to God, I will
call my dad's cell phone and I'll listen to those four rings and then
the words "Hi, this is Jack. I'm not available right now but if you
leave me a detailed message I'll call you right back." And I will
say, "Hi, Dad, I just wanted to thank you for teaching me about
love. I hope to see you soon."

I took a week off work after he died. The thing about grief is that it's
an emotional process that goes on with or without your active partici-
pation. You're still going to miss the person and question the meaning
of life whether you're convalescing at home or reading manuscripts
among the living, so you might as well go to the office, which will
require you to take a shower before reading the manuscripts.

Oddly, negotiating the aftermath of death wasn't as difficult as
I expected; in some ways, my life became instantly easier. For some
lucky reason, things seamlessly fell into place. We put Dad's house on
the market and it sold within a month's time. A windfall of life insurance money came through, and with it, a sudden financial security. I
could buy a dress at Barneys. I could pay off my student loans. I could
exhale and focus on the trajectory of my career.

Shortly after returning to work, I made my first book deal and effectively went from administrative-assistant-to-agents to agent myself.
It was a biography of one of the early pioneers of rock 'n' roll. In the
weeks after the funeral, I edited nearly a thousand pages of the author's research and helped carve out a proposal. I submitted the pitch
to a publisher on a Friday, and by Monday I had a buyer. It seemed
improbably easy. When the deal was announced in *Publishers Weekly*,

I was pleased, but I also felt a deep sense of disappointment that it hadn't happened before Dad died. At twenty-seven years of age I felt totally past my prime—a better daughter would have had it figured out by twenty-five. Now I'd never have enough time to undo what I saw as my childhood failures in the eyes of my father. I was haunted by the guilt that I could have hustled a lot more, that I could have been perfect.

At work I'd been idolizing my boss, consciously and unconsciously. This had been the case before Dad died but got more intense afterward. I just transferred all my needs onto a man ten years younger than my dad. I threw myself into accelerating my career and making him proud. Our little office felt like a band, and he was the lead singer we played backup for. In exchange for a job well done, we were treated to long boozy lunches seemingly every time someone sold a book or one hit the *New York Times* bestseller list. It was nearly impossible for me not to project a paternal role on the man who gifted me with cashmere mittens to get me through a New York winter.

———————

A month after Dad died, I turned on the *Today* show and they were playing "Here Comes the Sun." George Harrison had died of cancer. The novelty of my grief hadn't even begun to wear off. I was getting used to this idea that I was going to feel a terrible sadness every day. Depressed, restless, I was constantly reminded that my dad was dead. My grief had teeth. I thought of people in two groups—alive and formerly alive. John Lennon, Dad, and now George had gone and joined the Dead Dads Club. But something about Dad being in such good company made him feel less gone.

Grief made me a nicer person, more patient. I'd always tipped 20 percent even if the service was bad, but in grief I was angelic. I was tender. I was in a perpetual state of grace. At the agency, I answered the phone at the front desk, and every week some deluded sad sack would call the office line in order to get a message to the blockbuster author we repped. Sometimes the sad sack would be a little old lady in Duluth who wanted to know if Blockbuster Author could dedicate his next book to her daughter who was dying of something inevitable. Typically, I would politely listen and wish her daughter the very best. While grieving, I entertained all the sad sacks, invited their stories and gave them advice. I fretted with them over their losses and indulged their need to connect with someone they just knew would want to hear their story, too.

I saw Maggie once more, a few months after the funeral on a visit home. She still felt significant to me, and I thought maybe she'd stay in our lives. We'd agreed that she'd pick me up at my mom's and we would go for a drive. Maggie wanted to show me some of the places he loved. As she drove through Amish country, I asked if she had told her husband about my dad. Maggie stared straight ahead, her voice shaky when she answered, "Joe knows something's going on with me. I overheard him tell the kids that I needed space because I lost a patient."

"Sounds like a good guy," I said, immediately regretting it. "I'm sorry, that's really none of my business."

Maggie started to weep. "He is, that's the thing. He's a good father and a good man. I never expected to fall in love with someone else, but then I met your dad and I couldn't remember my life before him."

We had that in common.

When Dad had told me about Maggie, I'd asked, "Don't you feel bad about her husband?" He was disappointing me and I wanted him to know it.

He'd looked me in the eye and told me that he tried not to think about it. Sometimes love was worth the sacrifice. A year before he would never have considered getting involved with somebody else's wife, but this was different. Great love was worth it. She was the woman he wanted to be with for the rest of his life.

I felt sorry for Maggie, and grateful she'd made him so stupidly happy before he died.

"Of course, your dad always thought about my kids and their feelings. He would never pressure me about leaving. When you're a parent, you're a parent first."

She told me how they'd first met in a suburban bar among a loosely acquainted group of people who didn't want to go home after work, and Dad and Maggie ended up staying until the bitter end. They talked so long they were among the stragglers when the bartender announced last call, and so they decided to continue their conversation in Maggie's car, where they consummated their relationship. *Classy*. As she tore down back roads, I gripped the edge of the seat of the same car as she spoke, and calmly brought her attention to the speedometer: she was going seventy-two.

"I'm glad you told me," I said, even though I wasn't. I wanted to validate her feelings, but I also wanted to survive the afternoon.

I can accept that people go mad when they're grieving, but Maggie wasn't the only one who seemed to have no concept of boundaries with me: Dad had been the same way. When I had gotten the job at the literary agency, he'd confessed that he'd recently been flirting with writing fiction. Lately he'd felt like he really understood what undid his relationship with our mother, and writing it all down had been cathartic. The resulting short story was "pretty blue," he'd told me, but strong on subtext and insight into the sexual dynamics of a marriage after many years. I discovered the manuscript pages after he died, typed and double-spaced and fastened with a staple in the top left corner, in a folder labeled SHORT FICTION BY JCH. Inside was also a cover letter addressed to *Playboy* but appeared not to have been submitted.

The title was "Coming Back for More," a thinly veiled autobiographical short story about my mother and his paranoia that she was cheating on him. The story centers on a couple who have been married for fourteen years, a kind of sexually explicit revenge fantasy, the details of which I immediately and completely blocked from my mind. I tried to make light of it: *There Dad goes again, managing to be both creepy and embarrassing.* Worse on the disillusionment scale: the writing was terrible, simplistic, and the grandiosity of voice would never fly with *Playboy*'s fiction editor.

I didn't want to know the person who wrote like this, and yet I couldn't un-know my father. I set about trying to forget instead.

21

I WANT TO TELL YOU

WINTER TURNED TO SPRING AND THEN SUMMER. On day three of the four-day road trip from Ohio to Lake Powell in Arizona, my brothers and I were entombed in a '91 Accord plagued by electrical problems along with our father's ghost in a standard-issue tin box. This was a full two years before I'd be introduced to an actual selective serotonin reuptake inhibitor, and I was filled with anxiety about being locked in a car with my brothers, who didn't seem to like me as much as they liked the three alt-metal albums that played on repeat from Illinois to Colorado. The whole trip had the feeling of a ticking bomb. Which one of us would go first?

Once we hit the desert, the heat made everything surreal and hellish. I could taste the grit in the air. This was the landscape that Dad had wanted to be surrounded by; I tried to imagine a future for him there, but could only conjure him in a business suit.

We'd stopped in a little border town in Utah and purchased a clay urn made by a native artist, and somewhere outside Page, Arizona, we settled in early at a Holiday Inn for the night. We'd been staying in Holiday Inns exclusively like we thought he might have on a road trip.

Simon was lording over a pile of weed on the fake mahogany desk in our shared room, intent on rolling an arsenal of joints for our week ahead on a houseboat with nine other people. It seemed to me like as good a time as any to transfer Dad's ashes from their meager box to the clay pot. This was ill-advised for a number of reasons. Namely, since we were planning to *scatter* the ashes, it wasn't practical to house them in a heavy vase. We would be hiking up a steep cliff in order to disperse them, where hauling cumbersome pottery is not generally recommended. I did not think about this until I'd already started pouring the kitty-litter-like remains of my father from the untied plastic bread bag. Suddenly there was a mushroom cloud of Dad raining down on the pot. We decided to make the best of it and smoke it anyway.

"This is so cliché," we acknowledged, having each recently seen *The Big Lebowski*. But at least we didn't snort him. It seemed almost spiritual at the time, like something Dad thought a Hopi Indian might do.

"Dad would have done it for us." Greg said.

Even before the divorce, Dad had separate ways of communicating with each of us. Evidently he was much more casually transparent about his vices with my brothers than he was with me. Earlier that fall, about two months before he died, when I was in Cleveland for the visit after 9/11, he'd asked if I wanted to smoke a joint. I'd immediately burst out laughing at the look on his face—he was blushing. I was shocked, then I thought it was a trick, and then I was embarrassed for him.

"Are you crazy!" I blurted. "I'm still traumatized by your antidrug campaign when I was in high school." I was actually turned off pot in those days. It seemed to me a hopelessly uncool thing to do—something for the olds—maybe because it was my parents' drug of choice.

"And I don't even smoke that often. I'm certainly not going to smoke with someone your age," I clarified.

"Okay," he said. "Simmer down." We couldn't look at each other.

It was too awkward. We dropped the subject. I felt a fresh wave of annoyance. *Did that just happen?*

Now I was sitting in a hotel room with the brothers I hadn't spent any quality time with in years, smoking Dad's leftover schwag in a joint rolled with his papers, with some of his bone and tissue thrown into the mix. We got high with Dad one last time.

———————————

At Lake Powell, we set up camp at a cove surrounded by canyons and red sandstone cliffs. There was just enough gritty beach for a dozen friends and family to pitch lawn chairs. The landscape was insanely beautiful—blue sky, orange rock, blue water for miles—made all the more surreal by the fiercely dry heat. I felt locked in my body, but grateful somehow. In keeping with Dad's wish for this to be a celebratory vacation, the days were filled with adventurous activities. Mom and I went hiking in muddy clay up to our knees in search of otherworldly slot canyons to squeeze through and photograph, retracing Dad's steps in search of his greatest shots. In the canyons I was Alice in Wonderland looking up from the bottom of a giant piece of clay pottery. When the light pushed through the cracks at certain angles, as ephemeral as joy, I gasped aloud.

About four days in, there was no escaping what we were there to do. In late afternoon, Bob said, "Tonight, I want to say goodbye to my friend Jack." My brothers had scouted the perfect place to let the ashes go, a large boulder overlooking our camp about a skyscraper's distance above. As another exquisite purple sunset approached over azure water, it was now or never.

Simon and Greg scaled the beginning of the rock jutting above, a rope left by those who'd come before to help guide their way. They would be going it alone for the twenty-minute climb, Dad's two sons, and when at the top they would look down on us and let him go.

In pictures of the group of us standing below, we look as if we've just been visited by a spaceship. We were raw and wincing and staring slack-jawed at my brothers in miniature above us under infinite sky. Bob's daughter put her arm around my waist and laid her head on my shoulder like we did when we were small. Simon and Greg took the urn, which was filled with half of the ashes, out of the backpack. They made a gesture of acknowledgment to us below and let the contents spill down the front of the cliff. Without wind, in the clean, still air at dusk, they made streaks of pale against the rock.

The next morning, Mom and I made the exact same climb to the exact same spot, finding the place where they had made a marker the night before, JCH crudely etched on a boulder, with a view of Gunsight Butte and Navajo Mountain beyond. We spilled the remaining ashes out of their plastic bag in a circle around the rock.

This was the place he'd liked best, watching over the arteries of blue water that slipped through the desert in different directions while the sun baked the earth. I was sharing this with our mother, but I was sad that our family had not banded together after this crisis but grown further apart, angrier with time. A family should hold. The initials drawn on the boulder would surely wash away after it rained. I'd brought four small stones from Dad's collection—one for each of us—and placed them around the base of the rock. Obsidian, white gypsum, rose quartz, smooth and speckled blue. The lyrics to "Across the Universe" repeated in my mind like a prayer. *Limitless undying love, which shines around me like a million suns* . . . I would always remember this place, although I'd never come back. I would never be able to find it again.

He'll never get to see me get married, he'll never walk me down an aisle. When my father died these were among the first thoughts to cross my mind. This surprised me because I had made a vow to myself at sixteen that I would never get married, or at least I would strive not to see the inherently doomed institution as a life goal. I felt so strongly about it then that I had a ring sized to my left ring finger so that a man wouldn't get any ideas about asking for my hand, which was obviously already occupied. But there it was, the embarrassing truth—I wanted my dad to know that somebody wanted to be my husband. I wanted everyone to know.

Almost a year after Dad died, Paul and I were driving back from a visit home to Ohio. We'd been in the car for a good seven hours. Paul was driving through New Jersey while I simmered in the seat next to him. What was this relationship? Was this the man I was destined to be with? We'd been together then for three years, yet what did we have to show for it? If only Paul had been surer when I'd been sure—if we'd been engaged, or even pre-engaged, Dad might have been more at peace about my future. There was zero evidence that he had been worried about me in the slightest, but all I could think was, *If you could have just held out six more months. Six more months and I'd have had a real career and maybe a fiancé.*

Still, I worried that Paul wasn't the guy for me. He smelled so much like the past. We'd been arguing a lot—not about anything interesting, just arguing to argue. He was always talking about moving back to Ohio, the last thing I would ever do. If we were already making it in New York City, it would be a waste to leave. Now that we were finally happily together, how could he consider abandoning me?

I took my makeup bag out of the suitcase behind my seat and flipped down the visor for its mirror. When I was restless, I found it calming to do my makeup.

"Do you think we'll get married, ever?" I asked, rifling through some pencils.

Paul was quiet for a moment, then reached over and turned the music down. "Where is this coming from?"

Silently I gave myself a perfect black eye with pots of eye shadow and purple lipstick, dabbing the color out to my temple to demonstrate a realistic-looking bruise. Sometimes I liked to pretend I was a horror movie makeup artist, which was often the character theme I rendered best: "bad things to good girls," my annual Halloween costume since the late nineties.

Today, it matched my mood. I set my wound with a bit of yellow concealer in its violet center and stared hard at Paul until he noticed my work.

"Why did you do that to your face?"

"Just bored, I guess. It's how I feel on the inside."

"You know you're going to be twenty-eight this year," he said.

"So?"

"So, I'm just making an observation that you're getting older, and some people might think you act weird for your age."

"You're avoiding the question about marriage."

"That is my answer. We're not ready for that conversation. We live together—isn't that enough?"

I couldn't articulate what it was I even wanted. I wanted to be claimed. I wanted demonstration and reciprocity and romance. I wanted a family separate from the one that brought me into being. But Paul wasn't like Chris. He wasn't the guy who was going to tattoo my name on his body or loudly proclaim his love—I wasn't on a pedestal with him. What bonded us was mutual respect and familiarity. We didn't talk about the future, because he would change the subject.

At that time, I had a recurring nightmare where I dreamed that I was punching him in the face as hard as I could, and he was just ignoring me. My blows were too feeble, barely making contact. In the dream it didn't even seem like he could feel it. He didn't even know that my knuckles were bleeding.

We pulled into a gas station, and I unhooked my seat belt to go inside.

"Where are you going?"

"To buy some chips."

"People will think I did that to you," he said.

"Just tell them I did it to myself," I said.

———

I was having weeping fits on the packed train in the mornings. Paul seemed mortified by my open grief. "What's wrong?" he would whisper, trying not to draw the attention of bored-looking commuters. The trick to getting through rush hour on the train was to make oneself dead inside, and I couldn't hack it. *I don't know*, I'd mouth. I didn't. Lately I'd been grateful for any feeling at all. Most days I seemed to float between panic and surrender. I no longer understood that things would work out, that we were safe from immediate harm. Suddenly the past was in Technicolor, a bright stain spreading nowhere fast. I had the feeling that I was going to make some big changes, try new things, rebel. Saturn was returning. Now that no one was watching me, it felt like anything was possible.

We'd moved to a garden apartment in Fort Greene that we called the Tree House. Paul's career was thriving; he was well liked as a broker and he was making a lot of new friends at work. I encouraged him to go out with the guys or to go to shows without me, and I started spending more time with other people, too, throwing myself into the city like a drunken, stage-diving teenager.

I met a sculptor who reminded me of a young Matt Dillon (with less hair), especially when he smoked, which was constantly. He was the roommate of Andy, an old friend from school who was preparing for his first solo show at a gallery in Chelsea. The three of us spent weekend afternoons trying to stave off depression by digging through Dumpsters and junkyards in Bushwick, looking for found materials and art supplies. The commute to their studio was inconvenient, but I found a reason to go every week.

Eventually I started to wander over to the sculptor's side of the loft. I liked to watch him work. He was short, but he had this posture, like everything in his body was dying, he was fighting it with every movement, and he liked the way it felt to resist. Calloused hands. His T-shirts were full of holes from falling ash, so ubiquitous was the cigarette. He called me "baby." As in, "You gonna stand there watching all day, baby?" I could smell him from across the room, in a good way.

That's when I knew I was in trouble. I wondered if he actually knew my name.

One day he stopped circling the object in the middle of the floor—a ball of iron and wire that was slowly becoming a bigger ball of iron and wire. He turned to look at me sitting on the stairs that led to the loft where he slept. He pulled the cigarette from behind his ear and lit it. On the exhale he lifted up his T-shirt, showing one of those torsos that cut a V-shaped arrow down to the pelvis. He kicked off his boots and unzipped his pants, all the while boring holes through me with his eyes.

"Sometimes it helps the work if I'm not wearing any clothes."

My friend Andy's advice came too late: "Don't fuck him. I heard he threw the last girl down the stairs."

And so began my brief affair with the artist whose misery mined depths I'd not yet known existed. His mother was dying of cancer, and he was drinking a lot. Beer all day, bourbon all night. For a month we holed up weekly on his side of the loft for drunken, Xanax-fueled sob fests, and together we went insane. It wasn't an attraction; it was an infection. As soon as it happened, I regretted it. I was disgusted with myself for cheating on Paul, but it was a situation I believed I'd created and then felt powerless to stop. When we first kissed, it felt anemic and out of sync, as if underwater. Once he put his hands around my throat and marveled, "You're so small, it feels like I could crush your neck with my thumbs." He repulsed me, but I felt compelled to return a few more times.

The wake-up call came when, in response to the ongoing indictment of Michael Jackson as a pedophile on a recent cover of the *New York Post*, the sculptor told me that he felt sorry for pedophiles. I'd come to the loft once again to break it off in person, hoping if I could just level with him, make him see that what we were doing was making us both sick, then we could go on with our lives as if nothing had ever happened.

"You have to understand," he said, "inside, these guys are still little kids." He turned his head and spit a soaring stream of beer into the sink, a gargoyle in profile. "Imagine what it must be like to have impulses you can't control." He wasn't being sarcastic—he'd clearly given it a lot of thought.

His face looked made of rubber, a grotesque mask. His brow was furrowed with concern over eyes like glittering voids. I was glad for the table between us. I scanned the room for my bag as he rambled on about society's oppressive attitudes around sex.

"It wasn't so long ago that we stood in judgment of queers," he said. "We called that a choice and a perversion. I fail to see how this affliction is really any different . . ." He was still talking when I walked out the door.

"Where you going, baby?"

It scared me enough that I went right home and called a therapist. I did not ask anyone for a recommendation, I simply Googled "NYC psychotherapists" and took a chance. The woman on the phone was kind as she took my basic information and promised to fit me in that week for an intake. I had no idea what was expected of me, but I had enough money and the will to change. I hoped this person might have the answers I was desperate for.

The therapist's office was in a secure building on a cobblestone street in the Village. *Rothko, how original,* I thought when I saw the framed poster art on the wall across from the chairs. Worn copies of the *New Yorker* lay on a glass coffee table and small white noise machines hummed outside the office doors. I was edgy and hyperaware of my reason for being there. I picked up a magazine and turned it into a flip book. Tom Ford does caftans for YSL, a new offering from Design Within Reach's Allegro collection, Malcolm Gladwell asks the question "Are smart people overrated?"

And then a door opened and Ana emerged. She was tall, midforties, an Irish Carole King with wildly curly auburn hair, a darker shade of red than mine. She wore slouchy black layers of what looked like the work of a Japanese designer and clunky Mary Janes. We shook hands. She greeted me warmly and gestured for me to go inside and make myself comfortable on the midcentury modern couch (I will not call it a love seat), made cozier with velvet pillows and a cashmere throw. The light in the room was low, one step above birthday candles. No doubt it was meant to be womblike. I couldn't imagine a more feminine energy. I pictured her patients sitting there clutching the pillows, wrapped in blankets, sucking their thumbs. Next to a vase of white tulips sat a box of Kleenex and a bowl of Chinese ginger candies.

Ana sat opposite in a large velvet chair big enough for her and several pillows. I scanned the wall of literature behind her, wondering if we'd read some of the same books. She stared at me for a moment and asked how things had been going for me, what brought me to therapy.

I perched on the edge of the couch like I was in a job interview and listed my most immediate concerns.

"My life is out of control. I'm sleeping with someone I despise, I live with someone I love but I don't know how to talk to, and I feel really reckless and self-destructive since my dad died. Technically things are starting to work out for me in my career, but for some reason I can't really enjoy it as much because he isn't alive to see it."

Ana reassured me that she was here to help and that I didn't have to be alone with grief. She encouraged me to tell her about my dad. I told her about the day he died, and the way it brought my family together, and that the love for him from the community and his close friends had been so meaningful to me because it meant that we weren't the only witnesses. It meant that I'd been parented by a great man. I strove to be so loved again. My relationship with my dad had been closer in some ways than the one I had with my mother growing up. My mother had been so disconnected when I lived at home that I associated her with a heaviness I wanted to avoid, and him with a lightness and positivity I wished I could embody.

Ana leaned forward and offered me a tissue. "It sounds like you love him very much."

"That's just it." My eyes welled up. "I do. But it's confusing. My father wasn't perfect and he was often inconsistent. And a friend who has known me since I was a kid told me recently that he was surprised I was still so down about my father dying, since all I'd done was complain about him when he was alive."

Ana asked about my childhood experiences with "physical abuse." I immediately bristled. It wasn't like spanking was considered physical abuse by anyone I grew up with. Physical abuse was when a kid came to school with visible bruises and a black eye. And then I remembered Simon's.

"I guess, technically—my brothers and I were spanked when we were kids, but our family belonged to a church where that was the norm." She nodded, making a note. "It was the eighties."

"Did you ever feel like your parents were angry when they disciplined you that way?"

"Yes, but it was always characterized as disappointment in our behavior, which was considered sinful."

"Would you say your father had a temper?"

"For sure, yeah."

"Did you ever argue?"

"Yeah, I'm not one to keep my mouth shut. I was kind of rebellious in high school." I explained that while my father had often been furious with me, other times he treated me like he'd learned a lesson from a TV dad and was trying to be better.

"When I was in high school, he was the kind of father who made it clear he thought teenage girls who had sex were skanks, and two weeks later he's offering to pay for my birth control."

"I can see how that might be confusing."

"Look, if you're trying to say I was emotionally abused, I wouldn't put it that way. Maybe that was more my mother's issue with him, but both my parents told us that they loved us all the time, which is more than lots of kids get."

"That is true," Ana said. "I'm not here to condemn anyone, I'm here to support you. Just know that nothing you could tell me could shock me."

That put me at ease, and over time I did want to tell her everything. We focused at first on my most immediate problem—untangling myself from the mess I'd made with the sculptor, and figuring out why I had gone there in the first place. Ana challenged my decision-making without judgment.

"I told the sculptor I loved him, even though I don't," I said. "I thought I must have, if I was cheating on my boyfriend."

"So what?" she said. "So you felt love for him; it doesn't mean you're trapped for the rest of your life. You owe him nothing."

It was a strange concept at the time, owing someone nothing. I felt I owed everybody everything. I certainly owed Paul for sticking by me through this weird time out of mind, and since I'd started something with this other person, I felt I owed him, too. I owed my brothers for all the times I'd abandoned them, I owed my mother for being my mother, I owed my friends for putting up with me. I owed it to Dad to grow up and be a decent human being and inspire positive associations with the family brand.

"Maybe the question should be," Ana said gently, "what do you owe yourself? What kind of life do you want? It's okay to take some time to figure that out."

It was a revelation to hear that I didn't have to fix a mess that I'd made by turning it into something worth fighting for. Ana helped me see that I was attracted to the sculptor because he was obsessive where Paul was ambivalent, he was openly passionate where Paul was consistently unemotional. But the sculptor had a darkness and a mean streak, and though I was initially drawn to that personality because it was familiar, I had been looking for comfort that couldn't be found in another person. In the presence of either man, I felt totally alone. So much had changed, I would have to do the work of growing up on my own.

Paul and I wouldn't last the year, though our relationship didn't end so much as evolve. We waited for our lease to come up for renewal before separating and leaving the Tree House—he took the pullout couch, our first piece of grown-up furniture, and let me have the hundred-pound gilded antique mirror we'd found on the street, a prized possession. Paul would stay in the city and remain my dear friend, ultimately helping me move the mirror into every apartment I'd have for the next several years.

I thought it would be easy to find someone new in a city of millions, someone who didn't represent the past.

22

HELP!

SEX AND THE CITY WAS STILL HAVING ITS MOMENT: those four successful thirtysomething women at the height of their feminine power were carefree (and child-free), and so were my girlfriends and I. This was a few years before the economic recession, and we had expense accounts to burn. Usually we met for Hos Night, as we called it, at Angel's Share, a classy East Village bar you could enter only through an unassuming door in the back of a noodle restaurant.

There was Denise, now an art director, Jen the photo director, Vivian the beauty director, and me, the literary agent. We were obsessed with our work, our skin, and our relationships. One winter night after two or three plum wines, inspiration struck. What we needed was a vacation together, away from men and our high-pressure jobs. We wanted to go somewhere cheap and tropical, close enough that we could escape Manhattan but get the most out of five days and four nights.

One of our friends had been raving about an island in Puerto Rico called Vieques—aka the Spanish Virgin Islands, aka "Little Girl Island," alluding to its perception as Puerto Rico's little sister. Because it had recently gone from being a military base utilized by the U.S. Navy to a wildlife refuge, it remained relatively ignored by tourists and unspoiled by development. It was a place where the boys of summer rode wild horses on the beach, and the bay was bioluminescent, one of only a few on earth accessible to humans. It sounded like the perfect place for four women to go and lie in the sun, unencumbered by beauty regimens and bra straps—we could stock up on relaxation and jump-start our creative juices.

Despite a quick flight from NYC, the second leg of the trip foretold disaster. We were required to rent a car in San Juan to take us the hour's drive to a ferry port, where we would then travel another hour by boat to the island. But when we found ourselves surrounded at the loading dock by a sea of faces, we discovered the remaining tickets for boats to Vieques had all sold out. This was a national holiday for Puerto Ricans, similar to the Fourth of July. Hundreds of people sat sweating atop their luggage (which sometimes included large cages containing several crowing fowl). A man with a bullhorn made a series of ominous announcements in Spanish; many of us would be turned away this weekend, as the island had already reached full capacity.

"But . . . *una reserva*," we all said in unison, over and over to whoever would listen. "*Tenemos una reserva en el hotel.*" Being the only gringas at the rodeo, we launched a campaign in support of our cause and begged to trade seats with the travelers we found ourselves forced to compete with. Everyone said no. In the end, we split up and stormed the entrance to the final launch with a crush of travelers and stowed away, somehow making it on the last boat of the night. When we finally reached our rented flat in town, the landlady had gone home hours before, but had left the property unlocked for our arrival.

The next morning, we discovered what the bullhorn guy had meant by "full capacity." The island's resources were so taxed by the sudden influx of people that the whole place would remain without power and hot water for the entire four-day weekend. Had we booked rooms at the one reputable hotel in town, we would have had access to its backup generators and water heaters, but since we had insisted on roughing it to save money, it would be flashlights and buckets of cold water. (This might not have sucked so much if three of the four of us weren't menstruating.) Every meal seemed to lead to food poisoning, every sunscreen application somehow failed. The island was a three-personed god, battering our hearts, we complained, laughing at our own pretentiousness.

Our last night was reserved for the main event—the night kayak to the bioluminescent bay, where we would swim in seawater under a moonless sky lit from below by a million specks of glowing light, smaller than fireflies. Our tour guide, Larry, was kind of a douche who worked out of a tiki hut and wore shorts that would have been characterized in the late eighties as "jams." It was hard to know if he was thinking of our best interests, but there was no sense that anything could go wrong.

We were told to wear only our bathing suits and to leave our shorts and shoes in the truck we'd rode in on before walking a short distance to and from the kayaks. We all wore our bikinis, save for Viv, who had opted for an elegant white monokini by Tom Ford for Gucci that featured a large metal ring in the center of her chest. Her sunburn radiated off her skin even in the dark. We looked nearly nude in our suits, especially next to our tour mates, a troop of local boy scouts, who all wore matching red shorts and T-shirts to swim in. We soon figured out why we had been encouraged to leave our shoes back on dry land—the path to the docks was paved with muck. We trudged through a soup of mud, sand, and rainwater, its backsplash splattering our legs, as mosquitoes the size of dimes swarmed the air around us, the water's edge nowhere close. *Good*, I thought, *now we only have to paddle out a little ways to have the fun, and then tomorrow we leave this awful place.*

Larry, though mere inches away, blew his whistle to get our attention.

"People, listen up! The bioluminescence in the water is caused when we agitate the bacteria congregating there. You'll notice the change as we get farther out and you'll begin to see the movement in the water as it appears to glow. We are going to kayak together in a group. If for any reason you get separated from us, blow the whistle attached to your lifejacket and I will come back for you. Any questions?"

Just then it began to rain. Larry assured us that this intermittent tropical rain probably wouldn't hurt visibility. I squinted my eyes across the bay. It was difficult to see the horizon, but I couldn't tell if that was because of the rain, the dark, or the fact that I was using only one good eye to suss it out, having lost a contact lens earlier. It had dried up and folded itself into the corner of my eyelid while we were sunbathing and smoking a joint we got from an expat we met on the beach. In the haze of the afternoon, I hadn't missed it, hadn't needed two good eyes.

"Well, I guess this self-tanner isn't waterproof." We all turned to look at Vivian.

The edges of her white maillot (retail value: $690) were tinted a sad brown. (Thanks, Clarins.) Our legs were caked in mud so black it could have been blood. "You're conjuring Sally Hardesty in *The Texas Chain Saw Massacre* right now, minus the pants," I said, eyeing the identical yellow one-person kayaks we'd been assigned. On top of everything, the fish tacos we'd been subsisting on for days weren't sitting well with anyone.

She clutched her stomach and made a face. I worried about her. Viv was typically the most enthusiastic member of our party, but the last three days had taken a toll, and all the attempts to laugh were half-hearted.

We teetered into our yellow coffins, put our legs straight out, grasped our paddles, and after a short demo on how to maneuver our vessels through the water, we were off. What at first was a straight line of kayaking tourists soon grew fat and wobbly, with Larry and the scouts heading up the front, Viv and I somehow straggling a bit behind, her to my right. I felt I had to watch over her a bit, make sure she wasn't too woozy, since she'd said she wasn't a strong sea kayaker.

I had the benefit of experience from going with Paul on our first and only romantic holiday in the Bahamas, where he insisted I face my fears and snorkel a coral reef with him. My anxiety around sharing the water with the known predators indigenous to the bay, such as the stealthy tiger shark and the darting barracuda, was so intense that Paul suggested we try a dose of Ecstasy. As the drug took effect, we were successfully kayaking in shallow water, in tandem against the waves. The media's repeated assurances that I was more likely to be maimed or killed by my significant other than a rogue sea creature suddenly, finally sank in. Peaking under the influence of a powerful amphetamine while achieving a physical feat with my boyfriend made me feel very grandiose indeed. Then, I had been willing to forgive the eel for its terrifying lack of conscience as it snaked through the water, spineless. I wasn't jealous of the angelfish's nonchalance at living in an underwater death trap; in fact, I felt sexually aroused.

I assumed that this kayak experience would be just like that one, only this time I was alone in my plastic boat.

I looked over to my right and saw nothing but black water and a bit of horizon. Strange, since I'd been sure Viv had been right beside me the whole time, maybe even a little behind. But a cursory look only made me dizzy, and I tried to focus my one good eye on the place where I'd last seen the mass of little vessels, or heard them, anyway. I'd been paddling and paddling for a long time now and my arms were getting a little tired.

Just then it began to really rain. The water was suddenly choppier. For a moment I stopped the active paddling forward and let my arms rest at my sides. I decided to remain calm and call out for Jen, the most responsible member of our party, the oldest, in her thirties, and the one we all looked to for mothering.

"Je-en," I called, as if I were shouting at her third-story apartment window asking to be let up. The sound barely seemed to register in the night air. I tried again, this time attempting a staccato "JEN!" to no effect.

The rain pitter-patted against my plastic boat and the orange nylon of my life jacket. It was then I remembered the whistle attached. It was meant for blowing if you were separated from the group. Even if I appeared to be alone in the black, they couldn't be far away.

The sound produced by the whistle was one octave above the wind's, but not nearly loud enough to penetrate the sky. Some genius of engineering had outfitted my child-size life jacket with a kid's plastic whistle from Fisher-Price. Surely Larry had been using a metal version for his demonstration? I blew hard three more times, and each time I heard the interior of the chamber click as the magical bean inside bounced around on the strength of my breath, and the whistle eked out its sad song, barely audible above the rain on the water.

I paddled. I paddled and paddled. I vowed not to cry, and I kept paddling. I tried to focus on some horizon I thought should be there. I'd turned the kayak around and around, but couldn't locate the inlet where we'd launched, or anything but the choppy black water. Open water. Ocean water. Shark-infested water? *Be brave*, I told myself. *Don't worry about it, just be brave and wait for someone to realize you're out here. That's what Dad would do.*

I pictured him watching me from above, gentle and smiling down. *Turn off your mind, relax, and float downstream. You are not dying, kiddo.*

A movie montage played in my mind, as if for the last time before I died. It was a culmination of every humiliating moment of girlish inadequacy and human failure I'd experienced up to that very day. The time in junior high I was onstage at play practice and my fly was open and Jason Ballister yelled to the whole auditorium that he could see my "mole hole." The time I projectile-vomited in the aisle on an airplane while it was landing, flying by myself to Houston at age twelve. The wipeouts on the bike, the initial failure to pass my driver's test, my math shame. The time I drove Chris's truck into his best friend's parked car in our driveway completely sober. The time I walked *through* the screen door at my fancy new boyfriend's parents' house in Nantucket, not seeing the fine mesh in front of me until it was too late. The time I threw up on that guy while we were both naked during a very pivotal moment in coitus. The time I got so drunk I pissed my pants. The look on the face of the dentist when I opened my mouth for my last checkup.

I wanted so badly to be independent and never ask anyone for help, especially a man. Why couldn't I do the simple things that other people seemed to do with ease?

Finally I spotted something in the distance, a faint glow, a horizon. I steered toward what I hoped was the beach, then realized it was actually a ship. Should I move toward it and risk getting too close to its wake? Ugh, and how to be casual? *Oh, hi, yeah, I meant to be here, this is actually normal for me—part of my fitness regimen*. Humiliating. But moments later a spotlight bore down on me from above like a portal to heaven. It was a rescue mission.

"There's a girl!" I heard someone scream. And then a strapping young man was coming in a smaller boat, my hero. Another was swimming toward us: backup. The guy in the boat was there to transport me to the mother ship. I could leave the kayak behind, the swimming guy would take care of it. As we were approaching, I could see that the boat was full of people huddled together looking down on me with concern. *Thank you*, I prayed to Dad, *thank you*. Within minutes I was pulled up to the deck of the ship, a charter for tourists who wanted to tour the bioluminescent bay without kayaking there themselves. I was wrapped in towels for modesty and surrounded by kind women. "You're okay, now. You're okay" was their refrain. The captain told me I'd paddled the kayak out into open ocean, nowhere near the place I was supposed to be.

These tourists seemed angry on my behalf, not at all as disappointed in me as I was. (A couple of people even told me I was brave.) I was embarrassed but could hardly believe my good fortune. For the first time in my life, I'd been rescued.

I worried that my friends thought I had drowned, and I had no idea how to let them know I was okay.

"Can you take me to them?" I asked, first thing. They could not.

The captain explained that there was no real way to connect with the other group, though he would call the shack Larry worked out of to leave word that I'd been found. I would have to join the new party and they'd give me a ride back to the island on their chartered bus.

Meanwhile, I later learned, my friends were indeed concerned that I was lost. The entire troop of boy scouts had been dispatched to look for me. Larry told the group not to worry.

"We'll find her. She can't have gone far."

They didn't know what I was capable of. Nobody knew. I had paddled two miles outside the bay and out to sea. The people on the boat just happened to see me in the moonlight. If I had been a spiritual person, if I had believed in guardian angels, I might have imagined that my Heavenly Father had been watching out for me and put me in that ship's path. But that was too much to bear. My mother cried when she heard me tell the story for laughs. Not because I could have died, but because she suspected she knew how it had felt to be all alone in a kayak in the rain, in the dark, having no sense of direction, not believing she could ever save herself. *Only Jesus could save.*

The charter docked north of Esperanza, where we were staying, and I hitched a ride to town in an old bus, accompanied by hens and a lone rooster. I was still barefoot and wearing the windbreaker the captain had given me on the boat to cover up. The bus dropped me off in front of the local bar, where the story of my ordeal had already made the rounds. Kind strangers offered to buy me a drink, but I wanted to find my friends. I wasn't sure if they'd heard I was okay or back on dry land.

After twenty minutes, I couldn't wait alone any longer in a windbreaker and no pants, so I walked the half mile down the hill to our little rented house, feeling sorry for myself. Indeed, the girls had received word that I'd been rescued and spotted on dry land, unscathed. But I didn't know that when I spotted them walking several yards behind me, casually laughing and taking their time.

I sulked. Had no one even noticed I was missing? When we finally reunited they were full of reassurances. It was then that I slumped in a chair and cried like a little kid. Jen gave me a hug.

"We were worried when we didn't know you were okay, but we had faith in you. You got lost, but you're here now, and safe."

The next day nobody spoke much on the way back to Old San Juan, but I was relieved to walk its cobblestone streets. I needed to be close to a city, I decided, taking in the watercolor landscape. We toured a sixteenth-century cathedral while Jen spent an hour on the phone with the airline to move up our flights.

Arriving at JFK was the first time I really felt the pang of anxiety that accompanied not having a particular man in my life to come home to. A couple of years had gone by since the breakup with Paul, and though I liked living on my own, I wondered how long I could sustain the illusion that I wasn't lonely.

23

GOT TO GET YOU INTO MY LIFE

YES.

It's the word John Lennon saw at the top of Yoko's ladder the day they met at her gallery show in London. He saw it as a sign. If the word through the spyglass at the top of the ladder had been "No" or "Fuck You," he wouldn't have been so persuaded. It was like a secret message just for him. I had a similar approach when it came to relationships. On principle, I would never have committed myself to anyone who I didn't think was the be-all, end-all—life was meant to be lived in tandem with a soul mate. I was the opposite of choosy—I figured love chose you, that it was fated.

Sure, I'd heard the rumors that "love is an action verb that takes daily work," that you need to be pragmatic about who you choose to share your life with, that marriage is about endless compromise, that love is just *one* part of the equation, and that there's no such thing as a soul mate—but only from people in humdrum relationships with significant others they'd clearly settled for.

I knew there was another way to live. If I just held out for the John and Yoko mystique, for something pure, I could be part of a couple who treated every room like a cocoon, finished each other's sentences, wore each other's clothes, made work of equal importance in the eyes of the other, fought passionately, fucked constantly, made a child together on purpose, became the change they sought in the world, and embraced the same political and philosophical beliefs. Love was this magical thing that elevated and corrected itself: *Love is all you need.*

I took this further to include the smoking of French cigarettes, experimenting with different versions of sanity, mourning losses with illicit substances, a period of emotional regression, breaking up, indulging in a "lost weekend" and then reuniting, stronger than ever, till one of us died on the streets of New York City, a place that would remain forever haunted in elegy.

I was a very young thirty-three. I had a job I loved, helping make writers' dreams come true. I lived in a light-filled prewar apartment on my favorite street in Brooklyn. It had a claw-foot tub in a bathroom big enough to put a bookshelf in. My bedroom wall was festooned with the red zebra hunting print from Scalamandré—special-ordered at $200 a roll—the same vintage wallpaper featured in Margot's childhood ballet studio in *The Royal Tenenbaums*. I had a collection of vintage dresses and seven pairs of red shoes, one for every day of the week. All my best friends still lived in the neighborhood, and no one had kids yet. Every weekend we'd roll out of bed at eleven o'clock or later, and, feeling vulnerable from our Prosecco hangovers, meet for brunch to nurse bowls of steaming lattes and plates of specially cured bacon and three-minute eggs, crusty French bread and strawberry-balsamic jam. After, we'd go to films or readings or secret shows in tiny venues by bands we'd long admired, or to the park to read novels on blankets while contemplating later dinner plans. I was as free as I had ever been; it was time I adopted an expensive new habit.

The first time I'd discovered the joys of narcotic painkillers was right after my father's funeral, when a well-meaning friend threw in a few Percocets with a bag of sympathy pot. Two pills added an extra layer of lightness to the marijuana high I was beginning to find a whole new appreciation for in my thirties. My emotions felt both heightened and numb, like the sun was in my eyes, even if it was raining. I felt full of empathy for the people in the news. I was energized in a way I'd never been before. I actually looked forward to waking up in the morning, whereas before I had never wanted to get out of bed. What a perfect antidepressant. I was intrigued and made a mental note that Percocet agreed with me.

A few years later, a journalist friend wrote a piece for a fashion magazine about the latest trend in online delivery services—the online pharmacy. Back then, these too-good-to-be-true invitations would pile up in my email spam filter: "Vicodin, Percocet, Valium without a prescription. Call now!" For the story, my friend took them up on it, using the magazine's credit card to order a bottle of narcotic painkillers through the first website to solicit him. It worked. At the time, this wasn't legal, but it was everywhere and just under-the-radar enough to feel safe.

The journalist wrote a short piece about how easy the process of procuring drugs online was, but purposefully withheld details about exact websites, not wanting to blow their cover. Afterward, he brought home the research bottle of Vicodin, and he and I took all of them over the next few weeks. We discovered that if you increased your dose to two or three, the high lasted a good couple of hours and made you feel invincible in social situations because no one knew you were on anything.

It was so easy. Once a month from the office, I would make my credit card order through the pop-up website, and provide my cell phone number. A staff "physician" would call back within a few hours to ask about my pain on a scale of one to ten, my height and weight, and of course how many pills I wanted, and in what strength. Usually I said I was having excruciating back pain at level seven or eight, and two days later a bottle of thirty 7.5/500 hydrocodone would arrive at my desk via FedEx. After you'd ordered enough times, a "pharmacist" would call offering refills.

It would be a good two years before the DEA started cracking down on these online networks, and I took full advantage of the regular deliveries until they did. At first it was a weekend thing, something to do on a Saturday night. And then it was a Sunday morning thing, something to do to cure a hangover. After I got a dog (Sadie, as in "Sexy Sadie"), it became something to do after work when I was walking her, a way to bond with her, with Brooklyn itself. I cherished the Stepford-wife quality of my mood. Soon I'd be living out my own version of *Valley of the Dolls*.

A pill became the best way to start the day—not every day, just three times a week. In twenty-five minutes my face would flush hot and tight, and I'd feel a telltale thickening in my tongue. My voice took on a raspy quality and my breathing changed, getting slower and less necessary. Sometimes my heart would flutter. I knew I was high when I started skipping over words in my thoughts.

Before long my favorite feeling, my most selfish wish, was a stomach empty of food but full of Norco, washed down with a steaming café au lait. I took a continuing education class in art history that required my presence at the Met every Saturday to look at paintings for two hours. I don't remember a single thing I learned, but I think I had the time of my life.

I was flirting with disaster, but I justified my drug habit this way: It didn't interfere with my work—I was as productive as ever. No one could tell by looking at me that I was under the influence, including my therapist. These were FDA-approved pharmaceuticals. Sure, they weren't legally prescribed to me, but they were prescribed to millions every day. Most important, I had pain, and no one could convince me that I wasn't justified in alleviating it.

―――――――――

Julian Sean and I met again over the Internet—it had been almost fifteen years since our brief exchange from college when he'd quizzed me on my favorite Brontë sister. Last I'd heard, he'd broken up his band and abruptly dropped out of school to move to Chicago with a scarlet-haired fashion model who was going for a job in broadcast journalism. They'd made an unlikely couple—she towered over him physically, yet she had the disposition of a gentle fawn; he was destined to work in a record store. All these years later, Julian was still there and his girlfriend long gone. Now he was a burgeoning art star with a popular website, a highly entertaining tribute to his own ADHD and a place to sell his work—nonsensical pop art paintings crudely applied to plywood with latex house paint.

The subject matter of the paintings was pretty much dictated by our generation's unyielding appetite for irony-fueled decorative images of gibbon monkeys on skateboards. Julian made an average of five to eight paintings a day, and sold most of them on his website for twenty-five dollars. He was straightforward about his process: He'd scan an image that he liked—say, Nell Carter wearing a French maid's uniform—add a phrase like *Gimme a Break!* in black script underneath, clean up the scan in Photoshop, print it onto a transparency, project the image onto a board or canvas, and paint where the colors would be. After that dried, he'd outline the image in black, so the whole thing popped like a tattoo. Anyone could do it, but nobody wanted to—that was the secret of his success.

I emailed Julian through the site in an official capacity, wondering if he'd ever thought about doing a book. He had already received a fair amount of press for his creative antics, and it was my job to scout emerging talent. Julian was immediately responsive and suggested we speak further during his "office hours," late at night. I knew he loved to talk to people on the telephone and he was usually awake. He even advertised his home phone number as a psychic hotline, which included free advice, so there was never a shortage of strangers with interesting problems to keep him occupied. Sometimes Julian would post audio samples of these conversations, spliced together to make compelling monologues.

Though he loved to be the one asking the questions, he liked to tell stories, too. Growing up, he'd had the most cinematically hard-knock life story I'd ever heard. It had been just him and his mom, Rita, a complicated woman who didn't have many good things to say about the men in her life, fond as they were of fencing her in and using their fat fists to do it. Rita ran Julian's father out of town after she discovered he'd been feeding the baby a bottle filled with cheap champagne, and a stepfather didn't exactly cleave himself to anyone's heart. Rita took off a lot, too, leaving Julian to fend for himself for days at a time beginning at age five. He had to use a footstool to cook himself eggs. When he talked about Rita, it was as if she were a character in a novel, a wacky but lovable maniac who wasn't a good mother but sure did love her son a lot. For that, he'd remain forever loyal.

At night we would talk about our lives, our failed relationships, our friends and mutual acquaintances, our big dreams for the future. We talked about our vinyl trousseaus made of vintage 78s, so crucial to our understanding of ourselves and our parents. From Rita, he learned about Lou Reed and David Bowie, listening to their weird solo records when other kids were memorizing the *Free to Be . . . You and Me* soundtrack. Julian had an encyclopedic knowledge of music; it was the only constant in his life. Besides Ohio, that was our first common bond.

He had a hypnotic speaking voice, and a tendency to sigh into his words when he talked to me at night. During the daytime and in emails, he had a clipped, almost robotic affect and liked to communicate in as few sentences as possible. At night on the phone, no question was off-limits. Sometimes I suspected he was recording our chats like he did when strangers called the hotline, though he told me he wasn't. No matter how intimate our conversations, a part of me was always on guard—I was sure that if he was talking to me like that, there were others as well. Pictures of several pretty girls were always popping up on his site in photo essays—I thought of them as "the regulars."

We'd both make good pharmacists, Julian and I agreed. We'd simultaneously become ever more obsessed with the wonders of pharmacology. It wasn't always painkillers—it was fun to experiment with different feelings of all kinds. He took things like Prozac recreation-ally—only popping them on certain days to see if they'd have an ef-fect—and had been known to dabble in antipsychotics just to feel like he was walking through a wall of glue. We'd both discovered that a little blue Adderall could keep you going for the duration after a night of drinking or a marathon work session. Adderall was a drug to make you feel sober, cocaine without the comedown. Xanax, which every-body and their mom seemed to have a stash of, was a great way to take the edge off, as long as you didn't drink too much. (The trick was to never appear sloppy.) Soma, a muscle relaxer we loved for its name alone (though it wasn't quite the opiate of the masses like the version in Aldous Huxley's *Brave New World*), made for a lovely moviegoing companion. For me, all these pills were accompanied by a veil of mari-juana and the antidepressant Lexapro (via legit prescription), the only drugs I took religiously.

After a solid year of regular correspondence, I thought of Julian as one of my best friends. We made plans to hang out in Ohio when we were both home for the holidays. He would drive straight from Chicago to my mother's house to pick me up, then we would drive to Kent to drink at the same old bars, to reminisce with the die-hards and townies. When he walked through the door of my childhood home, I was relieved that I wasn't attracted to him—I was glad to see him, but I wasn't under some kind of pheromonal spell like I worried I might be. The feeling seemed mutual. We hugged like normal people and it was in that moment that I knew this was exactly the way it should be—of course two heterosexual, single members of the opposite sex could be friends. I told myself I'd much rather be his confidante than one of the many women he serially dated.

In town, everybody seemed to recognize him. We felt like celeb-rities, prodigal children who had gone away strangers but returned successful urbanites. Julian had an intensity, despite his unassuming looks—normal weight, five foot eight, thinning hair that he often cov-ered with a hat. He reminded me of Max Fischer from *Rushmore*, except thirty-four instead of fifteen. Julian wore a uniform—the same Buddy Holly glasses, Vietnam-era army fatigues, and lace-up Vans he'd been wearing since the late eighties.

We were inseparable that week. I appreciated his reverence for other artists, which I interpreted as humility. He always remembered the details of somebody's personal history or the content of their social media feeds. Whenever Julian said the words "That's cool," he always put an emphasis on the *cool*, as if whatever story you'd just told him was the most impressive thing he'd heard in a while. All of it had the effect of making me feel like I was the most captivating person in his life. I climbed back up on the pedestal and looked forward to higher self-esteem.

Julian and I kept in touch through the rest of the winter and spring. Then, the following summer, we spontaneously decided to take a ten-day road trip down south. I'd worked on a book with a close friend of Elvis Presley's who'd extended an open offer of a private tour of Graceland. Neither Julian nor I had ever been, but we had several friends in the region. Sadie and I would fly to Chicago, then drive south through Illinois, Missouri, and Tennessee, spending time in Memphis before continuing on through Georgia to South Carolina and then driving back again. Along the way Julian would document our experience on his website.

Basically we laughed for ten days, and fell in love in about five. It didn't start out that way—in every hotel room we stayed in on the road, we slept in separate beds. But in other ways we felt like a couple. Strangers treated us like we were when after three days, he started ordering my iced tea for me. "She likes three parts unsweetened, one part sweet," he'd tell the waitress at the Waffle House. "With lemon." He liked to drive for ten-hour stretches and insisted I nap in the back seat with Sadie as he did. "Nothing would make me happier than to just drive you around." He took pictures of me sleeping. Every day was a new opportunity to finish each other's sentences. Every look was a private joke.

Oprah says people always reveal their limitations right up front at the beginning of a relationship, and if you pay attention you can't miss them. In Julian's case, he laid bare to me every personal failure, every secret shame, every doubt he'd had about his impulses and his ability to love before we ever held hands in a photograph. His confessions were mesmerizing and framed in self-deprecation and survivor's guilt. He worried that he was programmed to repeat the sins of a father he never knew.

After he'd told me about all the horrible things that had happened to him and every tragedy he felt he'd caused, I only loved him more. He confessed that he'd knocked up more than one of his girlfriends and then become so anxious over the idea that he would be an absentee father just like his dad that he'd begged each to terminate the pregnancy. I was heartened that he'd always paid for the abortions. I could relate to his ambivalence; we had the same fears about having kids. The world wasn't fit for a child. At one point during a marathon stretch of driving, we made a list of all the wrong things that you could do to fuck up your kid, or by extension, how they could mess up your life. We went alphabetically: addiction, bullying, chimp attacks, death, Ebola, Facebook, GMOs, homophobia, injustice, Juggalos, kidnapping, lice, mental illness, nuclear war, Osama bin Laden, pedophiles, questions without answers, racism, suicide, terrorism, unemployment, violence, white people, Generation X, *you*. Parenting is a zero-sum game.

When we stayed with friends in Memphis, they offered me an air mattress and Julian the living room couch, but it felt wrong suddenly not to sleep in close proximity. We stayed up late talking, and when the sun rose I woke up to find him sleeping next to me, fully clothed on the slowly deflating mattress. By the time we were offered another guest room in Charleston, we took it gratefully, and that night I rested my head on his chest and didn't move until the morning.

Later that day we took a boat out into the cove where the dolphins slid through the water like sharks, and he and I were silent, trying to contemplate unknowable things. The next day we took a trip to look at a four-hundred-year-old oak tree that was rumored to be haunted. We stood under its arteries, staring at each other.

"Before you," he said, "I would see something beautiful and I'd have to wreck it. Like in kindergarten, if a kid took all of class to build a big fort out of blocks, I'd wait until he went inside to admire his work before I'd mow it down on top of him.

"But now, sitting here across from you, the thought that you could ever be unhappy, that anything bad could ever happen to you, it overwhelms me. I want to be a better person—for you. I want to make things with you, travel the world with you, team up. You're already my best friend. I don't know how I didn't notice how beautiful you are until this week. I think I just didn't want to see it because I have a habit of messing things up."

I could hardly believe what I was hearing. I could see myself from all angles in my mind, and from every one I was happy. It all made so much sense to me, that our lives had taken us on paths that in some ways perfectly mirrored each other's, and now we were finally going to merge. I felt certain that this relationship was it. Here was my dark, strange, funny, evil-genius man, my new best friend, the person who trusted me with all his sins and absolved me of mine. Julian and I were 100 percent about the experience. Together we were going to write ourselves into the greatest love story ever told.

That night when we went to bed we turned to each other in the dark. He touched my face and kissed me, and I laid my head on his chest and memorized his heartbeat. We wordlessly promised to take this seriously; it was time to grow up. I had the feeling he would always be there, no matter where I went or how long I lived, watching me, haunting me, becoming some theme in my life, the lesson that I never learn.

Julian proposed marriage through the mail, and I said yes via email. Instead of a ring, he sent a rare Beatles album from 1966, that highly collectable "butcher" cover version of *Yesterday and Today* known for its original album art depicting the band members adorned in raw meat and plastic doll heads. A limited number of copies had been shipped to the States before being returned to the record company by disgusted retailers. A new cover photo of the band sitting blandly among some luggage had been pasted on top of the returned albums, then they were shipped back. Industrious fans then steamed and peeled off the trunk covers to reveal the original image beneath, usually to disastrous effect. But the one Julian gave me was perfect. He said he'd found it in a bin in Chicago when he was first getting into collecting.

The plan came together so quickly it seemed one of us need only say aloud what we were both thinking and then it would be realized. If we wanted to make a whole new family, just the two of us, we could. The fact that we had to take flights to be together felt like a small price to pay. We could both work remotely, and Sadie didn't care where she was. We decided on an eventual commuter schedule of two weeks in his city, two weeks in mine.

Within days of getting engaged, we began to form a plan to start our lives over again, together, like the adults we were. Away from his mother and my family, away from our Ohio towns and our big-city successes. We would go east to New England, to a new place where we could start over, perhaps in a converted barn near an orchard, or in a cottage by the ocean. He'd make the paintings and I'd sell the books. We would live on love.

————————

"Hon . . ."

He was making my eggs over easy—Julian did all the cooking. It was the first morning of our time together in Chicago. He insisted on making every meal as beautiful as it was delicious. Big sunny yolks topped with cracked pepper, with arugula and a warm baguette and French butter on the side. NPR was whispering from the open bathroom door. Everything was radiant and alive and perfectly wonderful.

This is who we were, two working artists in love. Julian was looking at a town called Sandwich, Massachusetts. We would teach at the local university and open up a storefront out of which we would sell his paintings. I would write a book, a memoir with a happy ending. I folded my legs up to my chest in front of the walnut coffee table in the enormous kitchen, and noticed that he had added cinnamon to my coffee. I had just had an orgasm not ten minutes before. I could get used to this.

"Yeah, shug?"

We'd been trying out new terms of endearment for each other; we still hadn't settled on specific nicknames.

He turned away from the oven and walked some homemade potato bread toast over on a spatula.

"If I ever find out you've cheated on me, I'll cut off both your legs and throw them in Lake Michigan." He said it matter-of-factly, and then kissed me on the forehead. "Do you want me to make you some bacon?"

"What will you do with the rest of me?" I asked as I spread marmalade across my toast, its orange flecks dancing in the sunlight.

"I'm gonna get you pregnant."

I loved when he said shit like that. My heart swelled. This was what it was like to be taken care of. I didn't yet know that the man I was planning to marry would sometimes disappear for hours down in his basement, where he would paint, brood, and smoke; paint, brood, and smoke. Sometimes he didn't want to look at me, talk to me, or think about me being there. He shut down and closed off the world, everyone but his mother and his roommate. Sometimes he would pick a fight. Sometimes his manic episodes and the lack of sleep that fueled them rendered him psychotic, but he'd historically had a good sense of humor about them, and besides, when we were together our shared chemistry balanced us out. I helped him negotiate the world, so who needed meds? I was hoping he would be able to slow down and let me help him with his projects. There were so many.

Some part of me knew that he was heading for a crash, but he had enveloped me in mythology and I didn't want to miss the ride. Besides the creation of the paintings, there was the upkeep and management of his many online accounts, which included eBay, Etsy, Tumbler, Twitter, and Facebook; the management of his business; the constant planning and execution of the many pranks and stunts—the Banksy-level midnight marauding and public graffiti—necessary to keep Julian relevant in the eyes of his rabid fans. He was also deejaying regularly at popular bars that served cans of Pabst ironically. He was an ordained minister who would happily perform your wedding ceremony on the condition of two catered meals. He ran his own pirated DVD-sharing service called Julianflix. He could notarize your will. Once a month he threw blowout parties for the public at his place. He was often awake for thirty-six hours at a time, a product of his mania and various pharmaceuticals, then would induce sleep for twelve. He called the cycle "36/12." During the waking hours he would finish a dozen paintings of pink latex grizzly bears on old windows, organize and catalogue multiple playlists for friends, cook and photograph all his meals, deliver paintings to buyers, design an album cover, and watch a couple episodes of *Mary Hartman, Mary Hartman*.

Each day we were apart, he sent me messages through his work, hung flyers with my picture above the word MISSING around Wicker Park. One day he painted THE SPACE BETWEEN US IS KILLING ME in the street behind his house and posted it on the website. I lived for these public displays. I thought they were symbols of how perfect we were for each other. I had no idea it was the beginning of the end.

———————

We'd gone to Ohio to visit our mothers and to scope out places to get married the following fall. I thought having the wedding at David's house in the woods might be nice, and Julian agreed—having a ceremony there would keep things intimate. But as soon as Julian and I left one of the inns where friends were meant to stay when in town, Mom accidentally called Julian by another name.

"What did you think of the rooms, Jason?" she asked, totally oblivious to the flub. (To be fair, she had only just been introduced to him that morning.)

There was a pause. Julian stared at her, incredulous. "It's Julian," he said, his voice deadpan.

"Mom, his name is Julian, not Jason. Jason is Uncle Jason's name," I said, squeezing his hand reassuringly in the back seat.

"Oh, I'm so sorry, Julian," Mom said, peering at us in the rearview mirror and laughing it off. "I'm not so great with names, but I'll get used to you soon enough."

"That's good, because we're getting married," I said, trying to smooth things over, but I could tell he was fuming. When we got to David's house for dinner, Mom had to go on ahead because Julian couldn't get out of the car. He stared straight ahead through the windshield. I'd been so excited to show him the house, but he hadn't even looked in its direction.

"What's going on?" I asked, trying to sound casual. He didn't say anything, just sighed and hung his head. "What's wrong?"

He looked nauseated and sullen. Whatever light had been there before had abruptly gone out. He had completely shut down.

I pleaded with him. Could this really be about my mother? "She didn't mean anything by it—she just made a mistake. I love you and that's what matters, and she will, too, just as soon as she gets to know you. It's a running joke in our family that our mom can't even tell the difference between my brothers in old photographs."

He stared down at his hands. "I don't think I can do this," he said, then looked me in the eye.

I burst into tears. The night before, we'd been cuddled up in my childhood bedroom making a guest list, and now he was reneging. I knew it was bad, but I was determined to fix it.

"Please just give it some time," I said, hoping I didn't sound as desperate as I felt. "Don't worry about the wedding—what's important is that we're a team. We make our own family, remember?"

Julian nodded his head and squeezed my hand, and almost immediately started to come around. He was tired; he felt outnumbered by my family and stressed over the pace at which everything was moving—but he was in no way ambivalent about wanting to be with me. We agreed to table all the wedding talk for the night—there'd be plenty of time for that; what was important was just being together. After twenty minutes in the car, we emerged holding hands. At dinner, Julian made a toast, turning to my mother and addressing her by name. "I love your daughter, Paige. She's changed my life." I exhaled, touched that he would make such a declaration but unnerved by what had just happened in the car. It scared me that things could have so easily gone the other way.

In the six months we'd been together, these mood swings had occurred twice before, but they'd passed quickly. The first time it happened I was staying with him. It was late at night and he was downstairs in his studio painting. I went down to tell him something and accidentally startled him. When he saw me he actually jumped, then acted as if I'd meant to sneak up on him. When I apologized for scaring him he couldn't let it go. His entire demeanor changed, a dark cloud descended, and he turned cold. The longer I stayed in the basement and tried to smooth things over, to get "him" back, the more irritated with me he became. We ended up having our first argument, wherein he questioned my loyalty to him compared with that of an ex-girlfriend. It was confusing. I decided to give him some space and went up to bed, hoping he'd follow. He didn't.

The next morning he brought me breakfast in bed and apologized profusely for his rotten mood. He blamed it on nerves around his first solo gallery show, just a few days away—maybe I should avoid him altogether when he was painting on a deadline.

"It's a deal," I said in response, and just like that the cloud had lifted.

The day after our dinner at David's, we went to Julian's mother's house. Rita greeted us warmly, then returned to her work on the couch rolling a joint. She was excited to share some new strain she'd been cultivating since we'd last seen each other. Julian didn't smoke pot. It was the only drug he couldn't handle—it made him too jittery and paranoid. More for his mom and me.

"So, you kids just can't get enough of Ohio, huh? I wish you would have given me more of a warning that you were coming, Julian—I would have cleaned up the guest room," Rita yelled into the next room. Julian was already in the kitchen, compulsively cleaning out her fridge.

"Wait, you didn't know we were coming?" I asked, incredulous. I had been under the assumption we were there to start planning the wedding. I'd decided not to bring it up at all in front of Julian after his episode the day before, but was hoping Rita and I could engage in some girl talk about it when he wasn't around.

"Julian just told me yesterday that you all were in town. What's the occasion?"

"We came in to look at the property where we're thinking about having the ceremony," I said. I was surprised she hadn't even known we were in Ohio.

Julian came in from the kitchen to intercept the conversation. "So, Mom, there's something I wanted to tell you . . ." he said brightly.

Wait, what? We'd been engaged for four months. Julian and Rita checked in with each other at least once a week.

"Erin and I are going to get married," he said.

Rita sat straight up so fast that ashes from her joint fell on her lap. "But, Julian, what about your issues?!" Not what I was expecting her reaction to be.

"What do you mean?" Julian asked, laughing nervously.

"What do you mean?" I wasn't laughing.

Rita looked amused. Julian started talking fast. "This is different, I'm thirty-four and I'm ready for this. I'm different with Erin." (He was, he was different, but . . . what issues?) "I don't want Grandma to come to the wedding, though. She's so negative, and I want to keep it to just the inner circle."

"Whatever you want, baby. I guess congratulations are in order." She got up off the couch and hugged us both, but I could tell she wasn't convinced.

Later, when Julian and I were alone, I asked why he hadn't told her, especially when all our friends knew, not to mention the Internet.

"I just wanted to tell her in person. It's a big deal, and also I didn't want her to try to talk me out of it."

"Why would she do that? I thought she liked me."

"She does like you—she likes you a lot, and soon she'll love you, too. It's just, she's not the biggest fan of the institution, and I didn't want to get into it, you know?" He kissed me reassuringly. "This is really about our lives, and what we want to make of them. We don't need anyone's permission."

We went to Providence for Thanksgiving weekend to spend the holiday with my friends. He'd been quiet the whole week—still feeling out these new people—but I felt so close to him. Every night we walked the chilly streets lined with old Victorian houses, holding hands, and Julian said, "This is my favorite thing to do—just being with you. I can't wait to get to do this all the time." I was so excited, because we'd only have to wait a few more weeks to see each other for Christmas, when I'd come stay for a while and we'd do a longer trial run before I moved in for good.

I felt so certain I'd see him soon that I allowed myself to fall asleep on the train back to New York, and as a consequence missed our last conscious hours together before he had to go back home early the next morning. He looked sad when we said goodbye, which I took as a sign of our happiness.

A few days later, on my birthday, he sent flowers with a note to say he loved me "implicitly," and couldn't wait for me to get even older in his presence. He dedicated his website to me for a week and had his fans send me presents. Someone painted a portrait of the two of us, both of our heads thrown back in laughter. When we talked on the phone that night he sounded tired, mentioned he was feeling something coming on. I sensed he was probably coming off a 36/12 and really needed to rest. I told him to.

When I realized at dinner the next day that I still hadn't heard from

Julian, I figured he really might be sick, and when I still hadn't heard from him by midnight I was genuinely concerned. I couldn't remember the last twenty-four-hour period that had passed without us constantly in touch. I left a message letting him know I was worried. When he finally did call the next morning, he sounded out of it and depressed. He said he'd been sleeping too much. I asked if he was experimenting with psychiatric meds again.

"It's not that," he said. "You know I only take Benadryl now." (We'd made a pact: no more downers.) This, Julian said, was different; he was crumbling under pressure.

"What pressure?" I asked. "How can I help take away some of that for you?"

"I don't think you understand the amount of stress I'm under—I have this thing with the IRS . . ."

"Do you mean you have to pay taxes?" This was the absolute first time I'd heard him mention the IRS. We talked about money all the time—we had money, and now that we were going to join forces, we'd have even more.

"Very funny," he said, and then failed to elaborate.

"Babe, I know your tax bracket and it's going to be okay. On paper you're a starving artist. Whatever you're worried about can be remedied with the right accountant, or, like, your local H&R Block. I can help, and we can work it out in a few months. Please don't worry about it right now." He sighed into the phone. I didn't understand, he said, but he'd try to sleep off the anxiety.

On the third day he delivered a blow. He called sounding alternately listless and agitated, and when I suggested he make an appointment to see a doctor, he said he didn't think there was anything that could be done for someone like him. What ailed him wasn't physical but emotional. The reason he'd been so down the last few days was because he'd been feeling "bad about us." *But we would soon be hosting friends for Christmas dinner in Chicago. Rita was coming. I'd already booked a flight.*

"Define bad."

"I was up all night the last time we saw each other, and you just slept the whole time. Something about that makes me sad. I would have stayed up for you."

I apologized profusely. I hadn't realized . . .

Suddenly he blurted out that he'd been spending "too much time with someone else," for weeks now, and he was confused about his feelings for her.

"Her? Who?"

He said the name Lucy, a woman in a local punk band he knew socially.

"Isn't she married?"

"Not for much longer."

"Have you slept with her?

"Of course not, but I shouldn't be having these feelings for anyone else, and I am." He went on to blame the distance. He couldn't be alone. He needed constant attention. He'd thought he'd be able to wait it out, but being apart so much had caused his mind to wander. He wasn't sure he was going to be able to make so many changes. He thought he could share and be honest with me, but it turned out he couldn't. It just didn't feel good. And that was that, he had to go. This was too hard for him to talk about, he said, he had to get off the phone.

I sat upright in my bed trying to process what had just happened. Had he just broken up with me? I racked my brain for memories of my apparent rival. Lucy had come to our engagement party. Pretty, still in her twenties, quiet, always alone. Our conversations had been limited to small talk about pets.

Within days the truer story emerged: Lucy was in fact already staying with Julian, the two of them having been caught in his bed— our bed—by her husband. There had been a fracas, she moved out of her house, it was quite the talk of the town. A day after this reveal, Lucy's husband sent me a message via Myspace, wanting to make sure I knew my fiancé was an adulterer. I took a few days off work just to cry in the fetal position, and friends brought food to my apartment.

Denise holed up with me the first week so I wouldn't have to face the nights alone.

Every day he called. He was so sorry he had hurt me, he'd never meant for this to happen. We fought. I pleaded. Sometimes I ignored his calls, sometimes I called and left tearful messages. Some days I couldn't face the truth of what had happened and Julian played along. Sometimes he let me pretend that he wished he could take it back. But eventually, always eventually, he had to get off the phone. He had to stop analyzing what went wrong with us, he had to focus on his health and getting all the drugs out of his system—that was part of the problem, maybe it had all been a momentary lapse in sanity. He had to go to Home Depot, he had to get the supplies to make the paintings. Why didn't I get to focusing on my work, on selling the books?

Julian was moving on at lightning speed. Away from me, away from us, all our plans instantly erased. In retrospect I see clearly that every time I thought he was feeling guilt or remorse, in fact he was expressing concern that he actually wasn't feeling a thing. Sometimes he would call to ponder why he wasn't taking it harder—he would have expected more from himself, considering how much he'd felt for me in the beginning. "It seemed genuine at the time." I'd somehow made him want to marry me and just like that I'd made him want to call the whole thing off.

Just days after the breakup, Julian took on a new art project that involved helping people exact hilarious vengeance on those who had done them wrong. Have a grievance? Did a friend abandon you without warning? Somebody steal your man? For a fee, Julian would help conceive a personalized revenge package, which might include a half-eaten cheeseburger in the mail to the object of scorn, or a public lashing via memorable and permanent graffiti. This Robin Hood persona made me crazy. Couldn't people see that he was a bad person, that he was the one who deserved the most hamburgers through the mail? Online, his life looked palpably awesome. He threw himself a birthday party, open to the public, and simply replaced me with the new girl. Over Christmas just a month later, there were pictures of the two of them on his website, with Rita, eating what should have been *our* Cornish game hens, pumpkin mushroom stuffing, and what looked like my grandmother's recipe for green beans.

If not for the dog, I wouldn't have gotten out of bed—I preferred to spend a minimum of fourteen hours there, with occasional breaks for walks around the block and one meal a day. I avoided music like fire—every pop song a grating reminder that other people were happy, had ever been happy, would be happy forever, in their fulfilling, joyous, reciprocal relationships. How could I have fallen for this con artist, another man with two faces?

24

FIXING A HOLE

WHEN DENISE BECAME ATTACHED to the most charming, emotionally stable, attractive, and successful of all the men she'd dated in New York, she was concerned about their dissimilarities in musical taste. She preferred classic R&B and jazz and had an encyclopedic knowledge of the Great American Songbook, and she sometimes worried that her boyfriend's obvious affection for Coldplay might signify some insurmountable divide. She thought about it enough that she dedicated a whole session to the subject with her therapist.

"You will not believe what my shrink said to me when I told him I worried that I don't share a lot of Scott's taste." We peered at the dried ball of flower tea the waitress had set before us in a clear teapot as it throbbed at the surface, mesmerized as it sank and yawned into a giant purple posy, well worth its eight-dollar price tag.

"Let me guess, it's a sign that you're incompatible and he's not smart enough for you," I said confidently. Though I had no stable relationship of my own to reference, I felt I knew what was what on this particular issue. True love shared a soundtrack.

"No, but going in, I was sure he would think it was meaningful, which is how I broached the topic. I told him I've never been in such a healthy relationship, but I worry we don't get each other in a fundamental way—we don't like the same music, and I worry that our tastes aren't compatible. And that's when the shrink says that *he* likes Coldplay, does that mean he can't be my shrink? And I said that's different, and then he said it absolutely doesn't matter if your significant other has different taste."

"No!"

"I know. I was surprised, too."

And so began an ongoing debate with my own shrink.

Ana crossed her legs and peered down her glasses.

"Have you been using musical taste as a way to further distance yourself from men who might otherwise be good matches for you?" she challenged, knowing full well the answer.

"Why do you think it matters to you so much?" she probed.

"Because how do you know what kind of person they are? Whether or not they deserve to be loved?" I was only half kidding. "I don't know, I guess it matters like sense of humor matters, or good looks. It's attractive when you think the person you're with has that kind of intelligence, and conversely it's unattractive when you can't respect their taste. It's called a deal breaker."

"And what's a deal breaker for you?"

"Pearl Jam fans, people who attend raves or music festivals in Ibiza, and German disc jockeys who mix ambient techno. I don't like No Doubt or the state of California—both are too sunny. But experience has taught me not to trust a man who listens to the Smiths and Morrissey all the time, either, because it likely means he's still hung up on the first person to ever break his heart: his mother.

"I try not to get into it with people from San Francisco—the whole Bay Area has been bad news for me, same with Seattle and Portland. In Brooklyn, I'd prefer not to commute to the Williamsburg or Bushwick neighborhoods—the G train is really unreliable. Plus, I'm trying to avoid going out with actors, stand-up comedians, or writers of any kind. I won't date academics, not that one would feel the loss."

Ana raised an eyebrow. "Anything else?"

"I want a man to be excited about something—his hobbies or whatever—but not too excited. Too excited can be really embarrassing, like if they want to do a lot of karaoke or are really bad joke tellers or something. In general, I might have to be the chatty one in the relationship, but he should at least have read a lot of books."

———————

During the early weeks postbreakup, I comforted myself with the belief that Julian and I would eventually rise from the ashes. After all, even John and Yoko were separated for eighteen months. She had grown so tired of his constant neediness, his acting out, his philandering. She gave her blessing for his Lost Weekend, which included a move to Los Angeles with a new lover, knowing deep down that what was meant to be would be. Love was about trusting the inevitable. It was about the long haul. There was no doubt in my mind that if I could just hold out, focus on my own work and career, and truly learn not to care, we would work it out and find each other again. If Julian felt he needed to be with this other girl for a while, then that wasn't really about me.

But just as quickly as I had fallen in love, I fell into a depression. It was a feeling so heavy, I barely remembered my life before it. Had I always been so sad? I wanted to hide from the world, but New York City had no time for sad girls. And every day I knew that I'd have to truly learn to be alone. Yoko threw herself into her art, she made herself the focus—her work, her health, her dreams. As she got stronger, John changed, too. He became a man the minute he learned to shed the tough-guy veneer, his macho bullshit. As if by magic, Yoko had become pregnant with Sean almost as soon as she and John reunited.

By then she was forty-two. Anything was possible once you learned to let it go.

For weeks and then months, nothing felt good. Depression was like constantly being covered in slime even after I had just showered. And I took only baths because I didn't have enough energy to stand up for showers. I felt proud that at least I was making attempts to get clean. No matter how dark it got I always tried to project that lightness of the freshly washed, an unyielding positivity and softness. I talked myself into reasons for living and things to look forward to every day. *You never know who you'll meet*, I'd say to myself. *The love of your life, or the next great project, could be right around the corner.* But it was a hollow exercise. Julian had more than betrayed me; he'd shamed me, and worse, he took away any belief in love, the thing I most needed to believe in.

I didn't plan it, but a couple of times my use of pills would overlap with a session with Ana. I considered it a plus, as I would be showing her my best self. But one day I went and Ana asked me if I was on something.

She sat in her chair, studying me. Her head was cocked to the left. She clasped her hands over her knees and said bluntly, "Erin, I have to say that you seem different to me—not yourself. Something has dimmed the lights."

"What do you mean, 'dimmed the lights'?" I asked, incredulous. "I'm not any more depressed than usual, I can assure you."

"Really? Because, to me, your expression—your whole demeanor— is different. A little blank. What concerns me is that you might be taking painkillers again . . ."

I had talked to her the year before about a couple of instances when "I'd taken pills recreationally," trying to make light of it and normalize the necessity of anxiety relief. Everyone was doing it. I had not told her how much I was taking, before and throughout my time with Julian.

"You know, not all people who overdose die. Quite a few survive but with so much brain damage that they're never the same again, they're incapacitated. I don't think that's what you want. I understand why you're doing it, but I'm telling you that I'm concerned."

"Concerned that it makes me feel good?"

"Concerned that you feel so shitty in the first place. And I don't want you to die. You're in some trouble and I want you to acknowledge that."

I rolled my eyes like a teenager. "And I'd like *you* to acknowledge that just because I'm choosing to tell you this stuff now does not mean that I'm an addict, because that's not what's going on. I've never once experienced withdrawal."

I was angry with myself for telling her in the first place. It irritated me that no shrink seemed to be able to read my mind, short of noticing when I was depressed, and that was only when I allowed the person to notice. The therapist was there to mirror me, to help me analyze my patterns. But I only told her about some of them.

I didn't care that I was living a cliché: I had read a hundred recovery memoirs, and I knew exactly what I was doing to myself. I knew it couldn't last forever, that it could, in fact, be the death of me. I didn't care that there's an expiration date for everything. More than ever, I loved the feeling of lying on the floor of my apartment, *alone alone alone*, music blaring through my DVD player, too high, feeling my heartbeat, *slow slow slow*, as my breathing got shallower and shallower. My breath became a mantra . . . *he he he* . . . little Lamaze breaths. My tongue, a foreign thing in my mouth, thick like a cow's, a telltale ache in my jaw, a kind of warning, my ears ringing. Every day was a dare, and every day I lived.

Looking at Ana I was full of resentment. She was convinced that I wasn't feeling anything when I was on pills—who the fuck was she to say? I felt every emotion purely. The pills were in fact the buffer between war and peace in my mind. On pills = internal isolation; off pills = external degradation. The pills encircled me in a bubble of soft armor that would save me from myself. On pills I wouldn't pine for Julian, I wouldn't beg him to return, I wouldn't get on a plane to Chicago. On pills, I would do all the right things, preferably unconsciously. Now that everything had diminished to a reliable haze and I was blunt around the edges, there was no reason to stop yet.

"It was just a phase," I said. "I've already stopped."

———————

While waiting for Julian to come to his senses, I severed all contact with him, and did a lot of dating to distract myself. There was the surfer/medical illustrator with diabetes, there was the balding comedian on a hit TV show, there was the homeless artist I couldn't seem to stay away from, the pretty good actor who disappeared for pilot season, the earnest film editor married to his job, the *National Geographic* photographer, the famous-in-Brooklyn guitar player, and a bunch of randoms I met through six months of online dating. New York guys, actual men. I went to dinner with all my ex-boyfriends. *See how healthy*, I thought.

I watched Netflix. I wept and clung to hope. I obsessively checked Julian's website, which I was convinced contained hidden messages to me—here, a picture of the stoop on his block where just a year ago we'd passed out Halloween candy to sweet-faced children dressed as ghouls. There, a picture of a table set for two, double lobster tails, corn on the cob, wineglasses, candles. It was easy for me to ignore the context—a candlelight dinner for two by nature was romantic, but how could it be about anyone else but me, really? Who would be so cruel as to advertise the repeating of an old experience with someone new? What this was—I saw clearly—was a plea from Julian, a plea for understanding and forgiveness. He was remembering us.

While I continued bettering myself in order to get Julian to realize how much he missed me and come back, I became more productive. I decided to be a person who made things. I tried new media. I altered found objects, photographed them, mailed the pictures to strangers. I made a collage every day for three weeks. I kept thematic journals. I collected the work of other artists. I collaborated with others. I wrote a couple of television pilots. I went to the movies by myself. I threw a baby shower. I baked cookies. I dyed my hair as copper red as desert sandstone. I walked my dog past majestic prewar brownstones in Brooklyn and felt my feelings.

While I waited for Julian, I tried to stay off pills. In order to stay off the pills I preferred to be on, I took a lot of other pills. I took Cymbalta (for when "depression hurts everywhere") and tried Celexa and Prozac (for when it just hurt somewhere)—these were prescribed to me. Recreationally, I took Suboxone, an opiate blocker that I found made me feel just enough of Something Else that I could actually pretend I was still on opiates. Mostly this meant that I itched like my skin was made of wool. If I had them, I took Xanax and Klonopin and Ativan for anxiety and panic and the agitation that comes with sobriety and heartbreak, but mostly I used sedatives to block out my ability to remember. I found it a relief to realize that a whole week had gone by, which would therefore bring me all that much closer to the time when Julian and I would be together again—a time when consciousness actually mattered. If I didn't have the good stuff, I took Tylenol PM like they were vitamins. God forbid I wake up in the night. Waking up in the night was my worst nightmare.

I tried smoking cigarettes, smoking a cigarette first thing in the morning with coffee, not smoking cigarettes, and drinking beer in the afternoon. I read books about mental illness—about bipolar disorder and genius, about depression and suicide, about psychopathy and child abuse, about the effects of parental abandonment; I liked to think I knew as much as there was to know about broken people. I self-diagnosed. I tried rolling my depression into a ball and then kicking it into the abyss. I tried primal scream therapy in the dark by the river. I tried juicing and fasting and a ginger-turmeric infusion. I tried fish oil and vitamin D3 and gluten-free pancake batter. I tried essential oils in the bath. Once I added the cinnamon too liberally and broke out in a burning rash, for which I took Benadryl.

I took a break from therapy. I was disenfranchised with the entire concept. What kind of shrink saw a patient for the better part of seven years and failed to see the writing on the wall? Fuck therapy and its

$150-an-hour fee to feel like shit for an extra hour every week. My new mental health plan would entail smoking pot and watching *Intervention* marathons. I ceased to seek out all other illicit substances when I realized that I truly could no longer afford to take drugs. The choice was between switching to street heroin—a fiscal bargain—or abstinence and a return to relative health. I knew I didn't have the stomach to throw my life away for a slim chance at feeling anything like I once had. Too much had happened to ever go back.

Apparently it took a village to be my boyfriend, a whole mess of them to fulfill the various roles I now required. I had men who cooked for me, and good friends who helped me hang my chandeliers. I had guys I got beers with and ones I went to the movies with. There was the ex who seemed to have morphed into a friend with benefits, and Paul was still my emergency contact a good seven years after we'd broken up. Sex was always easy to come by, so to speak.

My type could be described as elusive—not necessarily on purpose—but busy or gone a lot, or like Julian, living in another city. He was smarter than smart, and he challenged me to constantly stay on top of my game. He was either attractive or charismatic—usually the most attractive or charismatic person in the room. He had dark mood swings, and had experienced a fair amount of trauma. He made me laugh. He took drugs recreationally, or was as in denial about his drinking as I was in denial that the sex we were having was transcendent. He had been to church but realized that God is dead. Most important, he inevitably had to leave me and find someone else, someone who wasn't me.

After Julian, it only got worse: *I'll open you up, get you to talk, listen to your story, heal you. Or you'll open me up, get me to talk, listen to my story, and leave.*

After Julian, every encounter with a new guy was muted. I didn't trust myself to know what to look for or how to be. I couldn't stand the dating ritual. Getting to know someone, becoming friends first, taking it slow, building a basis for a healthy relationship—these were not concepts that I'd been able to make work for me. Love meant periods of masochistic self-loathing mixed with manic sex. All you need is lust.

There were so many rules about what men could handle from women in terms of their personal histories. What was too much information to share? What was too little? According to myriad media on the subject, if you wanted to catch a fella, you were not supposed to disclose any major chinks in the armor until, like, the twelfth date. You were supposed to allow the subjective experience of your mental illness to unfold naturally. If by date twelve the guy generally seemed willing to continue sharing meals in your company, it was safe to say that he would be accepting of the disclosure of your particular personality disorder enough to handle the sight of your meds in the bathroom.

They tell us there are fundamental differences between the sexes—men are external, women are internal, men need to chase, women need to be wooed, men need mystery, women should talk less. The message to women is: if you want to be taken seriously in a relationship, it's best to hold off having sex with the guy you like for at least three dates or until you've agreed to be monogamous. You're expected to demur and wait for *him* to ask the questions. You're supposed to steer the conversation away from sex, or anything so fraught, yet stoke the subtext (subsex) that the answers are magically stored in your vagina. Woody Allen was wrong. The most powerful words in the English language are not "It's benign," but rather "The HPV has cleared up on its own."

For a while I tried doing everything I was supposed to according to experts. I went on dates with the same person for a couple of weeks, and flirted and texted and held hands under the restaurant table, invested in the narrative, and imagined integrating our friends. And then we'd sleep together and he'd spend the night, and there'd be snoring but also spooning, and maybe even brunch or a walk to the train.

And it would be fine, but not in any way life-changing. Soon enough, the conversations were always stilted, the sex uninspired, the revealed truths unspecial. The expectation I had that the best guys were hard to get inevitably led to them thinking I wanted too much from them or I was too much *for* them. And maybe I set it up that way, subconsciously, so they'd have to reject me, and I'd have to keep feeling that pain I knew so well.

25

YOU'VE GOT TO HIDE
YOUR LOVE AWAY

WHEN JULIAN GOT BACK IN TOUCH after two years of exile, every little insight I'd paid dearly for went straight to hell. He sent an email; it was plaintive: *I miss talking to you.* It was as I'd envisioned: he'd come home. He'd burned his life down, he said, during our time apart. He'd lost his mind for a while, and punished himself for the way he'd treated me. He got severely depressed, wondered what it was all for, thought about killing himself. The girl he'd left me for was crazy. She'd cheated on him. They'd lasted longer than we had by far, but he clearly hadn't been in his right mind. He'd been sick, he said, afraid of himself, not sure what he wanted from life. But most of all he was profoundly sorry for what he'd put me through—put *us* through—he wanted to understand why he always ran away from anything real in the end. With me it had been authentic, and I was the only person he couldn't lie to.

This made so much sense to me. Julian didn't know what it was like to be wanted. There hadn't been any people in his life that he could count on. His father abandoned him and his mother neglected him. He had a hard time disconnecting from a deep need to be Rita's son. She was his muse the way Julia was to John, or Ruth was to Dad. Rita had been the one who had questioned his intentions and ability to get married. That was probably it right there, the reason he fled just a couple months later: *he was trying to protect me.*

I was grasping for a scenario in which this two-year break was a perfectly normal thing for a couple to go through before reuniting forever. I willfully ignored the terrible feeling I had that I was being manipulated by a person who needed to constantly manipulate some-one—anyone—just to feel alive. I needed to believe I was special, and that all the pain had been worth it.

It was so good to hear Julian's voice, though it had changed. Now it was lower and softer and lacked the confidence I associated with him. He had been humbled, he said, by what he now knew he was ca-pable of, hurting the one person he had ever really loved. I was too sad to be angry anymore, and now I was worried about him. He sounded hopeless and clinically depressed. He'd recently been receiving treat-ment, but abruptly stopped all drug therapy, claiming it made him too tired to make the paintings. Every time we spoke, it was as if he was calling to say goodbye. After a couple of weeks of communicating every day, the pull to see him again was overwhelming.

I was planning a trip to Memphis to meet with a rock legend in need of an agent, which is how Julian and I concocted a plan to re-peat our epic road trip down south. I would take my meetings and he would be my chauffeur, and at night we'd see friends for dinner and stay in a quaint hotel. It seemed a fitting thing to do; there was a symmetry about it. All the same, I wouldn't be telling a single person that I was even speaking to him again. I knew such a thing had the air of the ill-advised and was undignified in its suddenness. I was walking back into the lion's den.

———————

A month later Julian picked me up at the airport in a rental car, and we got on the road straightaway. He looked better than I'd ever seen him look, physically healthier, and with longer hair. We'd both stopped taking drugs, so that helped. I could tell he was nervous. When we hugged hello, I felt the artery in his neck pulse and I had the urge to rest my head on his chest. I didn't, I kept it cool, but I already longed to know how the night would end. "I was so nervous about how this would be," Julian said, "but it's not so bad."

"This was . . . spontaneous of us," I said.

"It wouldn't be us if we'd planned it. We do know how to have adventures." Julian told me to open up the cooler in the back seat—he'd made us sandwiches for the road, displayed in neat little rows of Ziploc bags. We talked about all the weird places we might tour if we wanted to give the trip a theme. We decided on the tone of southern gothic—why not go ghost hunting in the most haunted region of America?

I caught him looking at me a lot in the car.

"What?"

"Nothing, it's just crazy to see you." Seeing him again had inspired a flurry of emotion in me, and I realized as soon as we were together that I wanted him back. I'd never wanted anything more.

His demeanor was more polite than passionate. We'd been talking about our time apart, and he complained a little too long about how Lucy had cheated on and abandoned him. The way I saw it, the fact that she selfishly drew things out so long with Julian was just another indication that something was very wrong with her, but it was over now, and we were back in sync, in a car, just the two of us. The irony of him complaining to me about the loss of his relationship with the person he left me to be with did not escape me—I was just that desperate to overlook it.

I focused instead on the thicket of choking kudzu, the plant so hardy it tended to take over existing landscapes that couldn't compete with its need for sunlight. The kudzu actually grew over the trees, killing every native plant beneath its vines. I'd never seen anything so lush. I felt my eyes sting with tears.

"Why are you talking about her right now?" I said, still looking out the window.

"Because I thought we were experiencing a really long car ride together and I have a lot on my mind." Julian was chewing gum, and his tone of voice was matter-of-fact. "I loved her, you know—we were together for two years."

Tears fell down my face. What was going on?

"Are you crying?" Julian pulled off the exit ramp into a mostly deserted rest stop. Its WELCOME CENTER sign looked sinister. We sat in silence for long minutes while the car idled. My stomach felt heavy with gravity and I wondered how I would get through four more days of this.

Finally, Julian spoke. "Did you think that we would just come down here and everything would be like it used to be?" he asked, baffled.

"Yes," I said, nodding vigorously. "Yes!"

"You thought . . ." he said, looking at me like he wasn't sure if I was being sarcastic. "We were going to get back together?"

"Why else would I come here with you, after not seeing you for two years? After you contacted me out of the blue to atone and tell me how sad you were about what you'd done to us and that it had all been the biggest mistake of your life."

"I didn't say that—I said I regretted the relationship with *her*. It was a product of my depression." He sounded exhausted—wasn't this the most obvious thing in the world?

"And what was your relationship with me a product of?" I wasn't angry yet, still clinging to disbelief.

"My mania, probably. It tends to feel like a good time—people like to feed off of it." Now his tone of voice was cold. "What happened with us is not really so different from what always happens with me: I see something; I want it; I get it by any means necessary; eventually I see something else I want, and I lose interest in the last thing. I thought it was different with you, but you weren't there enough—and it's not your fault, I know you wanted to be—but I couldn't wait. I couldn't wait, and I couldn't change, and you didn't deserve to be treated that way. I think on some level I knew that you didn't, but she did."

I didn't want him to say any more. After everything that had happened, and without the pills to sugarcoat the days, there was little between us but anger and resentment. He couldn't imagine how I thought we might be renewing anything but our friendship. I couldn't imagine how he didn't want to, but he didn't feel anything beyond a wish to be absolved. It was the norm for him to remain close to his former girlfriends, or at least the ones he'd initially left behind. If they couldn't have what he'd once promised, they'd take what they could get.

The next few days were a struggle. We were bound together socially, appearing to the world to be a couple. Julian was just as attentive as he'd always been—ordering for me at restaurants, singing my praises to any new acquaintance, flattering me. But at night, when we'd share a bed in the hotel room, he curled away from me toward his corner of the mattress, a pillow over his head. I lay in bed at five a.m. and counted my breaths.

When we were alone we tried to fill the hours with our haunted tours, but the process of walking in silence taking pictures of other peoples' forever losses tended to accentuate my unhappiness. We toured the crumbling remnants of an actual ghost town in Cairo, Illinois. Its once-thriving downtown streets were now lined with the carcasses of storefronts from the 1960s, the old signs in the windows long since bleached by the sun. It was as if Jesus had spontaneously instigated the Rapture in just this one city. As we walked past abandoned Queen Anne–style houses overrun with vines and decay, Julian wasn't taking pictures of me; it was the destruction he was interested in.

At one point we ended up at an unmarked graveyard for children in Greenville, South Carolina, regarded to be one of the creepiest places in America. A potter's field for orphans and the poor, it had gone untended for too many years. There were no headstones, and the tops of coffins jutted out of the earth. They let us know where we were. We walked separately, tiptoeing and wincing in silence.

Every place we sought out was barren and long past dead. On what would turn out to be the last night, Julian dived into the filthy Mississippi River near the site where Jeff Buckley had died. *This is our last goodbye*, I thought lamely while I filmed him, as instructed, from the rocks. On the drive home a day early, our contempt for each other was so obvious that we mutually decided after two hours of straight bitter silence that he should drop me at a hotel in Chicago so I could get through the next twenty-four hours with some dignity. I've never been so relieved to be alone in my whole life or happier to stay in a shitty Days Inn too many miles from O'Hare.

It never occurred to me when Julian was holding me that he might not have been giving something to me, but taking something for himself. In the beginning, I'd believed that we'd been drawn together by fate to heal each other and fix the thing that made us broken, that made me unlovable and him unable to love. Now that it was really over, I couldn't keep blaming the other side for my crappy choices. I had to take responsibility and break the pattern. I got back into therapy.

"Why is it taking so long for me to learn my lesson?" I asked Ana, exasperated with myself.

"Because sometimes it takes a lifetime. We have to bottom out before we're ready to change the course and stop repeating the essential tragedy of our lives."

"What's my tragedy?"

"You tell me."

"I have abandonment issues? I keep putting all my energy into keeping my relationship alive with someone who just isn't capable of going the distance or ever really connecting."

There were so many shared similarities among the men in my life. I needed them to have an essential vice or weakness, I felt most comfortable around intense, self-sabotaging, ambivalent smokers who underneath it all were smoldering in rage. It was kind of like looking in the mirror—I was a manic pixie nightmare. *Bring me your tired, your poor, your scruffified hipster with dimples. I'll take him under my wing. I'll teach him to fly, and watch him fly away.*

Then I thought about one of the darkest facts of my experiences with men: I'd intercepted the suicide attempts of three of them in the span of ten years. Even the first time it happened, I wasn't frightened, just relieved that I was there to intervene. During a mixed manic episode, a friend locked himself in a closet in my apartment and tried to hang himself by his belt. It was pure instinct to pull him down by any means necessary, though I ended up inadvertently choking him in the process. He was hysterical and angry, but I managed to convince him to call 911.

I knew it was an emergency when an on-again, off-again boyfriend left a voicemail wherein he told me that he loved me, his voice shaking. He'd certainly never said that before; that's how I knew something was wrong. I made a guess about where he was, and two hours later he was found overdosing in a bathtub. A third friend called me immediately after taking too many pills. He hadn't meant to die, but everything was beginning to go dark. With him there was already a protocol in place in case someone needed to find the Narcan shot to bring him back around. He knew I would always pick up the phone. I considered it a calling, saving lives, and I prided myself on being the person that friends gave their spare key to. I was unflappable in a crisis, a positive outcome of a chaotic childhood. I never considered that it might not be a virtue.

"All that saving the lives of the men in your life—I think you rescue because of a wish to be rescued yourself. You give them everything they need in the hopes that they'll reciprocate. After all, don't they owe you now? It's an unconscious currency of power and it almost never works." It was hard to hear, and I knew Ana was right.

"So what do I do?"

"You give yourself a break and stop blaming yourself for these perceived failures that are really just experiences. You have to work on cultivating a healthy sense of self again. Give yourself time to heal, and when you meet someone new, take it slow and listen to your intuition."

"I'm just worried I'll have to go through a sea of dicks to get to the other side."

Ana laughed. "You wouldn't be the first."

26

LET IT BE

IN THE SUMMER OF 2012, I went back to Fellowship Bible Church for the first time in eighteen years. Sarah, the daughter of my mother's longtime friend Jane, had died. My mother had called with the news three days before, and said she would be unable to attend the memorial service. She would be on her honeymoon with David and couldn't make it back in time. This was the church Sarah and I had grown up in, and the last time I had been there was for her dad's funeral. I felt a sudden urge to go in Mom's place.

Sarah was thirty-seven when her heart gave out. By then she'd been plagued with anorexia for more than fifteen years. She'd been in chronic pain since her father died from an aggressive cancer when she was a freshman in college. His illness and absence had affected every aspect of her life. Back then, she'd quit her liberal arts program, transferred to nursing school, and become an oncology nurse. She got married and divorced young, had no children, then got too sick to work. There were recoveries and relapses, too many to keep track of.

In recent pictures, she appeared hollowed out, waiting to be carried away. Mom told me that Sarah had tried to kill herself several times, the last attempt just two months before. In the end she was spared the choice.

During the eight-hour drive to Ohio, I felt the full narcissism of my survivor's guilt. I certainly hadn't been any kind of friend to Sarah since we were kids, and here I was missing her like I'd miss a sister. I'd never so much as written her a note or dropped her a line since I'd first heard she was struggling nearly ten years before, and by then she'd been in and out of treatment centers for years. At the time I was dealing with my own issues, but I remember wondering if her illness was somehow linked to the way she related to her dad growing up.

Sarah and I shared a quest for perfection rooted in a nagging wish for a do-over. From a young age we both woke up in the morning with the good-girl checklist in mind. If we could just get through the whole day without committing the number one sin of angering our fathers, that was a day worth remembering. Though my dad's toughness was more of a costume he wore, Sarah's dad was wild in the eyes and fearless on a motorcycle. I'd seen him body-slam his daughter until she cried when they wrestled, and carry her giggling out of the sandbox he'd built for her. I could relate to some of what she went through before and after her father died—the anxiety of constantly walking on eggshells, the need for order and control, the impulse to try to save others while losing herself. Fixer was our default setting. The difference was I had eight more years with my dad than she had with hers. I got the chance to break away while he was still alive. And now that he was gone, I was no longer hurting myself in order to prove I'd been in pain all along.

Though Sarah's inner circle had been small—a few close friends and family members—hundreds of people attended the service. Ever loyal to a fellow sister in Christ, it looked like the entire congregation turned up. A warm July rain steamed off the pavement of the church parking lot that reminded me of a Lexus dealership. In line to enter the building, I didn't feel good about the crowd. I'd always hated the sound of polite chatter in a receiving line at a memorial. I had expected more weeping women. *Mom would have entered the church crying,* I thought to myself.

The chapel itself was three times the size it had been in my day, and the decor had moved decidedly into the late 1990s. A supersized stage held an eighteen-piece drum kit encased in plexiglass, a grand piano, the ubiquitous organ, and a young Sandi Patty lookalike singing Sandi Patty–quality renditions of "Farther Along" and "We Shall Behold Him." A new pastor, younger and more vital, wore a lift in his right shoe and had a limp in his left leg, but had a handsome face and the confidence of a seasoned orator. From the vaulted ceiling in the foyer hung several pieces of barbed-wire-lined poster board featuring a color stock photo of a white man falling to his knees in front of an oak tree in the rain, highlighted by the word *iHOPE* in Helvetica typeface.

When the line moved inside, I saw some people I knew, but I felt a strong need to sit by myself. Jane sat in the front row, surrounded by supporters, wearing one of her hats. I waited my turn and then I took her hand in mine and I said what you say, *"I'm so sorry we're seeing each other for the first time in years under these circumstances."*

Jane blinked three times and stared at me. "Erin? Oh, Erin . . . not from New York City? Did you come from New York City?"

"I drove straight here. I couldn't stay away," I said.

Jane did a kind of bouncy dance in her theater seat. "Oh, sweetie, you've grown into such a beautiful young woman." Maybe we're always young women to our moms.

Jane said she felt so blessed, and I took my seat a few rows behind her. The Sandi Patty lookalike kicked things off with a little "It Is Well with My Soul" (*Whatever my lot / Thou hath taught me to say / It is well, it is well, with my soul . . .*) and I got that sinking feeling that I get at funerals when I can't believe the lyrics of the hymns that open them. It is so not well with my soul, thank you very much.

But then Jane stood up and she started talking and everything else fell away.

In a clear voice she said, "The story of my life is not at all how I would have written it." She spoke about losing her husband on November 10, eighteen years before, and the way the loss consumed her daughter.

November 10 had been the day our dad had died, too.

Jane told us that when Sarah and her brother were little kids, they couldn't really articulate their love for their parents, so they would use kid analogies to explain their feelings. Sarah would say that she loved her mother so much that her love could wrap around the Earth three times. And her older brother would one-up his sister by using the word "infinity." To prevent any sibling rivalry, Jane taught her kids that when anybody felt overwhelmed by the bigness of their love, they should simply say, "I feel like that." Two days before Sarah died, she gave her mother a no-good-reason card, a homemade thing made of construction paper and decorated with Magic Marker. The card said only *I feel like that.*

Jane told us that she'd always believed in the power of love. She believed if she'd loved enough, she wouldn't have had a dysfunctional family. If she'd loved enough, she could have saved her husband and kept her daughter alive. Her mother called Sarah a warrior, she fought so hard. Unfortunately, she found a way to cope that ultimately killed her. Jane realized she had to forgive her daughter for destroying someone she loved so dearly. And forgive herself, too. She'd been able to save her daughter's life before, just not this time.

"I've learned that my love is powerless over another person's choices," Jane said. "I couldn't love Sarah enough for her to choose life over her addiction, and I had to let her go. 'Let go and let God' has never meant so much to me. Now it means let go, and believe that when I do that I can trust God and His plan."

I'd never wanted to believe in something more than when she said those words. I prayed God's plan for Jane included sanity and peace. She closed by saying that the pain of loss was excruciating, but the joy of love was worth it. I felt the truth of those words.

The pastor spoke next. I braced myself for a speech that centered on anorexia as a metaphor for spiritual hunger, but I liked him immediately when he said that he wasn't there to paint some kind of Thomas Kinkade version of this tragedy. "All we have is hope, hope that a little girl will be reunited with her dad. Hope is what kicks in when optimism dies."

I allowed myself to imagine Sarah's reunion with her father in heaven, or at least in the corridor of light they say greets the deoxygenated brain. Was it his face she saw when she died?

"I want to see His face," Sarah's dad had told Jane when he was in the throes of his own death. I hoped that instead of Jesus, Sarah got to see her father unmasked.

On the drive home to New York, those last boxes from my childhood and Dad's records in the back, I wondered how old I'd be before I stopped looking for my father. I often recognized him in the faces of strangers on the street or characters on television. I saw familiar mannerisms in my brothers, who both stuck close to home to be closer to the memory of him, revisiting the same golf courses they'd always frequented together. I thought of him at the movies, at the ballet, at the museum, or whenever I was in Central Park, always ending up at the same spot—Strawberry Fields. I'd sit on the same bench across from the shrine to my father's favorite Beatle, the same spot where I sat with Dad the only time he got to visit me here before he died. Somehow being on the bench together that day felt like a fitting end to a coming of age for both of us. *The sun was up, the sky was blue,* we were doing just what we were meant to be doing together—paying tribute to our friend John in New York City, the place where he knew he'd always belonged, and the place where I felt free.

People forgive (or forget) the messy parts of John Lennon's life because his art changed the world and he wrote about aspirational themes like peace and love. But think about this: What do people who are full of rage *do* without a creative outlet? If John Lennon hadn't played rock 'n' roll, would he have been just another jealous guy who hit his kid and cheated on his wife, experimented with drugs and died young? It's been widely reported that the man who immortalized the lyric "Imagine no possessions" had a temperature-controlled room at the Dakota dedicated to his fur coats. Maybe Lennon was a peace activist *and* an asshole—I don't think the combination is uncommon.

Love, for a child, is implicit. Even the worst parent—whatever your definition of that may be—is a loved parent. I'm not talking about later, when an adult child has agency and can decide for herself how to respond and cope with the fallout of childhood; I'm talking about the imprint. A father at all is more than so many kids get, and a love between two imperfect people is still a love story.

I was with my dad the first time I saw the movie *Love Story* on television. He thought I'd like Ali MacGraw's wardrobe, and he was right, but the movie itself is pretty awful. The plot is simple. Oliver, the jock, and Jenny, the musician, meet at an Ivy League university, fall in love, and are each summarily rejected by each other's fathers for not being good enough. The couple decide to make do on their own while Oliver attends law school. Suddenly, Jenny falls ill and medical tests reveal she will die. (For some sexist reason Jenny's physician tells only Oliver about the terminal diagnosis, though she figures it out soon enough.) Her life-prolonging treatments are costly and Oliver must stoop to asking his father for money. Later, Jenny dies, and his father shows up at the hospital to support his son for the first time; he comes to apologize. And that's when Oliver shushes him by declaring, "Love means never having to say you're sorry," a sentiment he learned from Jenny.

As soon as Ryan O'Neal spoke the last line of dialogue, I turned to Dad and burst out laughing: "Oh my God, love means *always* having to say you're sorry!"

He was right there with me, and Dad said "always" at the same time I did, and we both had a good laugh. Years later I think I finally get the idea behind the schmaltz: when love is true for both parties—the mistakes we make, our human failures—nothing can erase the imprint. (However, you should still *say* you're sorry, and my little epiphany doesn't change the fact that the movie blows.)

On the road, I played a cassette copy of Dad's *Happy Sunshine Music* mixtape, his favorite, the soundtrack of his life since the sixties. This was the collection he'd played on the days when he was happiest to be alive. The last song on side two was "The End" from *Abbey Road*, incidentally the last song the Beatles ever recorded together; it features a final instrumental solo performance by each member of the band and manages to be the most upbeat song about confronting one's mortality I can think of. The word "love" appears twenty-six times, one for each of the years I had him in my life.

I had my dad for all those years, and I didn't know they would end just as my life was getting good, that it would force me to grieve for everything he never taught me and everything he did. Even with all that's happened, even after so much analysis and pain, I forgive my father. I like to believe that, had he lived, he would have asked me to, and I would have asked him right back.

I'll keep listening to the albums he passed on to me, and in that way, we'll continue our conversation. It's taken me a lifetime to figure out how to receive it, but I still believe that the love that matters is the one you give.

END SIDE TWO

ACKNOWLEDGMENTS

Writing a memoir has to be the loneliest collaboration. It takes so much assistance, and yet no one else can tell your story but you. Despite having worked in book publishing for so long, every aspect of this process has been somehow unexpected and extremely humbling. I am indebted to the many people who have been so generous through this too-many-years-long experience.

First I need to thank my dear friend Betsy Lerner, whose name is already a familiar presence in acknowledgments pages in books too numerous to count. B, I feel like I'm only courageous when you're watching. Your belief in me, support, and friendship have shaped my career and saved my sanity. Thank you for your patience and guidance these last nineteen years (at press time). I hope we die on the same day, of very old age, while watching the Oscars.

I'm so proud to be associated with Dunow, Carlson & Lerner Literary Agency. My colleagues inspire me every day. Extra thanks to

Arielle Datz for helping me balance it all. This book was originally championed by Leslie Meredith at the late, great Free Press before Atria picked up the baton. I am indebted to her and Dominick Anfuso for their early enthusiasm, as well as Judith Curr, and all the kind people at Atria who kept the faith and helped me through to the finish line, especially Rakesh Satyal and Loan Le.

I'm also indebted to the following people for their friendship, encouragement, and/or straight-up help over the years: Denise See, Paul Athens, John Chaich, Joshua Lyon, Erin Flaherty, Jody Kivort, Adam Ganser, James J. Williams III, Shya Scanlon, Adrian Todd Zuniga, Carter Edwards, Matthew Phillp, Steve Five, Janet Hicks, Brooke Ehrlich, Brannan Piper, Nadia Zazie, Scott Gardner, Kate Hagerman, Brando Skyhorse, Ben Schafer, Brad Listi, Edan Lepucki, Leigh Stein, Kristen Daniels, Margaret Wappler, Molly Schiot, Patti Smith, Patty Schemel, Lucas Hunt, Paul Florez, Margaux Weisman, Meg Leder, Elizabeth Thompson, Steve Burns, the great Bobby Zarem, Andrew J. Segreti, Rachael Butt-Saad, Alan and Lisa Carrelli-Kraus, Janyne Tucek, Dayton Manuel, Ryan Lewis, Ryan and Ceci Orvis, Ms. Carol Janes, Dolores Smith & Gigi, as well as the Steensen, Theis, Miller, Fowler, and Hosier families, and all the people who shared their memories of their fathers or mine.

This book couldn't have been written without the support of my mother and brothers, who have been generous with their permission in the face of the weird instinct some writers have to publish personal stories. Mom, you continue to inspire me with your strength, loyalty, and faith in love, not to mention your endless talents. You are the woman I aspire to become (except for the chopping-your-own-firewood part, because I'm lazy). Thank you for being so open in the face of every nosy question, and showing me that people can change and grow if they want to. Thanks to Papa Terry for being there all these years and loving me like your own.

Everyone said I'd have to finish the book before I'd be able to meet the person I'd been waiting to meet all along (something about getting on the other side of the past). It turns out that my dad's legacy was his optimism after all, because somehow I never stopped believing that peace and love are possible no matter how dark things can seem at the time. Chris Gelles, my love, you give me hope; thank you for saying *yes*.

ABOUT THE AUTHOR

Erin Hosier is a literary agent and the coauthor of the memoir *Hit So Hard* by Patty Schemel. She lives in Brooklyn.